DATE DUE

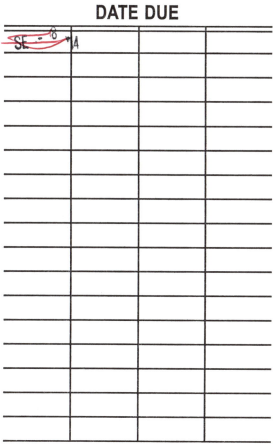

SE 8 A			

DEMCO 38-296

Performance in Life and Literature

Performance in Life and Literature

Paul H. Gray
The University of Texas at Austin

James VanOosting
Southern Illinois University at Carbondale

Appendix by
Robert Hopper
The University of Texas at Austin

Allyn and Bacon

Boston • London • Toronto • Sydney • Tokyo • Singapore

ɔh Opiela

rs

inistrator: Susan McIntyre
tle, Shaw & Wetherill, Inc.
Composition Buyer: Linda Cox
Manufacturing Buyer: Aloka Rathnam
Cover Administrator: Suzanne Harbison

Copyright © 1996 by Allyn & Bacon

A Pearson Education Company
Upper Saddle River, NJ 07458

Library of Congress Cataloging-in-Publication Data
Gray, Paul Havener.
    Performance in life and literature / Paul H. Gray, James
VanOosting.
        p.   cm.
    Includes index.
    ISBN 0-205-14045-9
    1. Oral interpretation.   I. VanOosting, James.   II. Title.
PN4145.G67   1996
808.5′4—dc20   95-41211
                                                 CIP

Printed in the United States of America
10 9 8 7 6 5 4 3 2   00 99 98 97 96

To
Tish and Brooks
Peter and Thomas
whose lives *are* poems

Contents

PREFACE

When accepting the Nobel Prize for Literature, Toni Morrison spoke as profoundly as in a Zen koan: "We die. That may be the meaning of life. But we *do* language. That may be the measure of our lives."*

This book is about *doing* language. It's about the *performance* of language in our everyday lives as well as in literature. These two kinds of *doing* are intimately connected. Words on the page of a novel, in the lines of a poem, or the dialogue of a play are exactly the same as those uttered by children on a playground, colleagues in a workplace, adversaries at debate, or lovers in moments of intimacy. Talkers and writers use language in the same ways; listeners and readers make sense of that language by the same means. The measure of our lives, in Morrison's formulation, is how we *do* language, how we *perform* words. She makes no distinction between literary art and everyday experience. Nor do we, in this book. Our purpose and our method affirm the continuity of language as performed in life and in literature.

"Conversation," in several senses of that word, is the informing model and metaphor for our thinking. At a literal level, conversation is the basis of all human communication. We understand words as a form of talk, a back-and-forth exchange, whether those words are sounded acoustically or printed on a page. This book contains many transcripts of real-life conversations as telling parallels to the language of literary texts. Likewise, we turn for theoretical insight to conversation analysts, particularly to our colleague Robert Hopper, whose research has become the close conversational partner to our own critical thinking. Metaphorically, this book can be read as an ongoing conversation between everyday talk and literature. Texts drawn from both sources are mutually informing and resonant.

Performance in Life and Literature began as a literal conversation, and a memorable one. We were walking together in the Garden District of New Orleans, admiring the residential architecture, and playing hooky from the obligations of a professional association meeting. We talked about the things we both love most: language at the crowded intersections of life and literature. For the next four years, we continued that pleasant conversation and, as a result, our thinking has become somewhat clearer on the subject. At the same time, we have garnered a more profound respect for the mystery and grace of utterance.

The conversation that matters most to us now is what can be extended to you, the student. We invite you to enter into genuine dialogue with us in this book. Bring your own voice, your own experience, and your own reading to the

---

*Toni Morrison, *The Nobel Lecture in Literature, 1993.* New York: Alfred A. Knopf, 1994, p. 22.

conversation. Argue when you will. Fume when you must. Celebrate when you can. All three verbs, along with many other performance possibilities, are ways of *doing* language.

As professors, we are usually involved in an intergenerational conversation with students, as often learning from our conversational partners as teaching them. We cherish the daily privilege of that dialogue. As authors, we have taken the liberty of dedicating this volume to four members of another generation with whom we are engaged in lifelong learning, our children.

Acknowledgments

We wish to thank many people for their kind assistance and wise counsel in preparing this book. Our colleagues Lynn Miller, Ronald Pelias, Nathan Stucky, Phillip Glenn, and Elyse Pineau read portions of early drafts and offered helpful critiques. John Anderson, Emerson College; Paul C. Edwards, Northwestern University; Mary Frances Hopkins, Louisiana State University; Jerry Krasser, University of Connecticut; James Pearse, William Penn College; Jerry Reynolds, Baylor University; Ron Shields, Bowling Green State University; Carol Simpson Stern, Northwestern University; and Kristin Valentine, Arizona State University, reviewed the manuscript, and their comments guided us through final revisions. Three graduate students at the University of Texas taught from various drafts and provided valuable feedback: Ed Smith, Claire Van Ens, and Joe Rice. Research assistants at Southern Illinois University helped with the task of securing literary permissions: Lori Montalbano, Tari Glaspie, and Beatriz Durán McWilliams. Rebecca Wolniewicz and Dan Fox read galley and page proofs. Carla Daves, Acquisitions Editor at Allyn and Bacon, has been very supportive of our efforts.

We would especially like to thank Carolyn Gray and Sharon Taylor, without whose consultation on matters from substance to style, we could not have written this book.

Chapter One

Everyday and Literary Performance

Reading Well/Performing Well

This book lays out an approach to reading well, which is the central skill required when performing the language of life or literature. In fact, reading well is critical to any understanding of human communication, whether it be face-to-face interaction, conversation over the telephone, writing or reading a letter, interpreting a novel, or listening to the beat of a rap lyric. Reading well is a fundamental metaphor for successful living. On the golf course, you learn to read the break in a putt. When forecasting the weather, you have to read the elements. If you know a friend very well, you might say, "I can read her like a book." Or, if you have some juicy story to pass along, "Here's one for the books!" The ability of coauthors to collaborate on a book, despite a physical separation by hundreds of miles, depends on one computer reading the language of another.

These instances of reading, drawn from the common images of casual talk, speak to its importance as a way of interpreting the world. Not only do you decipher print on the page, but you also read verbal and nonverbal cues, human and animal behavior, signs of nature, environmental change, and spiritual meaning. Some people read palms, tea leaves, or tarot cards. A baseball pitcher reads the catcher's signals; a batter looks to the third-base coach for a hit sign. Musicians read scores. Juries read faces. Physicians read symptoms. Apparently, if we believe the metaphors of everyday speech, you and I read continuously, and our reading material includes just about everything.

But what does it mean to read *well*? Here, too, casual talk makes some helpful distinctions. To get a quick overview of some situation, you'll *take a reading*. For a more thorough examination, you'll *read from cover-to-cover.* When an in-depth analysis is called for, you'll try to read *into* things or *between* the lines. How well you're able to read your own life, the behavior of others, and the changing environment can be a strong predictor of personal satisfaction and social success.

Reading well, no matter what the context, calls for you to step into some language system and look at the world from its perspective. The specific purpose of this book is to help you to read literature well, to get into its worlds of language and action, to see and feel its vitality from the inside. Through the examples studied here, you'll learn that everyday interactions share a great deal with the most profound utterances of classical literature. And we shall contend that *performance* is a unique and effective way of understanding the language of both life and literature.

If the idea of performing seems strange to you or even a bit scary, we ask that you try to relax, reflect a moment, and consider how well you already perform language in your everyday life. Whenever you lose yourself in a book, you're reading well on a performance level. Whenever there's a smudge on the page, and you don't see it, it's because you're immersed in the book's language world.

Whenever somebody in the room is speaking to you but you don't hear them, you're more attuned to the voices in the story than to your own acoustic space. Whenever you escape self-consciousness—an awareness of where you are or what's going on around you—and, instead, enter into the imagined landscape of a literary text, you're *performing*. Whenever the world of a thriller or a murder mystery, a poem or a comic book, is more real to you than the physical environment around you, it must mean that you're inhabiting the language of that literature and reading it well. If you have experienced such a sensation, even privately and silently, you already know what can be achieved when performing language. This same sense of immersion, shared with others, is the primary learning objective of this book—to help you make a literary world more tangible for yourself and your audience than the classroom with its desks and chalkboard, to invite you and your audience to care more about the heartache of a character than the headache of a hangover, to make the class feel more acutely the conflicts of a literary plot than the anxieties of their everyday relationships.

Most of the time you spend talking day in and day out you are actually performing language and doing it very well—whether on the telephone, over lunch, at a bull session, or in the grandstands of a football game. In fact, we expect one another to communicate effectively. Whenever someone doesn't perform language well, creating confusion in the listener and requiring some kind of correction, that person sticks out and the moment of incompetence is awkward. Most of us learn to perform language well from a very early age, perfecting the skill as we mature, and enjoying the results of interaction with others.

When learning the "new" performance skills introduced in this class, you'll probably be surprised time and again by how they seem "old" and familiar. Through common sense you can draw on a lifetime of experience that's applicable to performing literature. The procedure advocated in this book asks you to take stock of your inventory of performance skills to transfer them into literary experience.

CASE IN POINT: CONVERSATIONAL PERFORMANCE

The most familiar form of language is everyday conversation. It is the root of all other forms of language—both spoken and written. Conversation provides the infant's first performance challenge and, next to nursing or touching, affords the earliest pleasure of a human relationship. Infants learn how to perform conversation by murmuring nonsense syllables of real intimacy, by gurgling their sensuous satisfaction, and by crying out their demands. New parents are surprised and tickled to discover how well they can read their baby's performance behaviors. By paying careful attention, they begin to discern a whole vocabulary of infant experience and to share the way their baby perceives the world. Likewise, this baby learns from the parents' behavior, even when they don't realize it. The language of conversational performance begins at the painful joy of a birth cry and continues, without interruption, to the poignancy of a person's dying words. Between beginning and end, all of our personal dramas are enacted through innumerable conversational performances, replete with daily crises and occasional climaxes.

It is so easy to take everyday talk for granted that, perhaps, we should look more closely at this amazing human ability. Here is a telephone conversation between a college student and her mother. Because the telephone medium lacks

Key to Conversational Transcript

These scripts use markings devised by Gail Jefferson to describe conversation accurately in terms of timing, emphasis, and expression. Most of the scripts are in words, but laughter may be spelled out (e.g., hah hah hah). Sometimes audible exhaling is shown by **hhhhh** signs. The sign "**hhhh**" indicates in-breath. In addition:

TIMING	The scripts are like play scripts with speaker identification at the left margin.
A: ⌈no B: ⌊yes	Brackets indicate that two speakers were talking at the same time
A: okay= B: =alright	No pause
(.....)	Indicates a pause. Each period indicates about a tenth of a second; this pause is half a second.
	This sign: (......... ....) indicates a pause two seconds long. (.) indicates a very short pause
—	This sign indicates that some material was edited from the original at this point. Performers have the option to pause.
EMPHASIS	Some signs help mark vocal intonation.
no	Underlining indicates vocal emphasis or stress.
no::	Colon after a letter indicates that sound is stretched, lengthened. More than one colon is a longer stretch.
no?	Question mark indicates rising pitch
no.	Period indicates falling pitch
no-	Hyphen indicates abrupt sound cutoff

[Adapted from J. M. Atkinson & J. Heritage, eds., *Structures of Social Action*, Cambridge, 1984.]

the nonverbal cues of face-to-face communication, it provides a convenient starting point for our analysis of language in performance. The following transcription not only preserves a word-for-word dialogue but also attempts to code telling vocal behaviors such as pause, stress, and pitch. At first, these markings may seem confusing, but most of them will become clear as you analyze the conversation and talk about it together in class. We suggest that you read the transcript through to get the gist of it, and then return for a second, slower reading, paying attention to the markings.

It's Gun Be Hard to Do

(By permission of the University of Texas Conversation Library)

	D:	I don't know what to do, because I'm afraid I'll start cryin
		or somethin
		(..)
	M:	We:ll just try not to honey she thinks a lot of you
5		and she would love to see you I'm <u>su:re.</u>
		(..........)
	M:	It's gun be hard to do: I <u>kno:</u>w.
		(......)
	D:	We:ll, ·hhhhhhhh hhhh <u>I</u> just don't know what to do::
10		<u>I</u> get choked up over things like this.
		(...)
	M:	Yeah.
	D:	I: get choked up over things like this I can't-
		anybody that di:es that I barely even kno:w and hhh I me:an
15		especially fts somebody who I'm gonna be looking at
		and I <u>know</u> they're gonna be dead in a few months it's just
		·hhhh I don' know what to do, it's just horrible.
		(...)
	M:	We:ll just go and try to be as cheerful as possible
20		because that seems to be the attitude that Jan's taking
		(.....)

	D:	I know Mother but, maybe I'm jus- (..........)
	M:	And if you feel yourself- chokin up why just- you know
		kind of excuse yourself and (.......) and just- squeeze her ha:nd
25		and tell her how much y- you enjoyed workin with her
		up there that summer and ·hhhhh hhhh you know
		(.......... ....)
	M:	·hhhh just like tha:t is all I know to tell you to do:,
		(..........)
30	M:	It's har:d but they say the worst thing (..) u:h-
		(.....) is when people withdra-aw from terminally ill (..)
	D:	Yeah,
	M:	people like that you know and- and don't talk to em and
		don't- (......) you know just ignore em that's really hard.
35	D:	Yeah,
		(.......... ....)
	M:	⌊S:o do you wanna go to u::h (........) Llano with us tomorrow
		afternoo:n=
	D:	=No: Mother I ca:n't, I've got- u:h I'm meeting a gir:l at two:
40		and we've got to um (..........) study.
	M:	Yeah, okay.
	D:	So: there's no way I can go::
	M:	We:ll Timmy ca:lled you know Barry's uncle?
	D:	Uh huh=
45	M:	=And he has a ra:nch for us to look a:t so we're gonna go
		just look at it ⌈just
	D:	⌊How mu:ch
		(.......)
	M:	We:ll I- I don't know I don' know h- don't wanta dis- discuss it
50		on the telepho:ne=
	D:	=O:h.
		(...)

	M:	Bu:t u:h (..) We're gonna go over there and look at it
		just kinda get the lay of the la:nd, Misha said she didn't wanna
55		invest in anything that wasn't- on the- on the water you know
		either a ·hhhhh la:ke or something: recreational.
	D:	I: don't kno:w I don't a you just go:- and (......) cause
		John and I are planning on buyin some land,
		and we're gonna live on about ten acres.
60		(........)
	M:	At Llano:=
	D:	=No::. not at Llano, wherever we end u:p we're going to
		cause I'm gonna have a- all kinds of animals.
	M:	I:: see:
65	D:	I think it's important for children to grow up around
		animals.
	M:	I:: see: ⌈well
	D:	⌊And they can get married to each other you know
		like- (...) Tilly and Spike did.
70	M:	Uh: hu:h.=
	D:	=But anyway. ·hhhhhh u:m (.) what- tu:h- h:ow long
		are you gonna d- be down the:re.
		(..........)
	M:	Well? wi:hhh u:h we won't be gone- (....) if- Daddy
75		doesn't get away from the office till- (...) eleven thirty or
		so and it'll take us an hour and a half to ⌈get over there
	D:	⌊NO::::, I'm talkin
		about how long are you gu- are you going down to visit Jan?
		(........)
80	M:	I don't kno:w.
		(..........)
	M:	I don't- know whether I was invited or no:t.
	D:	Well- uhhh Mother if I:m invited you: are certainly invited.=

	M:	=Well maybe I wou:ld, maybe I would just go by the office and
85		pick Daddy up and that way we could just leave from there,
		som'in like ⌈that
	D:	⌊Well you're not gun be dressed up then?
		(.......... .....)
	M:	Well I don't kno:w. I'll pro ji- depends on what the
90		weather's li:ke tomorrow.
		(.....)
	D:	We:ll- I tell you what- You think about it and you call
		me back and tell me if you're gonna go visit Ja:n cause if
		you're no:t I wanna go to Jazzercise in the morning, cause
95		I'll be wastin a time. ·hhhh But- (........) I feel like I should
		go visit Ja:n because I feel like that's what God wants me to do.
		(..........)
	M:	We:ll do you mean you're not gonna go if I don't go:?
		(....)
100	D:	I don't kno:w. uh- I- uh no: I don't think I will, cause I don't
		know how to- ·hhh I feel real haw- uh awful about this but
		I don't know how to handle- I don't know how to handle it
		(..........)
	M:	We:ll=
105	D:	I'd hate to get in there and just- ba:wl in front of everybody
		(..)
	D:	Things like that- (......) I guess maybe it just shows
		that I'm insecure within myself because (....) it make- it
		(..) it offends me real- a whole lot
110		(......)
	D:	I ⌈know
	M:	⌊offends you:.
	D:	Death. (.) offends me, It really (....) bothers me.
	M:	Yeah.

```
115                         (..........)

      D:        And I guess it's afraid of- ·hhhh hhh I'm afraid of you
                kicking off some day or something I don know.

      M:        O:h. (....) we::ll (..........) well did you know Barry's si:ck?

      D:        Yeah I know I just talked to him.

120   M:        What'd he sa:y.

                         (....)

      D:        He just said that he threw up this morning when he got
                to wor:k, and (..........) I think uh- there's several people
                out at schoo:l

125                      (........)

      D:        I think it's maybe he may have a touch of the flu:.
```

Even on a first reading of this transcript, you'll notice its ordinary language and the everyday expressiveness of these two speakers. If you read the dialogue with a partner—one person being the mother, and the other the daughter—you're sure to sense an authenticity to their relationship in performance. Despite the ordinariness of this telephone conversation, we want to draw attention to how much *like* literature it is. Neither mother nor daughter sets out to create a work of verbal art, of course. Nevertheless, their dialogue displays many of the features we associate with literature.

First, the topics of their conversation—death, love, money, and God—are four of literature's favorite themes, resounding since antiquity, from Sappho to Seuss. Second, their conversation demonstrates compactness of expression as mother and daughter tear through ideas at a dazzling rate. This, too, is a quality cited to distinguish literary language from everyday talk. Third, the conversation is jam-packed with paradoxes, those opposite impulses that create tension on all sides and are hallmarks, theorists claim, of literary language. If you were to study this mother and daughter not as real people but as characters in a play, you'd find their motivations, interactions, and contradictions to be as complicated as those in Shakespeare, Lorraine Hansberry, or Tennessee Williams.

Notice how in lines 1 to 35, the mother urges her daughter to do the right thing by Jan, but then makes excuses herself for not visiting their terminally ill friend (lines 80–90); or how the daughter seriously weighs the benefits of going to Jazzercise versus following the will of God (lines 94–96); or the mother's willingness to discuss death and duty over the phone, but not money (lines 49–50); or the semantic spin the daughter puts on "death," as the idea shifts in her opinion from "horrible" (line 17) to "offensive" (line 113). In short, you'll seldom find characters in literature using language in any more complicated ways than we all do in everyday life.

Some critics argue that an important difference between the languages of life and literature is their various degrees of structural unity. They assert that literary language is more patterned, with the writer tying together plots and subplots, various motifs, and even apparent tangents into a coherent whole. By contrast, one usually assumes that everyday talk, lacking an author with an artistic purpose, remains comparatively unstructured. The conversation you have just read belies such an easy distinction.

If we envision this exchange between mother and daughter as a clash of wills—a classic conflict reenacted from one of the earliest Greek dramas, *Electra*, to the latest episode of *Another World*—with the mother determined to get her daughter to visit Jan and the daughter equally determined not to, then every exchange between them becomes a mini-drama of persuasion and resistance. For the first thirty-five lines, the daughter proposes reasons not to go, and her mother refutes them. Then the mother goes off on a tangent when she switches subjects from Jan to the upcoming trip to Llano, but, in context, we can see this as yet another tactic in her campaign to get the daughter to visit Jan. By the same token, the daughter's talk of her plans with John is actually an attempt to distract her mother's attention and to repel her persuasive force. Notice how the daughter keeps returning to the topics of death and dying by introducing such opposite terms as "live," "grow up," and "children."

By conceiving the transcript as a unified argument, dramatically enacted between mother and daughter, line 78 becomes its turning point or crisis. Until then, the daughter had been on the defensive, forced to rebut her mother's arguments. Once she realizes that her mother doesn't want to visit Jan any more than she does, the daughter manages to reverse roles and put her mother in the hot seat. From beginning to end, this whole episode can be read as a tightly unified dramatic conflict that reveals the complexity of both the characters and their relationship.

We've begun discussing the performance of language with this transcript of an actual telephone conversation to point out the similarity between everyday talk and the special utterances of literature. Our approach to learning places you squarely on the threshold between life and art. By inserting a literary *frame* around a real conversation, we've encouraged a *reading* of life as if it were art. As a result, we can observe a number of literary qualities in everyday speech that might otherwise be overlooked.

Performing Lived Language

Printed language can be read as a performance record of a lived experience, as the conversational transcript illustrates. In this class, you'll go one step further by actually lifting words off the printed page and returning them to the human body and voice through live performance. According to theorist Richard Schechner, performance is "twice-behaved behavior," which simply means putting words back into the body. When you see a live performance—whether in the theatre, on the concert stage, or under the circus tent—you expect it to be just that: *live.* If an actor's lines sound canned, if the singer is merely lip-synching, or if the sword swallower uses some trick device, you feel cheated. The first expectation of live performance is that it should be believable. Hence, when you perform literature, others expect your vocal and physical behaviors to square with what they already know about performance from everyday life.

Look again at "It's Gun Be Hard to Do," this time as an example of how people actually talk, and let's see what hints can be taken from it for the performance of literature. As an exercise, divide into pairs, and perform the first fourteen lines of this conversation, imitating the mother and daughter by doing everything with your voice that the script tells you to do. Take your time, and practice the exchange as many times as necessary to be sure you're including all the qualities marked in the transcript. After a dozen concentrated readings of these fourteen lines (just the length of a sonnet), your performance should begin to feel comfortable. You'll probably be able to do it without even looking at the page.

Observe how language is continuously inflected in this telephone talk. Some words stand out, while others get thrown away. When performers of literature began studying conversation, as far back as the eighteenth century, the first principle they noticed was variable emphasis on different words. They wanted to know how everyday communication is served by the voice singling out individual words for special emphasis. Their research concluded that volume, duration, and pitch are the major vocal variables. Notice in your fourteen-line performance how all three of these contribute to expressiveness.

Of equal importance to *how* speakers create emphasis is *why* they choose to punch certain words but not others. In our example, what does inflection tell you about this mother and daughter and their individual intentions? For starters, we can guess from the daughter's first emphasis (line 1) that she is worried about *doing* something, and her anxiety (line 2) is that she'll lose control or start crying. We know this not only from the words she speaks, but also from the *way* she says them. She reveals her attitude in performance as well as in words.

If you imitate the mother's response (line 4), you can't miss her peculiar emphasis on "well." In itself, this word wouldn't convey much meaning, but, according to the transcription, it gains significance from the mother's vocal stress and duration. Furthermore, "well" follows a slight pause in the dialogue (..). You may be tempted to ignore this data because no meaningful words are involved, but psychiatrists and sociologists insist that *everything* counts in the everyday performance of language.

The mother's vocal behavior might suggest that she's stalling. Maybe she can't think of a suitable response, yet feels that one is required. Hence, she pauses and draws out her "We:ll." In fact, the mother doesn't answer her daughter's fear that she might start crying, but simply instructs her, "just try not to." And, then, drawing on the intimacy of their relationship ("honey"), the mother dismisses her daughter's reservations and concludes with the double stress on "su:re," revealing her own self-confidence.

A long pause follows, almost a full second, during which we wait for the daughter to take her expected turn in conversation, responding to the mother's appeal. When she doesn't speak, the mother continues, this time in stressed vocalization of a phrase that *does* directly address her daughter's fears (line 7). Again, the mother's speech ends with a double-stressing of kno:w. If the "su:re" of line 5 expresses her confidence that she knows what will please Jan, the "kno:w" of line 7 asserts that she's also well aware of what her daughter is going through.

You can read the daughter's "well" (line 9), enclosed between two pauses and followed by her own extended sigh, as serving a similar function to her mother's "well" in line 4—stalling for time or, perhaps, gathering her thoughts and feelings. What's remarkable about her ultimate speech ("I just don't know what to do:: I get choked up over things like this.") is that, apparently, she has no new argument to offer or point to make. She seems merely to paraphrase her opening line ("I don't know what to do: because I'm afraid I'll start cryin or somethin."). However, her restatement cannot be heard as a simple echo. The words change slightly, but, of more importance, the vocal performance alters significantly. Now she emphasizes "I," a new performance that creates a new meaning. She contrasts herself with most other people and, certainly, with her mother. According to the daughter's inflection, her mother doesn't "kno:w" and shouldn't be so "su:re." In short, the persuasive contest between mother and daughter is played out not only in words but in performances.

We have analyzed just twenty seconds of conversation and, because it occurred over the telephone, we've attended only to matters of voice. Were this a face-to-face interaction, recorded on videotape, we could examine nonverbal codes of facial expression, gesture, and body movement to further enhance our understanding. We could find significance in every little movement by hypothesizing a motivation for its performance.

When the in-depth analysis of a poem reveals levels of complexity, some students may express doubt that the author really "meant all that." You might as well ask whether the mother and daughter in this telephone conversation were really aware of all the implications we have suggested when they made their original utterances.

Performance as a method of study helps to persuade us that the answer to all three questions must be a resounding "Y:e:s." In the mother–daughter conversation, for instance, each word and vocal inflection spoken by one person prompts a response from the other that seems to recognize the complex coding. This is nowhere clearer than in the exchange beginning with line 37, where the mother asks her daughter if she wants to go to Llano, and the latter responds,

"No: Mother I ca:n't (.) I've got- u:h I'm meeting a gir:l at two: and we've got to um (..........) study." Here it is the daughter's *performance* and not her words that conveys the real meaning. And the mother's response, with its falling inflections, "Yeah, okay.," makes clear that she is perfectly aware of what's really going on. If you look up "okay" in the dictionary, you'll be told it signals approval, sanction, or endorsement. But this mother's performance of "okay" signals no such thing. What she communicates to the daughter is the exact opposite of what "okay" is supposed to mean. Here, and again in line 41, vocalization, rather than a dictionary definition, prescribes meaning.

Realizing how complex this conversation is, we should be impressed by their high level of performance skill. Yet they don't display any expertise beyond that demonstrated by all of us in everyday talk. Indeed, because an author provides explicit cues within a literary text, you might argue that enacting a poem or story is a good deal easier than performing the interactions required in our daily lives.

The language of literature always derives from familiar forms of talk. Literature is a *found art*, made up of hand-me-down words well worn by previous users. Eudora Welty says, "We start from scratch, and words don't." More often than not, when a performance of literature fails to satisfy you, the performer has ignored the very skills perfected in everyday life. When you judge a play, movie, or TV drama as phony, you're comparing its performance to the standard of your own experience. The challenge of performing literary language is *not* to do something new or strange with it, but to tap into the depths of knowledge you already possess from a lifetime of using everyday language.

Performing Language: Four Principles

So far, we have been talking about the vocal features of an everyday conversation. By imitating them, you can experience how a mother and daughter used their performance skills to communicate shades of meaning as subtle as any encountered in literature. But how did they learn to perform language so well? Indeed, how do you and I know what to say and how to say it when communicating with each other? What principles guide the performative features of our everyday talk?

The first and most important principle of understanding language is to acknowledge the *world* in which it is situated. Words are intimately connected to the person who speaks them, the place and time they are uttered, and the identity of a specific listener. Or, to put it another way, language must be in context to make sense. Words point to the world their speaker lives in and, in some sense, they actually create that world. You know nothing about the mother and daughter in the telephone conversation apart from the language they perform. And yet their vocalized words are sufficient to invoke a sense of the world they inhabit. Simply from the performance of their language, you meet real people

(Timmy, Barry, and John), see real places (Jazzercise and Llano), and experience real events (illness, buying real estate, and rearing children). You couldn't make sense of this conversation without imagining the world in which it is situated. Chapter 2 explores the *worlds* of language and how they are constituted in performance.

A second principle for understanding language is to recognize that words, spoken in a specific context, always have some *effect*. Within the world of a particular utterance, a speaker's performance strikes the listener in one way or another and creates a response. Understanding language involves predicting its likely effect. What impression are you likely to make by choosing certain words, inflecting your intonation in a certain way, or adopting a particular form of talk? You always choose to perform one way rather than another in hopes of achieving some desired effect on your listener. If issuing a command, you want obedience. If asking a question, you want an answer. Of course, you don't always create the effect intended or get the response you want. Cause and effect in human communication are rarely linked in any simple or clear manner. This is so in part because the desired effect of any utterance is likely to be multiple rather than single. For instance, in a military setting, a superior may give an order and expect obedience from the subordinate, plus a little fear. If you get lost when traveling and stop to ask a stranger the way, you certainly want directions, but you may also want a little sympathy. When the daughter in "It's Gun Be Hard to Do" explains to her mother, "I get choked up over things like this," she wants more than understanding; she also wants her mother to show a little pity. The effects speakers hope for are coded by their language *in performance*. Chapter 3 examines the complexity of effect as a variable in understanding the language of life and literature.

The third principle is making *sense* of language. We put it third because you can't make sense without having some prior grasp of world and effect. The dictionary definition of words may create the illusion that language is static. We know it to be dynamic. Vocabulary, grammar, and voice are interrelated. More to the point, words make sense only in the context of a specific relationship between speaker and listener. The daughter in our telephone conversation can talk about going to "Jazzercise" only because she knows her mother understands the word. When the mother introduces "Timmy," she doesn't know for sure if the daughter remembers who he is ("you know, Barry's uncle"). Making sense is the focus of Chapter 4.

The final principle for understanding language is identifying its *genre*, or its category of talk. This is the subtlest dimension of analysis, and it leads us to consider problems of *form* in the language of life and literature. At a simple level, you differentiate genres of speech all the time. We all recognize that a *cheer* in a gymnasium is a different kind of performance from a *prayer* in a church. A politician's *campaign speech* is different from a professor's *lecture*. A *joke* is different from an *insult*. *Gossip* is different from *testimony*. The mother in the telephone conversation might have chosen the genre of command when telling her daughter to visit Jan. The language and tone of voice associated with issuing a command are different from the performance features of making a personal plea. When the daughter starts telling about the ranch she wants to live on with John, the mother says, "At Llano?" This response is in the genre of a tease, and the daughter recognizes it as such. In some circumstances, the meaning of language resides primarily in identifying its genre. We shall separate this topic into two chapters—5 and 6—devoted to poetry and narrative.

World, effect, sense, and genre are variables that interact during all performances of everyday talk. Taken together, they constitute what's *human* in human communication. Not only do they inform the language of life, but they also underlie the communication of poems, plays, and stories. The skills we already possess from personal experience are prerequisite to and sufficient for any satisfying performance of literature. They are the common-sense guides to appreciating human interaction in verbal art.

EXERCISE & DISCUSSION

Return to the conversational transcript on pages 5–9. In each of the following lines, describe the world evoked, the effect intended, the sense that's made, and its genre of talk. Be sure to take into account your cumulative knowledge of the mother and her daughter, as well as your knowledge of their relationship with each other. Support your discussion with reference to both the words and their performance.

   A. Lines 30–35
   B. Lines 37–38
   C. Line 61
   D. Lines 64, 67, and 70
   E. Lines 80–82
   F. Lines 92–96
   G. Line 113
   H. Lines 117–119

A Second Conversation

Your ability to communicate with friends, family members, and strangers—both as a speaker and as a listener—depends on understanding the dynamics of each different relationship. To comprehend the meaning of another's words, you must "consider their source" and account for their context. Language is rooted in experience, spoken by people, and understood through interpersonal engagement.

When failing to communicate an experience to someone else, you might express your frustration by saying, "I guess you just had to *be there*." In other words, language is inextricably bound to person, place, and time.

As we discovered through the analysis of "It's Gun Be Hard to Do," a whole world is evoked by the language inflected in conversation. As an eavesdropper, you *overheard* that telephone call. Nonetheless, without any further information, you were able to realize the thoughts, sensations, emotions, and motivations of a mother and her daughter. You came *to know* them by imitating their voices and imagining their relationship. You made meaning of their dialogue in the same way they did, by attending to language *in* performance.

Here now is a second conversation. It, too, presents a mother and daughter, this time in face-to-face interaction.

1	Daughter:	Well? (............) So? (.........) <u>how's</u> the <u>fair</u>.
	Mother:	hhh It was si:lly. Country fairs are si:lly. Nobody from
		the <u>country</u> <u>even</u> <u>comes</u>.
		(...........)
5	Daughter:	<u>Why'd</u> you <u>go</u>.
		(.....)
	Mother:	Agnes <u>likes</u> it, I guess?
		(.........)
	Daughter:	And you <u>like</u> Agnes?
10		(...)
	Mother:	<u>No</u> Jesse. Agnes is <u>crazy</u>, but Agnes <u>does</u> have a <u>car</u>.
		(.....)
	Daughter:	Is Agnes <u>really</u> crazy, or is she just <u>silly</u>.
		(........)
15	Mother:	She's <u>really</u> <u>crazy</u>.
	Daughter:	Mother:::
		(..................)
	Mother:	Jesse, <u>Agnes</u> <u>Fletcher's</u> burned down every house she's
		ever <u>lived</u> in <u>Eight fires</u> n she's <u>due</u> for a <u>new</u> one
20		any <u>day</u> now.
	Daughter:	No:::

	Mother:	Wouldn't surprise me a <u>bit</u>.
		(........)
	Daughter:	Why'nt you tell me this be<u>fore</u>.
25		(...)
	Mother:	The houses they live in? you knew they was gun fall down
		anyway so why <u>wait</u> for them was all I could ever make
		out about it (....................) Agnes likes the feeling of
		ac<u>co:</u>mplishment.
30		(..........)
	Daughter:	Good for <u>her</u>.
		(..........)
	Mother:	<u>Now</u> then <u>one</u> cup or <u>two</u>.
		(.....)
35	Daughter:	<u>One</u> (.....) <u>No marshmallow</u>.
	Mother:	Ya have to have <u>marsh</u>mallows. That's the <u>old</u> way, <u>Jes</u>.
		(.....) <u>Two</u> or <u>three</u>. Three:s <u>bet</u>ter.
		(.....)
	Daughter:	<u>Three</u> then. (...) Her <u>whole house</u> burns up? (..........) Her
40		<u>clothes</u> n <u>pil</u>lows n <u>every</u>thing? (softly) <u>I'm</u> not sure I
		<u>believe</u> this.
	Mother:	When she was a <u>girl</u>, Jess. Not <u>now</u>. A long <u>time</u> ago. (.....)
		She's still got it <u>in</u> 'er. I'm <u>sure</u> of it.
		(..........)
45	Daughter:	<u>She</u> wouldn't burn her house down <u>now</u>? Where would she <u>go</u>.
		She can't get <u>Bus</u>ter to build her a <u>new</u> one? He's
		dead. (...) <u>How</u> could she <u>burn</u> it <u>down</u>.
	Mother:	Be ex<u>cit</u>in though if she <u>did</u>. Ya <u>never</u> <u>know:</u>
		(.....)
50	Daughter:	You <u>do too</u> know Mama. She wouldn't <u>do</u> it?
		(..................)
	Mother:	I <u>guess</u> <u>not</u>.

	(.............................)
Daughter:	What <u>else</u>. (.............) <u>Why</u> does she wear all those <u>whistles</u>
55	around her neck.
	(...........)
Mother:	Why does she have a house full of <u>birds</u>.
	(...)
Daughter:	<u>I</u> didn't know she had a house full of <u>birds</u>?
60 Mother:	She doe::s. (...............) And she says (high voice) they just
	<u>foll</u>er her <u>home</u>. (normal voice) Well I <u>know</u> for a <u>fact</u>
	she's still <u>pay</u>ing on the last <u>parrot</u> she <u>bought</u>. (.....)
	(high voice) Ya gotta keep your life filled <u>up</u> she
	<u>says</u>. (normal voice) She says a lot of <u>stupid</u> things.
65	(.....................................) It's all that <u>okra</u> she <u>eats</u>. You just can't <u>willy-</u>
	<u>nilly</u> eat okra two meals a <u>day</u> and expect to get a<u>way</u>
	with it? (softly) made her cra:zy.
Daughter:	She <u>really</u> eats okra twice a day? (...............) <u>Where</u> does she git
	it in the <u>win</u>ter.
70	(.........................)
Mother:	Well, she <u>eats</u> it a <u>lot</u>. Maybe not <u>two meals</u> but=
Daughter:	More than the <u>average</u> person.
	(...........)
Mother:	I don't know how much <u>okra</u> the <u>average</u> <u>person</u> <u>eats</u>.
75 Daughter:	Do you know how much okra <u>Agnes</u> eats?
	(...........)
Mother:	No?
	(........)
Daughter:	How many <u>birds</u> does she have.
80	(...............)
Mother:	<u>Two</u>.
	(.............)
Daughter:	Then what are all the <u>whistles</u> for.

(...........................)

85 Mother: They're not <u>real</u> whistles. Just little <u>plastic</u> ones on a
                 <u>neck</u>lace she won playing <u>Bing</u>o. I only <u>told</u> you about
                 it because I <u>thought</u> I might get a <u>laugh</u> out of you for
                 <u>once</u>, even if it <u>was</u>n't the <u>truth</u>, Jesse. Things
                 don't have to be <u>true</u> to <u>talk</u> about 'em, you <u>know</u>.
90   (.................)

    Daughter: <u>Why</u> won't she come <u>over</u> here.
                 (.........................)

    Mother: <u>Well</u> now what a <u>good</u> <u>idea</u>. (...........) I should have had more
                 <u>co</u>coa (.......) <u>Co</u>coa is <u>per</u>fect.
95   (...............)

    Daughter: Excep you don't take milk?

    Mother: I <u>hate</u> milk. <u>Coat</u> your <u>throat</u> as ba::d as <u>ok</u>ra. (...........)
                 Sumpthin jist dow:nright dis<u>gus</u>tin about it.
                 (...........)

100 Daughter: It's because of <u>me</u>, <u>isn</u>'t it.
                 (...........)

    Mother: <u>No</u>, Jes.
                 (...........)

    Daughter: <u>Yes</u>, Mama.
105   (...........)

    Mother: <u>Ok</u>, <u>yes</u> then. She's <u>crazy</u>. She's as <u>crazy</u> as they <u>come</u>.
                 She's a <u>lun</u>atic.
                 (...........)

    Daughter: What <u>is</u> it exactly. Did I <u>say</u> something sometime, or (...........)
110   did she see me have a <u>fit</u> n's afraid I might
                 have an<u>oth</u>er one if she came <u>over</u> or <u>what</u>.
                 (...............)

    Mother: I <u>guess</u>.
                 (...................)

115	Daughter:	You guess <u>what</u>. (..........) <u>What's</u> she ever <u>said</u>. (........) She <u>must</u>
		have given you <u>some</u> reason.
		(...................)
	Mother:	Hhhh Your <u>hands</u> are <u>cold</u>.
		(..........)
120	Daughter:	What difference does <u>that</u> make.
		(........)
	Mother:	Like a <u>corpse</u>, she <u>says</u>. (higher voice) an' <u>I'm</u> gonna <u>be</u>
		one soon <u>enough</u> as it i:s.
		(..........)
125	Daughter:	I thought she didn't <u>like</u> me. She's <u>scared</u> of me.
		(..........)
	Mother:	<u>She's cra:zy.</u>
	Daughter:	Well <u>how</u> 'bout <u>that</u>. Scared of <u>me</u>. (.......................................)
		When <u>I'm</u> in the <u>hospital</u> does she come over <u>here?</u>
130		(..........)
	Mother:	<u>Her</u> kitchen's just a <u>tiny</u> thing. When she comes over <u>here</u>
		she <u>feels</u> like (..) Well, we <u>all</u> like a
		change o' <u>scene</u>, <u>don't</u> we.
	Daughter:	<u>Sure</u> we do. <u>Plus</u> there are no <u>birds</u> <u>divin</u> a<u>round</u>.
135	Mother:	I:: <u>hate those birds</u>. She says I don't under<u>stand</u> them.
		What's there to under<u>stand</u> about <u>birds</u>.
	Daughter:	<u>Why</u> Agnes <u>likes</u> them for <u>one</u> thing? (................) <u>Why</u> they stay
		with <u>her</u> when they could be outsi:de with the other
		<u>birds</u>? How much <u>water</u> they need? What their <u>singing</u>
140		<u>means</u>? How they <u>fly</u>? What they think <u>Agnes</u> is?
		(...................)
	Mother:	Why d'you have to <u>know</u> so <u>much</u> about things, <u>Jesse</u>?
		<u>There's</u> just not that much <u>to</u> things that <u>I</u> could ever
		<u>see</u>.
145	Daughter:	That you could ever <u>tell</u>, you mean. (.....) <u>You</u> didn't have

	to <u>lie</u> to me about <u>Agnes</u>?
Mother:	<u>I</u> didn't <u>lie</u>? (..............) You never <u>asked</u> me before.
Daughter:	<u>You lied</u> about settin <u>fire</u> to all those <u>houses</u>, 'n bout

<u>You lied</u> about settin <u>fire</u> to all those <u>houses</u>, 'n bout
how many <u>birds</u> she had? (.....) bout how much <u>ok</u>ra she
eats? 'n why she won't come <u>over</u> here? (.............) If I have
to keep dra:gging the <u>truth</u> out of you, this is gonna
take all <u>night</u>.

150

(..........)

Mother: That's fi:ne with me, I'm not a <u>bit</u> sleepy.

Read this conversation at least three times to differentiate the two speakers, get the gist of their conversational topics, and sketch the contours of their emotional relationship. Then, as you did with the earlier transcript, try pairing up with a classmate to perform the conversation aloud. Use the vocal markings to guide inflection, pause, and emphasis, imitating the original utterances as best you can.

This conversation has a lot in common with the first one. Here, too, the interaction is between a mother and a daughter. Both relationships are stretched and tested through instances of harmless deception. Both touch on the topics of money, death, sickness, and gossip. Notice, too, that this mother and daughter use many of the same performance techniques in face-to-face conversation that their counterparts did over the telephone. Once again, you will find the principles of *world, effect, sense,* and *genre* informing an understanding of this language and its performance.

However, there is a big difference between the two conversations. The first one came from life; the second one came from literature. The telephone call was naturally occurring talk, tape-recorded, and only then looked at through the frame of literary performance. The kitchen conversation *began* as dramatic art, was preserved on film, and only now offers itself as an instance of everyday interaction. In the latter case, words were *written* by Marsha Norman, *published* as a play called '*Night Mother*, and *spoken* by professional actors Ann Bancroft and Sissy Spacek in a movie.* Vocabulary, syntax, and grammar were penned by a playwright; inflections, pauses, and emphasis were performed by actors. Even though one conversation involved the language of life and the other the language of literature, notice that you make sense of both in precisely the same way. Vocalized words are situated in the complex dynamics of a human relationship. When you perform another's language, precise distinctions begin to blur between reality and fiction, ordinary and literary, life and art.

*With permission of Universal Studios.

Making a Difference

In our two examples you can see important differences, as well as similarities, between the languages of life and literature. First, let's catalog some interesting distinctions between the naturally occurring conversation of "It's Gun Be Hard to Do" and the artistically constructed dialogue of 'Night Mother. Before paying attention to the words themselves, take careful note of the performance markings in these two scripts. The first mother and daughter use more complicated vocal techniques than do their counterparts in the play. The characters in 'Night Mother never speak simultaneously, and only once (line 118) do they communicate through nonlinguistic noises. Both things happen often in "It's Gun Be Hard to Do." Note, too, that conversational repair, or self-correction, occurs frequently in the live talk (e.g., in lines 13, 14, 15, 25, and 39) but only once in the film scene (line 132).

These observations are drawn from only two transcripts and are not meant to suggest defining differences between the vocalizations of everyday and literary language. We can generalize from them, however, that literature, when it attempts to imitate real-life conversation, is likely to *simplify* the complexities of everyday talk. The difference between the two is not one of kind but of degree. Professional actors who are trained to give voice and body to literature do not rely on any techniques other than those used by all of us in life. Authors and actors merely *select* from the inventory of naturally occurring speech those performance techniques that suit their artistic purpose.

Consider now the overall organizations of these two conversational transcripts. In structure, as well as in performance, the literary selection is simpler than everyday talk. Topics of conversation in the real-life example shift much more rapidly than in the movie scene. The first mother and daughter juggle at least four subjects: (1) visiting their friend Jan, (2) looking at a ranch, (3) life with John, and (4) Barry's sickness. They alternate easily among them, but not in any straightforward or simple way. In the second example, taken from literature, only three topics—Agnes, cocoa, and lying—are fitted together, and in a much simpler progression. Even the introduction of the third topic, the mother's lying, might be seen as an extension of the first, Agnes. This playwright's structure, like her actors' performance, borrows techniques from everyday communication. However, the artistic treatment simplifies what occurs naturally. Neither author nor performer adds a single new strategy to the catalog of everyday communication techniques. Rather, the verbal art of literature, whether presented on the page or on the stage, is constructed of hand-me-down materials drawn from common human experience.

But what of the characters themselves? Are the fictional characters in 'Night, Mother really more complicated than the real ones in "It's Gun Be Hard to Do?" Richard Stern, novelist and literary critic, maintains that even here art simplifies life:

Fictional characters are simpler than the simplest real person; every day contains so many thoughts, impressions, and gestures that the most complicated character in literature can never be given a hundredth of them. The made-up characters of fiction . . . are made to appear complex and complete because they answer every—narrative—question asked of them.

(One Person and Another, p. 3)

J. L. Austin, a philosopher of language, described literature and its performance as "parasitic" to the language of everyday life, deriving its essence from the ordinary. He argued that the literary parasite caused no damage to its host but, at the same time, returned nothing *new* to it. We emphasize the same point when we suggest that the performance of literary language calls on no *new* skills other than those used to communicate the language of life. Our entire approach demonstrates that performing the languages of life and literature can be mutually enhancing, that a knowledge of one can enrich the other.

We've begun this study of language with examples of dialogue in the forms of a telephone conversation and a filmed scene, because drama seems to bear the closest resemblance to our everyday talk. Later, when we include lyric and narrative interactions in our analysis, you will still require no new knowledge or skill other than what you already possess. By heightening the awareness of your everyday performance skills, you can select those that are most applicable to a particular work of literature. You can draw on personal experience to gain entry into the literary worlds of plays, poems, and stories.

Realizing Language

"To realize" something can mean (1) to grasp it or to understand it clearly, (2) to make it real, or (3) to bring it vividly before the mind. All three senses of the verb describe the aim of performing literature. To take lifeless print from a page and to convert it into human speech is what we mean by realizing language. To know what a character is thinking, how she feels, and what motivates her when saying, "You lied about settin' fire to all those houses," claims a different level of knowledge than merely reading words. This more intimate realization is available only through enactment. Performance is a method for improving your ability to realize the language of literature. When performing a dramatic dialogue before the class, you are uttering (that is, "outering") the work of your imagination, revealing to others the strengths, weaknesses, and idiosyncrasies of your reading. But performance does more than show how well you've read. In rehearsing for public performance, you realize aspects of the literature your silent reading neglected. Performance, then, is both a method of discovery and a means of demonstration. Ann Bancroft and Sissy Spacek realized the words on the page of Marsha Norman's script by finding in them the reality of a human relationship and by adding to them the nuance of human speech.

The worlds of "It's Gun Be Hard to Do" and 'Night, Mother are entirely the products of language in performance. You have no other access to them apart from the words on the page. We stress this point because good performance depends on a reader's ability to evoke an entire world from, through, and in language. Words trigger your senses, emotions, memories, and thoughts. With the aid of these invisible tools, your imagination creates a highly visible world. Performance is our method of construction. The worlds of literature, like the everyday world, are composed fundamentally of *people, places, things,* and *events.* Language points to all of these and, in doing so, allows our imaginations to realize them. Performers are more apt to describe these elements as *characters, scenes, props,* and *actions.*

By reading and enacting the words of 'Night, Mother, you have already begun to conceive its people, places, things, and events. No doubt, you have a mental image of the two main characters—what they look like, what clothes they are wearing, how their voices sound. If you compare these mental images around the class, you may not find full consensus, but you are likely to reach fundamental agreement. Although you may not agree on the daughter's exact age, for instance, no one is likely to argue that she is a child. Although you may differ in characterizations of the mother, no reader of this scene is likely to find her cold, hard, or vindictive. You will probably agree, as well, that this conversation takes place in a kitchen. Whatever action may be going on, it will be action appropriate to a kitchen.

From these fairly easy observations, you have probably taken the creation of a literary world beyond what's certain to what's probable. The kitchen, in your imagination, must be located in a particular house of a certain design, style, and period. You may even have determined, consciously or unconsciously, that this home, with these characters, may be located in a specific state or region. Here's a simple test of the work already conducted by your imagination. If we were to assert that the conversation of 'Night, Mother actually takes place in a school cafeteria in Hong Kong, you would probably revise your mental images radically. This indicates that your imagination had already constructed a world.

The reality evoked by the talk of these two women includes all the elements constituting a world: places, people, things, and actions. We come to know Agnes so well, in fact, that you might even envision her physically, although she is not actually present in the scene. This world is cluttered with things (houses, cars, birds, fairs, and plastic whistles) and teeming with activities (attending fairs, burning houses, visiting friends, and keeping birds). When conceiving the world of this conversation, you are not engaged in some passive activity. Your imagination has done something rather spectacular; it has created a world from nothing more than words and a few traces of performance.

To get *inside* the world of this drama, you need to take on the personalities and perspectives of the two characters by enacting their voices and bodies. Look again at the opening of this conversation. Try two different performances of the first three lines, and listen to the changing effect of language.

Daughter: Well? So? how's the fair.

And now try this version:

Daughter: Well? (...............) So? (..........) how's the fair.

Compare the two performances of the daughter's opening line. In the first version, the absence of pauses suggests that the daughter is eager for news of the fair. In the second performance, the daughter's pauses are there perhaps because she wants to get the conversation going. To merely say, "Well? So?" without giving the mother a chance to respond is not an invitation to casual conversation; it is a demand for information.

To determine the effect of language in a particular situation, you must ask the question why: "Why does this speaker say these words in this way at this time?" Or, to put it another way, "What motivates the speaker?" For example, in the short exchange quoted above, why does the mother respond immediately to her daughter's question: "How's the fair?" Why does the daughter pause after her mother says that country fairs are silly? What motivates the daughter to ask, "Why'd you go?"

Pause is just one performance clue to an intended effect. Another, as in line 16, could be the way a speaker draws out a particular word.

Mother: She's really crazy.
Daughter: Mother:::

Your already acquired command of everyday language should suggest *why* the daughter performs "mother:::" and what effect she wants that word to have.

So far in this discussion of effect, we have been examining individual lines. But these lines always reflect an overall effect, a goal or intention a speaker has throughout the conversation. In "It's Gun Be Hard," the mother had an overall intention: to talk her daughter into visiting Jan. In 'Night, Mother, the mother indulges in a wildly exaggerated description of her friend Agnes. In lines 86–88, she explains her own strange performance by specifying the effect she wants her words to have: "I only told you about it because I thought I might get a laugh out of you for once." Such explicit statements of effect are rare in conversation and only occur in this situation because the daughter demands some explanation.

As clear as the mother's desired effect may be, it's harder to determine when that intention begins to take control or shape the conversation. At the beginning, it's the daughter who works to get things going. Somewhere in the first twenty lines the mother seems to formulate her intention. Can you say precisely when, in Bancroft's performance, the idea of cheering her daughter up occurs to the mother? What significance do you attach to each of the mother's pauses in those first twenty lines? Why do you think they diminish in length and frequency after line 18? Can you explain how the mother's overall intention affects performance of particular lines in this conversation? Our transcript records the decisions of one performer, Ann Bancroft. If you were to develop your own performance of Marsha Norman's play, as opposed to imitating Bancroft's, the mother might realize her intention at a different moment or in a different way.

Turning to the daughter's overall intention, we discover that she wants more than a cheerful conversation with her mother. She wants the truth. As early as line 16, she begins to insist on it. The daughter's frequent pauses, every time her mother tells something new about Agnes, coupled with her insistent questions, demonstrate a relentless determination to produce her desired effect. Like the mother's admission of intent in lines 86–88, the daughter is frank about the effect she wants in her last line.

In two different conversations—one drawn from everyday talk and the other from literature—we have witnessed a clash of wills between mother and daughter. Your analysis of effect or motivation is probably the most important key to unlocking the structure of each dialogue. In whatever literary genres you perform—drama, narrative fiction, or poetry—a speaker's intended effect always serves as a crucial clue to realizing literature.

In addition to constructing the world of language and determining the intentions of its speakers, you should also note how performers communicate sense. Although performers use a number of different techniques to control sense, for now we want you to focus on just one—*emphasis*. In both the conversations we have been studying, the speakers give words emphasis by (1) the use of force (_____), (2) length (:::), and (3) rising pitch (?). In everyday talk, we don't consciously think about force, length, or pitch. We think about the idea being communicated, and let our language habits take care of technical matters. Most performers of literary language follow the same rule.

Performers know intuitively *how* to emphasize words. Their problem is not how but *what* words to emphasize. Three rules or factors usually determine where emphasis falls in everyday talk. First, speakers tend to emphasize words that carry what one textbook writer, Wayland Maxfield Parrish, called "the chief freight of meaning."

We:ll just go and try to be as cheerful as possible

I'm meeting a gir:l at two:

It was si:lly.

Second, speakers tend to emphasize words that introduce some new idea, as in

> how's the fair
>
> Country fairs are si:lly

The daughter's forceful rendering of "fair" in the first line represents a change of subject in the conversation; "fair" is a new idea. Her mother's repetition of the word, lacking emphasis, acknowledges "fair" as an echo idea, rather than a new subject. She emphasizes si:lly instead. Repetition often de-emphasizes a word, but it may also deliberately underscore an idea as in "It was si:lly. Country fairs are si:lly."

A third reason for stressing particular words is to strike a comparison or contrast with some other idea, as in

> Now then, one cup or two
>
> They're not real whistles. Just little plastic ones
>
> I thought she didn't like me. She's scared of me.
>
> Why they stay with her when they could be outsi:de

Unlike sense, genre (a particular *kind* of talk) is not indicated by any of the transcription markings. In the dialogue from '*Night, Mother*, the speakers draw on three different genres. Lines 1–7 display the kind of talk we often use to get a conversation going, what theorists call "phatic discourse." This genre contains very little information. Nonetheless, it is important because phatic discourse sets things into motion. A standard opening to conversation,

> Hi. How are you?
>
> I'm fine. And you?

is an instance of phatic discourse. Such greetings usually function simply to get the conversation started without really meaning to inquire about a person's well-being. Sometimes, depending on the circumstances and the relationship, the same words could be loaded with intent, however. Imagine you have recently heard that a friend is seriously ill and decide to call him or her on the phone. "How are you?" in this situation requires quite a different performance than a casual greeting. The difference is one of genre.

After line 7 in the scene from '*Night, Mother*, the genre shifts from phatic discourse to gossip and continues in that vein almost to the end. At least, gossip seems to be what the mother is performing. The daughter participates whole-heartedly, too, until lines 40 and 41, when she steps outside the story being told to her and questions its veracity. It is almost as if she were speaking to herself, rather than to her mother, in a more reflective genre. For the remainder of the conversation, two different kinds of talk weave in and out. The mother tries to stay at the level of gossip, but the daughter shifts to interrogation, and does so with increasing intensity (see lines 45–47, 50, 68–69, 72, 75, 79, 83). In the mother's long speech (lines 85–89), she abandons gossip and yields to her daughter's forceful interrogation, a genre that dominates their conversation up to the moment of highest intensity in lines 145 and 146.

Genre can be a subtle guide to understanding the language of our everyday talk, as well as literature. Until you know what *kind* of talk you are engaged in, you may not be able to say for sure what another person's words mean. When eavesdropping on someone else's conversation (and that's how literature often feels), you may not have a clue to its meaning until you can determine the genre of talk. Is it banter? Scolding? Ridicule? However, once genre provides its frame of reference, communication—both naturally occurring and artistically created—becomes comprehensible.

Good Reading

We began this chapter with some examples of "reading" and "reading well" to demonstrate the pervasiveness of the reading metaphor in our everyday lives. But now, after analyzing two examples of talk, we want to complicate the matter. In fact, there are many kinds of good reading. If your objective were to do well on an examination, then good reading of a textbook might mean selecting the right words to highlight. Such a definition would be too simple for our purposes. Or consider reading for self-improvement. Here you might search the text for some lesson or moral to apply to your own life. This approach comes closer to what we mean, but, as a definition, it still falls short. Good reading *for performance* demands vivid realization of what's happening, when, where, why, and to whom. Good reading, for performance, takes us on a journey whose success could never be measured merely by reaching a planned destination. The goodness of reading, as we use the word, depends on the performer's engagement and the intensity of the journey itself.

Good reading, whether of literature or of life, must situate you *inside* the vitality of a particular world, and performance is a literal means of getting you there. The language of our everyday conversations, as well as the words in literature, make reference to a concrete world. In a sense, we could say that language *creates* that world. More precisely, *you*, the reader, create a world through language.

When two or more students perform the same conversation in class, it becomes apparent that each has read the passage somewhat differently. Performance, because it makes a reader's constructed world plain for all to see, can reveal the relative strength of one conception or another. But what makes for a stronger or weaker imaginative creation? To answer this question, let's look again at 'Night, Mother and focus on one specific action.

If we believe this conversation is taking place in a kitchen, mother and daughter have to be doing something. Our knowledge of everyday life tells us that people seldom stand around in a kitchen talking for as long as this without doing something else. If you are performing the mother, you might imagine that, while talking, she's putting away some things she had bought at the fair. When reading line 33 ("Now then, one cup or two?"), you must go back and revise your conception of the action. The mother wouldn't say this line, in all likelihood, unless she had been making some kind of drink for her daughter all the while they'd been talking. By line 35, you come to realize that it's not soup or coffee or tea that she is making; it's possibly hot chocolate. Not until line 94 can you be certain that the drink being prepared is definitely cocoa.

As simple as this example may be, it illustrates one fundamental principle of performance: an individual reader's creation of a world must accommodate what is given in the text. If you want to enact *this* conversation, the mother cannot be making Cup-of-Soup. She must be making cocoa. That's a given. If, on the other hand, you are performing the daughter, it's quite possible that you may be folding clothes, helping your mother, or engaged in some other plausible action. The text doesn't specify what the daughter is doing. At the same time, you couldn't imagine her doing just anything. What you come to know of the relationship between these two characters rules out certain things. For instance, because we know that the daughter is intent on learning the truth from her mother, she probably wouldn't be sitting casually in a chair and thumbing through a magazine while talking.

A particular language world—constructed from the given circumstances of a text supplemented by the fillings-in of your imagination—provides cues to its own strong performance. From within the language world, you can determine not only *what* to do but *how* to do it. Once again, if you are performing the mother, you are making cocoa from the beginning of the scene until the moment when you determine that she finishes the task. But *how* you prepare the cocoa makes a difference. It makes a difference to the daughter, who is the mother's audience within the scene. It also makes a difference to your audience. How you prepare the cocoa should underscore what's going on in the relationship between characters. If a performer were to subordinate language to the activity of making cocoa and, thus, communicate to an audience that this scene is *about making cocoa*, we should agree that such a performance is weaker than another where making cocoa helps us understand the scene as being *about a mother and daughter relationship*.

Physicalizing a text takes rehearsal, and your rehearsals of action should concentrate on two objectives: (1) to repeat the action often enough that it becomes natural and easy for the character to do, and (2) to use the action in every way possible to underscore the meaning of words. Ultimately, your concentration must be where the character's attention is. In this conversation, both mother and daughter are concentrating on each other. Our interest as audience is in the unfolding of that relationship. Language and action are intimately linked in the creation of their world.

A performer needs to be double-minded, believing in the scene being performed and, simultaneously, standing back from it to communicate with an audience. For the character in the scene, cocoa goes into a *pan*. For the performer on stage, a prop (cocoa) goes into another prop (pan). Pan/Prop is an instance of the performer's double-mindedness. It points to the larger principle we have been pursuing: believing and communicating are inextricably bound together in the performance of literature, as well as in everyday interactions.

EXERCISE & DISCUSSION

Return to the first twenty-five lines of the conversation from *'Night, Mother*, and imagine you are performing the mother. The text dictates that you are making cocoa, but how you do this is entirely your decision. Assume that, just before delivering the first line, you have added the final ingredient to the cocoa pan on the kitchen countertop. Now you have several actions still remaining—stirring, turning on the burner, lifting the pan to the stovetop, placing it on the burner, more stirring, and, perhaps, tasting. Rehearse the mother's first six speeches, and decide exactly when you wish to execute each action.

Through experimentation, trial and error, decide when to stir, when to stop, and when to stir again. Remember, you want the action to be a communication aid. Let your cocoa-making reflect and underscore the changing dynamics of conversation. (For instance, is there ever a moment when the mother would stop her action, as if in freeze-frame, to give full attention to the daughter?)

Then, after rehearsing the scene privately, let several pairs try their performances out in front of the class. Discuss the communication impact of various approaches to cocoa-making. Concentrate, attaching meaning to even the smallest physical action.

Rehearsing Life

We close this chapter by returning once again to lived experience. By considering two commonplace interactions, we may illustrate the lively interplay among world, effect, sense, and genre in the daily performance of language. First, imagine yourself falling in love with someone. The two of you are well-matched, enjoy sharing your lives together, and take pleasure in a growing intimacy. It feels as if you're committing yourself to something long-term, but that subject has never come up explicitly in the relationship. So, you decide the time has come to address the issue openly. Your intention is to pop the question: "Where are we heading in this relationship?" And, more important, your desired effect is to reach a positive agreement: "I want to make a long-term commitment. How about you?" Hence, long before you enter into conversation with your partner, you have formulated a specific intention and calculated a desired effect. Then, your challenge is to orchestrate an interaction that is most conducive to a positive outcome.

Well in advance of the actual conversation, you begin trying out possible approaches in your mind, finding just the right words to make plain sense and to communicate your feelings and thoughts. For such an important occasion, any old language won't do. You can't risk being misunderstood, so you revise endlessly in your imagination: Shall I begin with this sentence or that? If I use this particular word, what will he or she think? Maybe it would be better to begin another way and lead up to the question. As you contemplate all the options, your trial language and revisions are guided by an overall intention and the sense your partner is likely to make of the words.

Somewhere in this creative process, your concern with individual words enlarges to a consideration of genre. What *kind* of talk will further my intention most effectively? Shall I start off casually and then shift subtly toward seriousness? What if I were to lay an ambush and just fire the question off out of nowhere, bang? What would be the comparative advantages of approaching the subject like a debate case? Maybe I should frame the issue in narrative terms, chronicling the history of our relationship and demonstrating the logic of the next step? Or should I go for the old-time romance of Hollywood, getting down on one knee? Each of these alternatives (and many others come to mind) suggests a different genre of talk. After deciding on your basic approach to performance, more revisions of language are required.

In this hypothetical situation, your intention (effect) has driven you to choose words (sense), and to select a style or kind of talk (genre) to enhance communication effectiveness. All of these decisions demand analysis. They are conditioned by the dynamics of a specific relationship. And, recall, all of them occur in advance of the actual interaction. But you're still not ready to go into action.

This performance, because its success is *so* important to you, requires rehearsal. In fact, you're likely to rehearse for days before the event. When trying things out aloud or in your mind, you imagine all the circumstances of the interaction down to the smallest detail. You choose a setting where the conversation might best occur: in the living room of your apartment? in your car? at a restaurant? You fantasize the best time of day: late at night? early evening? noontime? first thing in the morning? And you imagine some action. Shall I bring up the topic while playing cards? over cocktails? at halftime of the ball game? between the entree and the dessert tray? Oh yes, and what shall I wear? These details, and a myriad of others, create a *world* in which language may become situated and find meaning. Finally, then, you imagine the scene over and over again in your mind, trying out every nuance of expression, moment of timing, gesture or wink, pause or sigh until you get the thing as perfect as possible in rehearsal and feel ready to risk performance.

Apparently, in our everyday communication, the more important an interaction is, the more likely we are to treat it as a performance event: creating world, considering effect, choosing words with care, and determining genre. The more committed we are to achieving an intention, the more driven we are to rehearse.

If you're willing to grant that we approach important moments in everyday relationships as performance events requiring rehearsal, you may still hesitate to draw the full analogy to performance of literature. After all, the argument goes, literature involves a world of make-believe, not *real* life. Consider, then, a second commonplace situation. For this example, you need to reenter the mind of a ten-year-old child.

Imagine a fifth grader, boy or girl, who is told by mother and father to come straight home after school. "No detours to play with friends. No stopping by the park." Despite the stern warning, this child finds it irresistible to spend thirty minutes in the park with friends on the way home. He or she didn't exactly *decide* to break the rules. It just happened. Now, imagine further, that this child doesn't want to pay the price of disobedience when arriving home. He or she decides it would be better to make up some plausible explanation, an alibi that might be believed.

To escape parental wrath, the child composes and rehearses a lie with all the same intensity and creative commitment as the lover in our previous example or the professional actor preparing a part. In the child's case, believability is everything. To produce the desired effect, the child must choose just the right words, deliver them in just the right tone of voice, and display just the right attitude. While hurrying home, the child rehearses every detail in the imagination: how to walk through the back door, what greeting to offer to mother or father, how to begin the story, when to end it, and how to make an exit. The alibi's credibility depends on creating an entire world in language. One mistake of analysis, rehearsal, or performance, and the jig is up.

If you've ever told a calculated lie, recall the painstaking process of composition and execution by which you created the make-believe world in hopes of winning an audience's belief. We suggest this example *not* to recommend an analogy between literature and lying. We suggest it as a commonplace experience in which a child draws instinctively on the same impulses required for adult literary performance. A child, when telling the whopper alibi, demonstrates at least three basic competencies for the performance of literature: the right attitude (wanting to convince an audience), the requisite skill (finding just the right words), and the creative stamina (rehearsing a desired effect).

Summary

Literary performance, like everyday conversation, situates language in the dynamics of a human relationship. The mother–daughter dialogue in Marsha Norman's 'Night, Mother displays the same features of sense, effect, genre, and world as the interaction of "It's Gun Be Hard to Do." Ann Bancroft and Sissy Spacek drew on the same performance techniques to realize language as did the real-life dyad in the first example. The major difference we observe between these two performances is that literary enactment appears somewhat simpler than the everyday exchange.

By juxtaposing everyday and literary performances, our hope has been to establish some basic principles of congruence between life and art. As we turn attention in other chapters to the worlds of literature, we ask you to bring to bear the full inventory of your everyday communication experience, from the automatic dialogue of phatic discourse, to the personal intrigue of gossip, to the calculated risks of lovemaking and lying. The languages of life and literature create their worlds and produce their effects by means of the same basic principles. In both, communication must be embodied in individual human beings. Understanding emerges by grasping how language works within relationships.

Chapter Two

Performing in the World of Language

In the middle of his routine, a popular stand-up comic pauses, stares into space, and then apologizes to the audience: "Excuse me. I just drifted off into my own little world. . . . But it's OK. They know me there." The audience laughs appreciatively, recognizing that we all drift off into our own little worlds, and that people know us there. This comic is not using "world" to mean the earth or the globe. He's referring to what the dictionary describes as "any sphere, realm, or domain, with all pertaining to it." This is the sense in which we shall approach the worlds created by, through, and in language.

How Language Creates Worlds

As anyone knows who has ever enjoyed a story, literature can create an entire world out of language—a sensuous world of space and time, peopled by characters in action. Indeed, a single work of literature can create several worlds. *The Wonderful Wizard of Oz* is a story known to most Americans either in book form or through the movie adaptation. It creates two distinct worlds, Kansas and Oz, which bear no resemblance to each other. Each is a unique "sphere, realm, or domain, with all pertaining to it." The world of Kansas includes cyclones, but it has no bad witches or poppy fields. These are right at home, however, in the world of Oz.

The Wonderful Wizard of Oz is *about* these two different worlds as they are experienced by one character, Dorothy. Throughout the story, the reader or viewer shares Dorothy's perspective, looking at Oz through the more familiar lens of Kansas. The world of Kansas *frames* the world of Oz. Dorothy tries to make sense of her new world in terms of the old.

> *The Witch of the North seemed to think for a time, with her head bowed and her eyes upon the ground. Then she looked up and said, "I do not know where Kansas is, for I have never heard that country mentioned before. But tell me, is it a civilized country?"*
>
> *"Oh, yes," replied Dorothy.*
>
> *"Then that accounts for it. In the civilized countries I believe there are no witches left; nor wizards, nor sorceresses, nor magicians. But, you see, the Land of Oz has never been civilized, for we are cut off from all the rest of the world. Therefore we still have witches and wizards amongst us."*

The two worlds in *The Wonderful Wizard of Oz* are "high definition" because the story gives so many specific details about both Oz and Kansas. Other works of literature, however, may give very few concrete details. A world is only implied, setting a context or frame in which the reader can make sense of the speaker's words.

Our first conversation in Chapter 1, "It's Gun Be Hard to Do," was an example of a low-definition world. The words didn't point directly at a world so much as stand out against an implied setting. Because both mother and daughter were inside their world, they had no need to describe it. As an invisible participant overhearing their conversation, you were left to *infer* a world from clues and hints as they became available. Such inferences are essential to understanding any spoken or written language.

If you read a simple, declarative sentence—"Don't touch that bat!"—without any notion of its context, you can't be certain what the words mean. Place it in some world, however, and the sentence makes sense immediately.

- "Don't touch that bat!" the veteran barked at the rookie, spraying tobacco juice onto the floor of the dugout.

- "Don't touch that bat!" shouted our guide through the Twin Caves.

In some instances, "world" may be the focus of literature or, on other occasions, merely the backdrop for clarifying a speaker's words. In either case, you cannot do without the orienting compass of some explicit or implicit world when coming to terms with language.

Many theorists argue that a reader begins projecting possible worlds from the very first words of a literary text. These projections may require revision as more information becomes available, but you can't enter another's language—whether in literature or in life—without projecting some sense of world. No theorist has ever figured out exactly how readers manage this mysterious construction. For nineteenth-century Romantics, *imagination* was the key for both writer and reader to make something out of language, to give concrete and sensuous form to the words.

It is not surprising that the nineteenth century became one of the great ages of the performer—in music, in theatre, in dance, and on the reading platform. Nor is it surprising that the period produced the most famous acting teacher of the modern age, Konstantin Stanislavsky. Early in his career, Stanislavsky realized that the method by which he had been taught to develop a performance (that is, by imitating other performers) could never produce anything but a pale copy of the original. He believed that the performer should be an active, creative participant in the literary experience. He taught his performers to flesh out the language of literature by reference to their own memories and emotions, and by use of their own bodies and voices.

Many current literary theorists insist, as Stanislavsky did for performers, that any good silent reader must be an active participant in the creative process. Thus, for instance, the German theorist Wolfgang Iser says:

> *A literary text must therefore be conceived in such a way that it will engage the reader's imagination in the task of working things out for himself, for reading is only a pleasure when it is active and creative.*
>
> ["The Reading Process," in Jane Tompkins, ed., *Reader-Response Criticism* (Baltimore: The Johns Hopkins University Press, 1981), p. 51.]

And the American theorist Norman Holland agrees:

That is, all of us, as we read, use the literary work to symbolize and finally to replicate ourself. . . . We interact with the work, making it part of our own psychic economy and making ourselves part of the literary work—as we interpret it.

["Unity, Identity, Text, Self," in Jane Tompkins, ed., *Reader-Response Criticism* (Baltimore: The Johns Hopkins University Press, 1981), p. 124.]

Another American theorist, Stanley Fish, sounds exactly like Stanislavski when the Russian theatre director rebelled against performers imitating each other:

In the old model utterers are in the business of handing over ready-made or prefabricated meanings. These meanings are said to be encoded, and the code is assumed to be in the world independently of the individuals who are obliged to attach themselves to it (if they do not they run the danger of being declared deviant). In my model, however, meanings are not extracted but made and made not by encoded forms but by interpretive strategies that call forms into being.

[*Is There a Text*, pp. 172–173]

The difficulty with all of these statements is their suggestion that you are conscious, while reading, of what the text gives you and what you add to it. In most cases, however, you create an entire world, unconsciously filling in the gaps between what's given. Two different readers of the same text are unlikely even to pronounce all the words in the same way, much less inflect them with the same vocalization, or attribute to them the same meanings.

Nowhere is the creative participation of a reader more apparent than in the performance of literature. Read the following selection from L. Frank Baum's *The Wonderful Wizard of Oz*, and collaborate with its language to create mental images of the world described:

The cyclone had set the house down, very gently—for a cyclone—in the midst of a country of marvelous beauty. There were lovely patches of green sward all about, with stately trees bearing rich and luscious fruits. Banks of gorgeous flowers were on every hand, and birds with rare and brilliant plumage sang and fluttered in the trees and bushes. A little way off was a small brook rushing and sparkling along between green banks, and murmuring in a voice very grateful to a little girl who had lived so long on the dry, gray prairies.

While she stood looking eagerly at the strange and beautiful sights, she noticed coming toward her a group of the queerest people she had ever seen. They were not as big as the grown folk she had always been used to; but neither were they very small. In fact, they seemed about as tall as Dorothy, who was a well-grown child for her age, although they were, so far as looks go, many years older.

Three were men and one a woman, and all were oddly dressed. They wore round hats that rose to a small point a foot above their heads, with little bells around the rims that tinkled sweetly as they moved. The hats of the men were blue; the little woman's hat was white, and she wore a white gown that hung in plaits from her shoulders; over it were sprinkled little stars that glistened in the sun like diamonds. The men were dressed in blue, of the same shade as their hats, and wore well polished boots with a deep roll of blue at the tops. The men, Dorothy thought, were about as old as Uncle Henry, for two of them had beards. But the little woman was doubtless much older: her face was covered with wrinkles, her hair was nearly white, and she walked rather stiffly.

If you have seen the film adaptation of *The Wonderful Wizard of Oz*, chances are your visualization of Baum's description resembles the scene in the movie when Dorothy steps out of her house. If so, your experience is testimony to the power of that particular performance of the world of Oz. Your visualization is evidence of how much your reading is influenced by your remembrance of past experience. If you read hastily, what you visualized may have looked exactly like the scene in the movie. If you read carefully, giving yourself over to Baum's description, there were probably moments in the text that didn't quite fit the memory of the film you were superimposing. If you have never seen the movie, the mental picture sparked by Baum's words was still animated by the particular experiences you brought to the text, though the extent of your contribution may be harder to detect.

What you bring to the words on the page constitutes the creative contribution of the performer. Those influenced by their experience with the movie version can testify to the creative contribution of the makers of that movie. One of the satisfactions of performing literature is the knowledge that you have brought an audience into communion with your own reading of a particular piece of literature. And the *power* of the performer is such that your audience can never encounter that text again without being influenced at least a bit by your performance.

Your creativity as a performer does not give license to present the worlds of literature in any way you want. Nor does the fact that every performance is unique lead to a conclusion that all performances are equally good or valid. No audience can experience your performance of literature unless they can believe in the worlds you create through language. More accurately, they must believe that the world you communicate actually *is* the world of the literature. They needn't believe yours is the only world, but they have to believe it is a possible one. And that can only happen if *you believe* the world you are creating in performance is the world of the text.

"World" is a large category. It includes everything in language, from setting to scene to action. To appear real, any language world must include at least four elements—space, time, a speaker, and a listener. These are the focus of the remainder of this chapter. Refinements of all four elements, as well as their necessary interdependence, are offered as we move to subtler levels of effect, sense, and genre in subsequent chapters.

Space in the Worlds of Literature

Space and time, Einstein taught us, are sometimes impossible to separate. This is so in language as well as in physics. Although intimately connected, space and time manifest themselves in distinct forms and, for the sake of introduction, we'll discuss each one in its own terms. Read the following paragraph from *The Wonderful Wizard of Oz*. It's how the book opens and, except for incidental markers, time seems to stop as the description unfolds.

> *Dorothy lived in the midst of the great Kansas prairies, with Uncle Henry, who was a farmer, and Aunt Em, who was the farmer's wife. Their house was small, for the lumber to build it had to be carried by wagon many miles. There were four walls, a floor and a roof, which made one room; and this room contained a rusty looking cooking stove, a cupboard for the dishes, a table, three or four chairs, and the beds. Uncle Henry and Aunt Em had a big bed in one corner, and Dorothy had a little bed in another corner. There was no garret at all, and no cellar—except a small hole, dug in the ground, called a cyclone cellar, where the family could go in case one of those great whirlwinds arose, mighty enough to crush any building in its path. It was reached by a trap-door in the middle of the floor, from which a ladder led down into the small, dark hole.*

Space, in the world of literature, usually presents itself in the homelier notion of *place* or a succession of places. In the first sentence of the paragraph quoted, three characters are introduced in relation to the region where they live, namely the great Kansas prairies. If you know the plot of the whole story, you can appreciate how much information Baum packs into these opening words, and how necessary it is for the reader to pay close attention. The paragraph deals with the house, but this is no *mere* description. Inside the world of the house live three people, and outside the house swirls the violent foreshadowing of a future dis*place*ment. Soon enough, Dorothy and her whole house will be carried into a different world.

When an author presents such details, it is hard to believe he didn't intend for you to construct a precise mental image of the house situated in its Kansas landscape. Baum uses the lens of your imagination to snap a sequence of pictures, with the words pointing first here and then there. His first photograph is of the house from a distance, with the viewer standing outside it. Then he moves inside the house to see the single room from various close-up angles. He arranges an album of very specific still-shots—stove, cupboard, chairs, table, beds—and then stands back to snap a picture of the whole room.

A camera analogy, although admittedly crude, may be helpful for understanding one type of creative collaboration between writer and reader in the imaginative construction of space. We must move beyond it, however, to appreciate the dynamism and flexibility of your mind when responding to the spatial representations of language. When Baum describes the cyclone cellar, apparently incidentally, you must leap away from the immediate scene to consider the prospects of an actual cyclone. This movement is accomplished so easily that you're probably unconscious of how language has transported you. If a camera tried to achieve this in such a short time—even a movie camera—the jump-cuts from cellar to cyclone and back again would draw undue attention to themselves.

The kind of reading we're describing notices detail and takes time. Speed-reading or skimming may be beneficial for other purposes, but a performer is obliged to read slowly. Collaboration with a text is impossible at the breakneck rate of speed-reading. In performance, the goal of reading is not to see how quickly your mind can absorb information, but how thoroughly your senses can integrate language into the construction of an entire world.

Studying the language of everyday life can help you understand the slower motion of literary performance versus rapid reading. When you engage in casual conversation, your rates of delivery and listening are measured by the clock of *speech* communication. Rate is determined by the speaker's desire to focus a listener's attention, by intuitive strategies for leading the listener to follow what you're saying. Our description of one reader's attention to the opening sentences of *Oz* argues for an understanding of the paragraph as human speech, not as print on a page. A reader's mind, when co-creating a literary experience through language, is engaged in a performance, not a rapid calculation.

Return momentarily to a scene from "It's Gun Be Hard to Do," and listen to the mother describing one sense of place:

Mother: =Misha said she didn't wanna

invest in anything that wasn't- on the- on the water you know

either a ·hhhhh la:ke or something: recreational.

Like the author of *Oz*, this mother is trying to get her listener to visualize a specific place. Her spontaneous way of doing this is to visualize the scene for herself. Obviously, she hasn't thought out this description in advance because her attempt is full of pauses and corrections. The point is that she could not hope to get her daughter to see *what* she means unless the mother herself sees *where* she means. The clear hint for you in this example is to learn to see what language describes for yourself, in the moment of performance, to invite the co-creation of place with an audience.

So far, we have talked about language and space as though visualization were the sole concern of a speaker. Visualization is not the end but the means of communication, however. Notice the daughter's reactions in the following exchange with her mother:

Daughter: (........) cause John and I are planning on

buyin some land, and we're gonna live on

about ten acres.

(........)

Mother: At Llano:=

Daughter: =No::. not at Llano: Wherever we end u:p

we're going to cause I'm gonna have a- all

kinds of animals.

Ignore the mother's teasing for a moment, and focus on the daughter's performance. She begins by suggesting a general space and specifying its size, "about ten acres." She stops. Then the mother fills in the gap with a concrete place, Llano, which the daughter rejects emphatically. Instead, she offers additional details about the place she has in mind. The daughter seems to be impressing on her mother that the specific place isn't so important as its character or ambience. She cares most about what the place is going to *feel* like.

Llano is all wrong from the daughter's point of view because her mother isn't getting into the quality of space that she is visualizing. There must be room to raise animals there. That's what's important to the daughter. She isn't trying to communicate a specific scene so much as to create an imagined space large enough to accommodate the kind of life she and John are planning.

In literature, no less than in life, writers hope to convey more than a snapshot of a place. They want to create its ambience. To understand any speaker's language, you must enter fully into his or her world, inhabiting a specific place with *all that pertains to it.*

Here's a poem which, by its title alone, you might predict features place. Read it through slowly, paying particular attention to the sensuous details. Gather an insider's feel for the world co-created.

"At the IGA: Franklin, New Hampshire"

by Jane Kenyon

(Copyright Jane Kenyon, 1989. Originally published in Ontario Review *and, subsequently, in the* Pushcart Prize Anthology, XV, 393–394.)

This is where I would shop
if my husband worked felling trees
for the mill, hurting himself badly
from time to time; where I would bring
my three kids; where I would push
one basket and pull another
because the boxes of diapers and cereal
and gallon milk jugs take so much room.

I would already have put the clothes
in the two largest washers next door
at the Norge Laundry Village. Done shopping,
I'd pile the wet wash in trash bags
and take it home to dry on the line.

And I would think, hanging out the baby's
shirts and sleepers, and cranking the pully
away from me, how it would be
to change lives with someone,
like the woman who came after us
in the checkout, thin, with lots of rings
on her hands, who looked us over openly.

Things would have been different
if I hadn't let Bob climb on top of me
for ninety seconds in 1979.
It was raining lightly in the state park
and so we were alone. The charcoal fire
hissed as the first drops fell. . . .
In ninety seconds we made this life—

A trailer on a windy hill, dangerous jobs
in the woods or night work at the packing plant;
Roy, Kimberly, Bobby; too much in the hamper,
never enough in the bank.

From the title and first line alone, we know that place will play a major role in the world of this poem's language. One good starting point when you're developing a performance will be to concentrate on *where* a poem is set. In broad strokes, you could divide up the lines in this poem according to changes of scene:

1. This is where I would shop if my husband worked felling trees for the mill, hurting himself badly from time to time; where I would bring my three kids; where I would push one basket and pull another because the boxes of diapers and cereal and gallon milk jugs take so much room.

2. I would already have put the clothes in the two largest washers next door at the Norge Laundry Village. Done shopping, I'd pile the wet wash in trash bags

3. and take it home to dry on the line. And I would think, hanging out the baby's shirts and sleepers, and cranking the pully away from me, how it would be to change lives with someone,

4. like the woman who came after us in the checkout, thin, with lots of rings on her hands, who looked us over openly.

5. Things would have been different if I hadn't let Bob climb on top of me for ninety seconds in 1979. It was raining lightly in the state park and so we were alone. The charcoal fire hissed as the first drops fell. . . . In ninety seconds we made this life—

6. a trailer on a windy hill,

7. dangerous jobs in the woods

8. or night work at the packing plant;

9. Roy, Kimberly, Bobby; too much in the hamper,

10. never enough in the bank.

Arranging the poem like this, as a sequence of different places, helps one to see the picture album of this woman's existence. When you begin rehearsing the lines, however, you must climb inside each photograph to become fully aware of its sense of place. Let's walk through one approach to preparing this literature for performance.

Start by finding your own space—someplace at least as large as the performance area in your classroom where you'll present the poem. Choose a spot where you think the speaker could be to say the words in section 1. Standing in that spot, try to see what she must be seeing when she speaks. Don't settle for the first image that comes to mind or for some out-of-focus picture. Experiment with different, specific images, filling in the gaps inferred by what the language gives you.

Move (literally walk) to a new spot each time you get to a new place in the poem. Try to identify each performance area with a particular scene in the poem. Hence, sections 1 and 4 will be played in the same performance space. By this rehearsal technique—and it's only one of many you could try—you are equating performance spaces with poetic places. The exercise feels awkward at first, as when a play's director blocks a scene ("cross downstage left," or "take three steps right"), and the movements feel mechanical to the actor. Repeat the poem, using your assigned spaces, as often as necessary to make the movement flow smoothly and feel natural for the speaker. Even if your actual performance uses none of the space assignments or blocking movements of this type rehearsal, it helps you sort through the spatial dimensions of the poem.

No matter how many times you practice, some of the movements we're recommending are likely to remain awkward. This is so, in part, because some of the places referred to in the poem are more vivid to the speaker than others. They are not all equal. Nor is she seeing things with equal vividness in each place. For instance, in sections 9 and 10, it's doubtful that the speaker takes much effort to visualize Roy, Kimberly, Bobby, the hamper, or the bank in very specific terms. These are not such concrete visualizations as, say, the Norge Laundry Village, the gallon milk jugs, the baby's shirts and sleepers, or the thin woman in the checkout line with lots of rings on her hands. To shift places literally between sections 9 and 10 in the final performance may not help your audience, because it draws their attention not to the change of place, but to the communicative strategy itself. Still, many experienced performers find it helpful to exaggerate scene shifts at first, and then experiment with less obtrusive strategies later.

In section 1, on the other hand, literal movement may be important to getting a feel for the poem's language world. The first word, "This," is a demonstrative pronoun pointing the audience's imagination to a specific place. You needn't handle all shifts of space in the same way in performance. The poem itself offers instructions and clues to your common sense when assigning relative values to different places.

The first scene shift, between sections 1 and 2, presents a special problem for the performer. If you moved at the beginning of section 2, locating the speaker in an area representing the Norge Laundry Village, then the phrase "in the two largest washers next door" wouldn't make any sense. You *are* next door already. On the other hand, if you merely gesture to indicate "next door," then the audience sees you remaining in the IGA. As a third possibility, you could wait to move until "done shopping." But this presents a problem, too, because you haven't enough words to cover a long move to a new place.

One solution to the dilemma might be to perform the reference to the laundromat by a shift in posture or attitude of the speaker's body. In section 1, you could indicate place by looking around and pretending to see what the woman describes. In section 2, while remaining in the same space, you could gesture to the store next door after the words "done shopping." Using this strategy, you would need to perform in such a way that your audience knows the speaker has left the IGA mentally and is now imagining another scene.

This single example of spatial performance actually raises a major problem in the poem as a whole. Not only is the speaker in the IGA when she imagines the laundromat next door, but physically she remains in the grocery store from the beginning to the end of her poetic utterance. In her first sentence, the speaker establishes a conditional mood: "This is where I would shop *if.* . . ." For the entire first half of the poem, everything expressed points to a condition contrary to fact. Her statement implies that the speaker doesn't, in fact, shop at the IGA, isn't married to the husband referred to, doesn't take her laundry out, and so forth. By the end, of course, you can feel more certain that the speaker is describing herself, the earlier conditional mood notwithstanding.

Given the complex weave of verbal, mental, and spatial dynamics in this poem, what's a performer to do? Should you place the entire poem in the IGA? How faithful should you remain to your literal analysis of scene shifts in the poem? One answer may lie in what we saw Frank Baum doing in the opening paragraph of *The Wonderful Wizard of Oz*. He invited the audience, in the fashion of a roving camera, to see the scenes he was describing. We were not so much in the presence of the speaker as in the place to which the speaker referred, namely, Dorothy's house.

While "At the IGA" poses challenges a bit more complicated than those in Baum's opening paragraph, the audiences for both speakers give over their imaginations to the language presented by the texts. The literal scene in the IGA starts the speaker thinking. You, as audience, go where the speaker's thoughts take her—to the laundromat, to the clothesline, to the state park. The poem's structure lays out a roadmap, which helps you go with it. Your ultimate performance choices have to establish the reality of several imagined locations while, at the same time, allowing the natural fluidity of this speaker's thinking.

After the last words of the poem have been uttered, it's probable that the speaker's consciousness returns to the literal IGA, and it might be a nice touch for a performance to return to that scene just after the final words. By such a strategy, you would reinforce the IGA as a frame for all the other scenes in the poem. This is a common ploy in movies that begin with someone telling a story, dissolve to enactment of the tale being told, and then return to the scene of the telling at the end.

Explorations of space lead inevitably to other dimensions of a literary work. Even in this discussion of a first rehearsal, we have had to consider elements of the poem and of its performance beyond place. It was easy enough, in this poem at least, to spot where changes in location occur. However, as we saw in sections 2 and 10, whether or not you choose to perform those changes through movement depends on what's happening in the speaker's mind and where you want to concentrate the audience's attention. And none of our considerations of place answer the question of why the first half of the poem is presented as condition contrary to fact, while the second half isn't. Space can never be fully isolated in a literary analysis or performance because, in literature as in life, place is the stage setting for human action and perception. Space is where living *takes place.*

As one indication of just how important place is to human experience, you need only remember the terror of waking up from a nightmare. Your heart races. You perspire. You're disoriented by the horrific images of your dream. The way a person calms down from a nightmare is *not* to ask what it means, at least not initially. One does not even ask "Who am I?" The way a person calms down from the terror of a nightmare is to ask, "*Where* am I?" Only when you can answer that question—I'm in my own bed, or I'm in a hotel room in New Orleans—can you put a frame of reference around the nightmare experience and see it for what it is. Where am I, a question of *place,* is fundamentally linked to Who am I, a question of character.

Exercise & Discussion

Try an approach similar to the way we walked through "At the IGA" with the following piece. After reading it several times, divide the prose into shorter sections depicting shifts in place. Then, as a class, improvise a workshop in movement, blocking your understanding of place in this piece. After rehearsal, discuss the questions that follow the story.

From "I'm Bound to Follow the Longhorn Cows"

by Dave Hickey

(Copyright © Dave Hickey, first published in Riata, *Spring, 1963. Anthologized in* South by Southwest, *University of Texas Press, 1986.)*

When the white sun had spun into the pupil of the sky, as it hung at the top of its trajectory between the two horizons and then began to fall into early afternoon, the old man found himself trapped in a bathtub of tepid water on the second floor of his ancient house. He flailed about for a few moments and then he became quiet and listened to the long winds shushing through the empty corridors and rooms of his house, which was Victorian in design, having two stories, an attic, a storm cellar, spires, lightning rods, weather vanes, cupolas, traceries, and an occasional leaded window; it rested on the plain like a child's block dropped on an immense crazy quilt, patched with green and yellow, an old house, but the interior had been completely modernized, and the bathroom in which the old man sat was paneled with cool blue tile.

He had seen ninety summers, as the Comanches, who were gone now, would say, and he was the only person in the surrounding country who was older than the house. On the old man's first birthday his father had driven four stakes into a bald ridge on the prairie, and began to lay the foundation, and the old man had grown up with the house. It was part of all his memories, the nucleus of his childhood, the point of departure and the point of return for the many journeys of his youth and manhood, for, during his first half-century, the old man had been a rambler and a heller. But unfortunately, unlike his house, the old man could not be modernized, except by the use of what he called "contraptions," his false teeth, his electric wheelchair.

QUESTIONS FOR DISCUSSION

1. At the beginning of this chapter, we talked about space in *The Wonderful Wizard of Oz* in terms of photography—both still-shots and motion pictures portraying a descriptive passage. If you apply the camera analogy to this section of "I'm Bound to Follow the Longhorn Cows," what pictures seem most vivid to the speaker? What pictures are most important to the reader? If you were assigned to create a pictorial representation of this part of the story, would you choose to shoot a photo album of still-shots or a motion picture using filmic techniques? What is it about the narration of the story that leads you in one direction or the other?

2. Regardless of whether you choose to think of the imagery of this passage in photographic or cinematic terms, *sequence* is a major strategy for telling the story. Can you explain why each new picture or image occurs when it does? If you were making a photo album, what difference would it make to the passage if you changed the sequence of pictures? If you were editing a movie, what difference would it make to the final cut if you altered the sequence of shots? Speculate on the logic informing this author's choices of imagery and sequence.

3. Divide the class into teams of four or five students each, and experiment with rehearsal possibilities for this scene. How might you perform it, paying special attention to space? Are there points in your rehearsal of the passage where movement from one place to another seems awkward? Seems excessive? Why is this so? (Try a rehearsal using two performers, one playing the old man and the other playing the speaker of these words. As the speaker, where would you stand in relation to the old man? Would you stay there from begin-

ning to end?) In class discussion, compare the approaches taken by each rehearsal team.

4. Can you describe the difference in the feel or function of the settings in this passage from the feel or function of place in "At the IGA?"

Time in the Worlds of Literature

Language is inextricably bound to time. Words shed old meanings and take on new ones over time. Sentences demand verbs and, at least in the English language, verbs always mark time. The very utterance of words, whether through speaking or writing, takes time. You cannot write or read, talk or listen outside of time's constraints. Likewise, time measures both the segments and the continuities of our everyday lives, no less in literature than in life. The world of a poem, a story, or a play is as dependent upon time as upon space. Space is easier to talk about because it displays itself in the tangible form of place, but time is invisible. We mark its passing but never its presence. Eudora Welty, the American novelist and short story writer, spoke to the relationship between time and space in the language world of a novel:

> Time and place, the two bases of reference upon which the novel, in seeking to come to grips with human experience, must depend for its validity, operate together, of course. They might be taken for granted as ordinary factors, until the novelist at his work comes to scrutinize them apart.
>
> Place, the accessible one, the inhabited one, has blessed identity—a proper name, a human history, a visible character. Time is anonymous; when we give it a face, it's the same face the world over. While place is in itself as informing as an old gossip, time tells us nothing about itself except by the signals that it is passing. It has never given anything away. *

We manipulate time in conversation with such apparent ease that it may be difficult to notice. For instance, in the telephone call "It's Gun Be Hard to Do," the mother and daughter began their talk about visiting Jan, which projected them into the future. Then they inserted into that dominant time frame several references to what Jan and the daughter had done together in the past. The conversational tangent about ranches skips into the future again. When the mother speaks of Barry's sickness, she's in the present. Her mention of when he became ill takes her back into the past. This kind of time-shifting goes on continuously in everyday talk and proceeds smoothly. Only if you're trying to

---

*Eudora Welty, "Some Notes on Time in Fiction," in *The Eye of the Story: Selected Essays and Reviews* (New York: Random House, 1979), p. 163.

get a particular story straight, as when comparing the conflicting tales of two witnesses at a criminal trial, are you likely to pay specific attention to time shifts. During conversation, you can bend and fold time. You can run it forward or backward, fast or slow, and even give the illusion of suspended animation or stopped time.

Literary language imitates the power of everyday speech in its manipulations of time. Read through the following poem and note the ways the writer frames and re-frames his imagined world with time.

"The Sudden Appearance of a Monster at a Window"

by Lawrence Raab

(From What We Don't Know About Each Other *by Lawrence Raab. Copyright © 1993 by Lawrence Raab. Used by permission of Viking Penguin, a division of Penguin Books USA, Inc.)*

Yes, his face really is so terrible
you cannot turn away. And only
that thin sheet of glass between you,
clouding with his breath.
Behind him: the dark scribbles of trees
in the orchard, where you walked alone
just an hour ago, after the storm had passed,
watching water drip from the gnarled branches,
stepping carefully over the sodden fruit.
10   At any moment he could put his fist
right through that window. And on your side:
you could grab hold of something like
this letter opener, or even now you could try
very slowly to slide the revolver
out of the drawer in the desk
where you're sitting, where you were writing
a letter which is there in front of you.
But none of this will happen. And not because
you feel sorry for him, or detect
20   in his scarred face some helplessness
that shows in your own as compassion.
You will never know what he wanted,
what he might have done, since
this thing, of its own accord, turns away.
And because yours is a life in which
such a monster cannot figure for long,
you compose yourself, and return

30 to your letter about the storm, how it bent
the apple trees so low they dragged
on the ground, ruining the harvest.

We start consideration of time by tracing *its* shifts, as we did when analyzing space in a literary world. And, of course, verbs are the most dependable markers of temporal shift.

The poem begins in the present and remains there until the middle of the sixth line, when it moves into the past. "Just an hour ago" marks this shift precisely. Line 10, then, takes the reader back to the present. Lines 16 and 17 ("where you're sitting, where you were writing a letter which is there in front of you") continue in the present, except for the four-word shift into the past. Line 18 moves into the future and remains there until the last word of line 23, which signals a return to the present. The final lines of the poem carry the speaker back in time to "just an hour ago."

When we assigned this poem for performance in one class, students developed various strategies for marking time's passage. One chose to restructure the poem on the page, as we did with the earlier example of space, noting shifts in time rather than place. By such a logic, the poem would look like this:

1. Present
    Yes, his face really is so terrible you cannot turn away. And only that thin sheet of glass between you, clouding with his breath. Behind him: the dark scribbles of trees in the orchard,

2. Past
    where you walked alone just an hour ago, after the storm had passed, watching water drip from the gnarled branches, stepping carefully over the sodden fruit.

3. Future
    At any moment he could put his fist right through that window. And on your side: you could grab hold of something like this letter opener, or even now you could try very slowly to slide the revolver out of the drawer in the desk where you're sitting,

4. Past
    where you were writing a letter

5. Present
    which is there in front of you.

6. Future
    But none of this will happen. And not because you feel sorry for him, or detect in his scarred face some helplessness that shows in your own as

compassion. You will never know what he wanted, what he might have done,

7. Present
   since this thing, of its own accord, turns away. And because yours is a life in which such a monster cannot figure for long, you compose yourself, and return to your letter about the storm,

8. Past
   how it bent the apple trees so low they dragged on the ground, ruining the harvest.

This student, in her first rehearsal, decided to distinguish the present time frame from all others by literalizing what is described in the present, as if to demonstrate "this is what's happening right now." Both the past and the future, in her rehearsal, took place in the speaker's mind as a memory or a projection.

In her first rehearsal, this student performed section 1 by literalizing the speaker's situation. Sitting at a desk, writing a letter (action that precedes the first words of the poem) with a letter opener beside it, she looked up, saw the face in the window, and spoke her first words, rising and moving back from the desk as she realized that "only the thin sheet of glass" separated her from the monster. Moving only slightly to see "the dark scribbles of trees behind him," she turned away from the window, speaking the words of section 2 to herself. At section 3, she returned her gaze to the window again, sat down, and imagined the acts described rather than literalizing them. At section 4, she saw the letter; at section 5, she touched it. She performed section 6 as if thinking aloud. She paused before section 7, without changing her stance, until, at the first complete sentence, she returned to her letter writing. At section 8, she looked up and remembered the final image of the poem.

Starting with time gave this student a way into the performance of the poem. In rehearsal, she let her voice and body enact the discoveries of her grammatical analysis. And, like most first rehearsals, this one raised as many questions as it answered. First, she found that not all shifts to the past could be handled in the same way. She felt more comfortable literalizing the actions and attitudes depicted in the present than she did by leaving them implicit in the speaker's recollection. Sections 2 and 8 are so much fuller than section 4. For her, they felt qualitatively different, as well as being longer than section 4.

When trying to understand such differences, she turned to the performance of past-tense experiences in everyday talk. Moments such as sections 2 and 8 are like trying to explain a dream to someone, or asking a friend to visualize a beautiful place you once visited. Recalling the behavior appropriate to this kind of remembrance is easier than recalling the nearly unconscious reference to writing a letter (section 4). This is so not because it's difficult to recall how one writes a letter but because the recollection occurs and passes so quickly. She realized that the time shift felt awkward because she was overperforming it compared to everyday talk. The conversational transcript of "It's Gun Be Hard to Do" includes several instances of rapid time travel, some explicitly marked by a speaker's delivery, and others hardly noted in performance. From that conversation, we might offer a performance generalization applicable to this poem: the more conscious effort is demanded of a speaker to make a time shift, the more that shift should be marked by specific performance behaviors.

Further, this student discovered in her first rehearsal that not all references to the future in the poem are the same. The more she thought about section 3, the less she felt it was referring to some real future time (even though the speaker later identifies these events as future in line 18). Instead, she concluded that section 3 represents an alternative version of the present. "At any moment," the performer reasoned, is just another way of saying, "right now he could." All the things she imagines doing as a response to the monster (using the letter opener, reaching for the revolver) are not so much future events as possible options for the present. In performance, she could *imagine* doing all these things as she describes them or, alternatively, she might act out each possibility, treating the future as the present. This situation is not unlike the mother's in "It's Gun Be Hard to Do," when she details different options the daughter could enact if she were to visit Jan.

This student's third realization in her first rehearsal of the poem was that time, as an analytical tool, has its limits. The temporal element of a poem provides one beginning, one way to get started. But it's only one point of entry into the language world of literature, just as space opens another window onto an imaginary landscape. Neither is sufficient in itself. Both time and space lead a performer to consider other aspects of the literary world.

EXERCISE
&
DISCUSSION

Now try a poem on your own. Read the following work and experiment with the rehearsal procedures and problems that follow.

"A Supermarket in California"

by Allen Ginsberg

(From Collected Poems 1947–1980 *by Allen Ginsberg. Copyright © 1955 by Allen Ginsberg. Copyright renewed. Reprinted by permission of HarperCollins Publishers, Inc.)*

What thoughts I have of you tonight, Walt Whitman, for I walked down the sidestreets under the trees with a headache self-conscious looking at the full moon.

In my hungry fatigue, and shopping for images, I went into the neon fruit supermarket, dreaming of your enumerations!

What peaches and what penumbras! Whole families shopping at night! Aisles full of husbands! Wives in the avocados, babies in the tomatoes!— and you, Garcia Lorca, what were you doing down by the watermelons?

I saw you, Walt Whitman, childless, lonely old grubber, poking among the meats in the refrigerator and eyeing the grocery boys.

I heard you asking questions of each: Who killed the pork chops? What price bananas? Are you my Angel?

I wandered in and out of the brilliant stacks of cans following you, and followed in my imagination by the store detective.

We strode down the open corridors together in our solitary fancy tasting artichokes, possessing every frozen delicacy, and never passing the cashier.

Where are we going, Walt Whitman? The doors close in an hour. Which way does your beard point tonight?

(I touch your book and dream of our odyssey in the supermarket and feel absurd.)

Will we walk all night through solitary streets? The trees add shade to shade, lights out in the houses, we'll both be lonely.

Will we stroll dreaming of the lost America of love past blue automobiles in driveways, home to our silent cottage?

Ah, dear father, graybeard, lonely old courage-teacher, what America did you have when Charon quit poling his ferry and you got out on a smoking bank and stood watching the boat disappear on the black waters of Lethe?

Thus far, we have been underscoring your need to be aware of precisely where jumps in space and when breaks in time occur within a piece of literature. This is necessary because, unless you can make it clear to an audience when these occur, they won't be able to follow your performance. But the procedure we have been discussing can also help you understand *why* the poet orchestrates time in a particular way.

Break the poem up into individual time units (see pp. 51–52), but don't number them. Next, rearrange them chronologically, noting what would follow what, had the poet begun with the first thing that happens and ended with the last. (Don't worry if you aren't certain about where a particular item goes. Start with the ones you're sure of, and add the uncertain item wherever it might possibly fit.) Then, without referring to the original poem, rearrange the items again in the poet's order as you recall it. As you put these pieces back together, ask yourself why the poet introduced a time shift when he did. (Don't worry that your reason may be "wrong." What is important here is that your reason makes sense to you.) Check back to the original to see if there are discrepancies between it and your rearrangement. If there are, try to explain why the poet might have put the item in question where it is. Finally, perform the poem, noting not just where time shifts occur, but why they are necessary. If you understand why the poet arranged the temporal structure of the poem as he did, your performance not only avoids being mechanical, but you have a sure guide to which time shifts are of minor value and which are crucial to your communication with the audience. Note also those instances where a particular item *must* come in its given order so that the audience can understand what follows. (Sequence is one of the major temporal aids to any reader's understanding.) What does this tell you about the relative importance of various items in the poem?

This exercise can also be used to analyze shifts in space, but it requires modification. In the time exercise, you rearranged sections chronologically, but no such obvious principle is available for reordering shifts in space. Performers often find it more helpful, after dividing the text into scenes (see page 44), to note the relative specificity of each. For example, compare the lack of information about the setting Ginsberg gives you for the first clause of the poem ("What thoughts I have of you tonight, Walt Whitman . . .") with the specific detail he provides about the neon fruit supermarket. Again, the most valuable question the performer can ask is *why*. Why doesn't Ginsberg tell you where the speaker is when he says those opening words, and why does he give you so much information about the world of the supermarket? Trying to figure out why writers choose a *low definition* (little specificity) for one scene and a *high definition* (more concrete detail) for another is a good indicator of the relative importance of various settings. This difference, in turn, should influence how you perform the poem.

Return to the first clause of the poem, a low-definition scene. In performing this language, do you fill in the missing details, in effect making up a plausible place? Or do you perform these opening words giving no clue to your listeners where the speaker is? You can't answer this question satisfactorily until you try multiple possibilities in rehearsal. Only by *doing* can you discover what works.

Theory and Practice

The American philosopher William James sometimes urged his lecture audiences to think of different theories as so many tools in a toolbox, and to think of the practitioner as a pioneer trying to solve problems on a frontier farm. As often as not, the available tools in the box won't quite fit the problem at hand. The pliers aren't the right ones to repair the barbed wire fence, or the wrench doesn't fit the broken pipe. To survive, James observed, the practitioner has to be able to improvise.

As a performer, you are a practitioner, too. This book can equip you with some versatile tools, but sooner or later, like the pioneer, you are going to have to improvise when the tools don't quite fit the problem at hand. For example, read again the final sentence of Ginsberg's poem:

> Ah, dear father, graybeard, lonely old courage-teacher, what America did you have when Charon quit poling his ferry and you got out on a smoking bank and stood watching the boat disappear on the black waters of Lethe?

If you were to assign this section a chronological place, it would have to come well before any other part in the poem, because Whitman died in 1892. And if you tried to arrange it spatially, it wouldn't relate to any other place described or implied in the poem. It is outside the world created by the rest of the poem. Everything else is in California, but this is as far from there as Oz is from Kansas. Distance, in this case, isn't a question of miles or direction. The final lines evoke an entirely different world. Your problem, as a performer, is to devise a communicative strategy to signal that the poem is ending in another world. What can you *do* in performance to solve this problem? To find the answer, you have to improvise and experiment, and no two performers solve the problem in exactly the same way.

Remember that theory exists only as an aid to help you make a performance work, and performance, in turn, aims at making the worlds of literature seem real for an audience. When performing, you should be no more concerned with demonstrating that a given theory works than a pioneer, when mending a barbed-wire fence, intends to demonstrate the usefulness of a pair of pliers.

Speakers in the Worlds of Literature

"Speak that I may see thee."
Ben Jonson

In literature, as in everyday conversation, one can't conceive the meaning of words without locating them in some *place,* grasping them at a particular *time,* and hearing them from the voice of a specific *speaker.* "Consider the source" is a commonplace qualifier in everyday talk, pointing up the close link between any story's credibility and its speaker's identity.

The language of a literary text may be spoken by a single voice or by multiple speakers. It may emanate from a character with a distinctive personality or from a stock type. For example, much of the poetry written before the nineteenth century put words into the mouths of the lover, the sage, the clown, or the gossip. Even drama, the literary genre most associated with individual speakers of distinct personality, has not always been understood through character psychology. Samuel Johnson, the most penetrating reader of Shakespeare during the eighteenth century, displayed none of our contemporary need to identify characters as unique personalities. In his famed *Preface to Shakespeare*, Johnson wrote:

> *Shakespeare is above all writers, at least above all modern writers, the poet of nature; the poet that holds up to his readers a faithful mirror of manners and of life. His characters are not modified by the customs of particular places, unpracticed by the rest of the world; by the peculiarities of studies or professions, which can operate but upon small numbers; or by the accidents of transient fashions or temporary opinions: they are the genuine progeny of common humanity, such as the world will always supply, and the observation will always find. His persons act and speak by the influence of those general passions and principles by which all minds are agitated, and the whole system of life is continued in motion. In the writings of other poets a character is too often an individual; in those of Shakespeare it is commonly a species.*

Writing in the 1700s, Johnson spoke from a world we might be able to imagine, but hardly the one we live in. Ever since the Romantics, we have been preoccupied with the uniqueness of literary characters and their idiosyncratic psychology. And yet, our conception of "characters," both in literature and in life, may come closer to what Johnson was talking about than we think. The conversation analyst who transcribed "It's Gun Be Hard to Do" didn't name the two speakers, but referred to them as what Johnson might call "a species," Mother and Daughter. Much of our dramatic interest in that conversation is in how much those two specific speakers act like mothers and daughters generally.

Listen to yourself or others complain about a character on TV or in a movie as "unbelievable," and, more often than not, what is meant is that the character doesn't conform to "a species." As you move through a day, you play different roles in different circumstances and various relationships. You are the adult with one friend, parent with another, and child with a third. With a teacher, you may play student; with your beloved, a lover, and so on.

Speakers and Their Listeners

All utterance, both literary and everyday, is rooted in conversation; therefore, one of the best places to begin any analysis is to identify the relationship between the speaker and the listener. Personality and characterization cannot be apprehended directly; they become manifest only in the context of some relationship. Even in the apparently solitary world of a play's soliloquy or a poem's lyric contemplation, where speakers talk to themselves, we still gain access to character only through understanding some relationship, in these cases an interior one.

One powerful criterion for determining the believability of performances is whether their speakers sound and act as if they were talking to real people (a mother, oneself, a lover). This is so in the performance of everyday life as well as in literature:

A: Hello?

B: Hey!

A: Hi.

B: Are you ready yet?

This short exchange—two utterances each, by two speakers—conveys little information about its world. The words make no reference to where or when they are spoken, and they tell nothing directly about the speakers themselves. Nonetheless, the words do contain information about a relationship.

Speakers A and B must know each other. B only has to make a sound ("Hey") to be recognized by A. Furthermore, A and B have made plans to do something together that are so recent or so important as to need no reference. You don't have to be absolutely certain about a language world to perform its words believably. Sometimes when you are given as little specific information as this, you are left to invent plausible worlds and to choose the one that provides the richest context for understanding. Here you might guess that A and B are close friends. On the other hand, it's possible that B is house hunting, A is a real estate agent, and the last line refers to an appointment they've made to look at a condo together. Our point is that each possible relationship suggests a different way to perform the same words. In this example, your ability to guess the relationship between two unknown speakers means that you have some standard to apply that can guide performance options.

Analyzing the relationship between speaker and listener can provide important clues to what motivates a character. We'll have much more to say about this in Chapter 3 on effect. At this stage, however, it's important to grasp the centrality of relationships when mapping the worlds of language. Notice in the following two examples, one taken from life and the other from literature, how performance is controlled by the response the writer wants from the reader and the implied relationship between them:

> *Mom,*
>
> *I've thought over what you said, and I still think you're not being fair. When have I ever been irresponsible with the car? The state of Texas gave me a license, so they must think I can handle city traffic. I'm going to Betty's house right after school. Please, change your mind.*
>
> *Rob*

Doctor,

The pills are good for nothing—I might as well swallow snowballs to cool my veins—I have told you over and over how hard I am to move; and at this time of day, I ought to know something of my own constitution. Prithee send me another prescription—I am as lame and as much tortured in all my limbs as if I was broke upon the wheel . . .

(From Tobias Smollett, *The Expedition of Humphry Clinker*)

The first example, taken from a real-life note, is clearly a son–mother relationship, but this category is too broad to be of much help to the performer. What's more telling is the particular role this speaker plays with his mother. Rob isn't a whining adolescent. In the language of the note, he's an adult, advancing a reasoned case for getting the car. In the second example, taken from literature of an earlier era, the speaker is a patient and the listener is his doctor. Their relationship tells us something of the power differential between them, as did realizing that the previous conversation was between mother and son. But within the general parameters for playing a "patient," many different roles are possible.

Return to "A Supermarket in California," (pp. 53–54) and focus this time not on the physical and temporal dimensions of its world, but on its characters, and particularly, on the relationship between its speaker and his implied audience. The poem's most important listener is Walt Whitman himself—so important, in fact, that the speaker identifies Whitman in the very first clause of the poem. Whenever a literary work draws this much attention to the person whom the speaker is addressing, you can be sure that analyzing their relationship is going to reveal much that's useful to a performer.

In this poem, notice specific hints the speaker gives of his relationship with Whitman. He addresses Whitman at one point as "dear father, graybeard, lonely old courage-teacher." Clearly, this is a loving relationship. The speaker identifies Whitman as both father and teacher. We know from the opening of the poem that Whitman is a confidant of the speaker, someone with whom the "I" of the poem wants to talk over his experiences. Such intimacy should imply a tone of voice for the performer, one you might use in your own world to "open up" with a friend you respect and love.

When analyzing a relationship, beware of oversimplifying it. The one between the unnamed speaker and Walt Whitman is son to father, as well as student to teacher, and the poet emphasizes these relationships at both the beginning and the end of the poem. These relationships literally frame everything else that happens between beginning and end. But notice how the speaker addresses Whitman inside the supermarket:

I saw you, Walt Whitman, childless, lonely old grubber, poking among the meats in the refrigerator and eyeing the grocery boys.

I heard you asking questions of each: Who killed the pork chops? What price bananas? Are you my Angel?

What a different picture we get of their relationship here. Suddenly, the tone has gone from the deferential respect of a student toward a teacher, to teasing. We could hardly have predicted this turn from the earlier description.

EXERCISE & DISCUSSION

In working out the shifting relationship between speaker and listener in a particular literary selection, you might find it helpful to start with broad, general categories. One procedure popular with performers is to collapse all possible relationships into three basic roles—adult, parent, and child. That is to say, we relate to one another as one adult to another, as a child to a parent, or as a parent to a child. Performers are attracted to this system, because each of these roles suggests a particular tone of voice and even a physical stance.

1. In the note from Rob to his mother (page 58), the speaker is literally a child talking to a parent. Is that actually the relationship Rob is performing? Can you demonstrate the differences in tone of voice if Rob were performing in each of the three roles?

2. In the literary note on page 59 from Smollett's "Expedition of Humphry Clinker," is the speaker playing child talking to parent, parent to child, or one adult to another? Is it possible that the speaker might shift from one role to another during the course of the note? Demonstrate how these shifts might affect your performance.

3. In the first line quoted from the Ginsberg poem (page 59), the speaker makes reference to Whitman's homosexuality. We have suggested that the speaker is teasing his listener here. Do you agree, and if so, can you show this critical judgment in your performance of the line? If you disagree, can you demonstrate the tone you do hear when you read the line?

4. We are not told what the speaker's sexual orientation is. If you decide that he, too, is gay, how does it affect the relationship between speaker and listener? How does it affect tone of voice? Now, does the relationship between speaker and listener seem to be one of child to parent, parent to child, or adult to adult?

5. In the second line quoted (page 60), does the speaker think the questions Whitman asks are silly or profound? Comic or serious? Does the speaker address Whitman as a parent, as a child, or as an adult?

Speakers and Space / Time

To see how world helps to reveal character, you need to examine speakers' attitudes toward the places they inhabit. What does a speaker value about a particular place? What are the clues, both obvious and hidden, that depict attitude? Is the speaker aware of limitations in the world?

Here are two different perspectives on character and place. The first, a poem by William Stafford, celebrates rootedness. The second, taken from an essay by Wallace Stegner, reflects on rootlessness.

"One Home"

by William Stafford

("One Home" copyright © 1977 The Estate of William Stafford. Originally published in Stories That Could Be True, *Harper & Row, 1977, and is used by permission.)*

Mine was a Midwest home—you can keep your world.
Plain black hats rode the thoughts that made our code.
We sang hymns in the house; the roof was near God.

The light bulb that hung in the pantry made a wan light,
but we could read by it the names of preserves—
outside, the buffalo grass, and the wind in the night.

A wildcat sprang at Grandpa on the Fourth of July
when he was cutting plum bushes for fuel,
before Indians pulled the West over the edge of the sky.

To anyone who looked at us we said, "My friend";
liking the cut of a thought, we could say "Hello."
(But plain black hats rode the thoughts that made our code.)

The sun was over our town; it was like a blade.
Kicking the cottonwood leaves we ran toward storms.

Wherever we looked the land would hold us up.

From "The Sense of Place"
in *Living and Writing in the West*

by Wallace Stegner

(*Wallace Stegner*, Where the Bluebird Sings and the Lemonade Springs: Living and Writing in the West. *New York: Random House, 1992, pp. 199–200.*)

[If] every American is several people, and one of them is or would like to be a placed person, another is the opposite, the displaced person, cousin not to Thoreau but to Daniel Boone, dreamer not of Walden Pond but of far horizons, traveler not in Concord but in wild unsettled places, explorer not inward but outward. Adventurous, restless, seeking, asocial or anti-social, the displaced American persists by the million long after the frontier has vanished. He exists to some extent in all of us, the inevitable by-product of our history: the New World transient. He is commoner in the newer parts of America—the West, Alaska—than in the older parts, but he occurs everywhere, always in motion.

To the placed person he seems hasty, shallow, and restless. He has a current like the Platte, a mile wide and an inch deep. As a species, he is non-territorial, he lacks a stamping ground. Acquainted with many places, he is rooted to none. Culturally he is a discarder or transplanter, not a builder or conserver. He even seems to like and value his rootlessness, though to the placed person he shows the symptoms of nutritional deficiency, as if he suffered from some obscure scurvy or pellagra of the soul.

Whether from Stafford's or Stegner's point of view, place is intimately linked to character, providing the staging points for self-discovery and self-revelation. Time, then, spotlights the meaningful behaviors of a character taking place on that stage. Ultimately, you will find that time and space are inextricably bound up with action. That braiding together is the focus of later chapters, but it is necessary to mention it now to underscore the interconnectedness of all aspects of world.

Speakers and Action

Time and space are not static in a language world, providing some mere background for character development. Nonetheless, it is hard to see their motion and dynamic interplay. Time and space become visible in dramatic fashion, however, through the action of characters. Action *takes place*. Here's a poem in marked contrast to Stafford's "One Home." In "The Whipping," action predominates. In fact, action shapes this world, as well as defining its characters.

"The Whipping"

by Robert Hayden

The old woman across the way
    is whipping the boy again
and shouting to the neighborhood
    her goodness and his wrongs.

Wildly he crashes through elephant ears,
    pleads in dusty zinnias,
while she in spite of crippling fat
    pursues and corners him.

She strikes and strikes the shrilly circling
    boy till the stick breaks
in her hand. His tears are rainy weather
    to woundlike memories:

My head gripped in bony vise
    of knees, the writhing struggle
to wrench free, the blows, the fear
    worse than blows that hateful

Words could bring, the face that I
    no longer knew or loved . . . .
Well, it is over now, it is over,
    and the boy sobs in his room,

And the woman leans muttering against
    a tree, exhausted, purged—
avenged in part for lifelong hidings
    she has had to bear.

So far in this chapter we have used poems to illustrate the importance of world in the performance of literature. Our final illustration is written in prose. Develop a performance that communicates the times and places in this story's language, the speaker's relationship to her listeners, to her world, and the events that transpire in it.

"Admission of Failure"

by Phyllis Koestenbaum

(Originally published in Epoch, *Vol. 40, No. 1, p. 19, and subsequently in* Best American Poetry 1992, *New York: Macmillan, 1992.)*

The hostess seats a girl and a young man in a short-sleeve sport shirt with one arm missing below the shoulder. I'm at the next table with my husband and son, Andy's Barbecue Restaurant, an early evening in July, chewing a boneless rib eye, gulping a dark beer ordered from the cocktail waitress, a nervous woman almost over the hill, whose high heel sandals click back and forth from the bar to the dining room joined to the bar by an open arch. A tall heavy cook in white hat is brushing sauce on the chicken and spareribs rotating slowly on a squeaking spit. Baked potatoes heat on the oven floor. The young man is eating salad with his one hand. He and his girl are on a date. He has a forties' movie face, early Van Johnson before the motorcycle accident scarred his forehead. He lost the arm recently. Hard as it is, it could be worse. I would even exchange places with him if I could. *I want to exchange places with the young armless man in the barbecue restaurant.* He would sit at my table and I would sit at his. After dinner I would go in his car and he would go in mine. I would live in his house and work at his job and he would live in my house and do what I do. I would be him dressing and undressing and he would be me dressing and undressing. Our bill comes. My husband leaves the tip on the tray; we take toothpicks and mints and walk through the dark workingmen's bar out to the parking lot still lit by the sky though the streetlights have come on as they do automatically at the same time each night. We drive our son, home for the summer, back to his job at the bookstore. As old Italians and Jews say of sons from five to fifty, he's a good boy. I have worked on this paragraph for more than two years.

SUMMARY

In this chapter, we have introduced the first of four dimensions of language, namely the *worlds* created by and through words. A reader or performer cannot begin to assess the *effect* of language (the subject of Chapter 3), or even to grasp the *sense* of words (Chapter 4) without first locating language in a specific context, some concrete world. In literature, words do not only describe the worlds of their speakers. For the reader or audience, words actually create those worlds, as we witnessed in the mirror images of L. Frank Baum's Kansas and Oz.

The worlds evoked by language—both in our everyday conversations and in our encounters with literature—take up imaginary space, contoured to the topography of a concrete place (for instance, "At the IGA"). The worlds of language take up time, as well, whether marked by the twinkling of an eye, the warp speed of intergalactic travel, or the telltale beat of a heart (as in "The Sudden Appearance of a Monster at the Window"). At the intersections of space and time emerge the speakers and listeners of language, whose presences we have introduced here and who are featured more centrally in Chapter 3. Through your performance of a speaker's words in the context of a relationship with some listener, you can invite an audience to inhabit the world's space and feel its passage of time.

We close this chapter by yielding the stage to a new voice. Nobel laureate Toni Morrison is an author of keen insight to the collaborative performance of writer and reader in the language worlds of literature:

> The imagination that produces work which bears and invites rereadings, which motions to future readings as well as contemporary ones, implies a shareable world and an endlessly flexible language. Readers and writers both struggle to interpret and perform within a common language of shareable imaginative worlds.*

---

*From Toni Morrison, *Playing In the Dark: Whiteness and the Literary Imagination* (Cambridge and London: Harvard University Press, 1992), p. xii.

Chapter Three

Three

Performing the Effects of Language

The worlds of language—whether homegrown in everyday conversation or composed in literature—are constituted of space and time, with the presence of at least one speaker in a relationship with some listener. That sentence is as far as Chapter 2 took us theoretically, and, as it closed, we were just beginning to cross the border from *world* toward *effect*. Here, we discuss that dimension of language concerned primarily with the relationship between a speaker and a listener, namely, the intended and perceived effects of each participant's words. In literature, as much as in everyday life, characters talk to each other (or to us) with the express purpose of producing some effect, whether or not they succeed in that intention. The inherent drama of human interaction can be described as a tension between the effect intended and the effect achieved.

In Chapter 1, we analyzed two mother–daughter conversations for the effects each participant wanted her words to have on a listener. To study effect, we suggested, you must pose the question *why*. Characters themselves ask this question continuously. In "It's Gun Be Hard to Do," the daughter was just as focused on her mother's intended effect as was the mother herself. In *'Night, Mother*, each character asked the other one "why" while listening. Both sets of mothers and daughters heard each other with suspicion, just like Mr. Allen in the following telephone exchange:*

Mr. Allen: Hello?

Tracy: Hello Mister Allen?

           (......)

Mr. Allen: What can I do for you.

Tracy: Okay, this is Tracy from Carpet Colors ((Mr. Allen hangs up))

The most telling moment in this brief exchange is the 0.6-second pause, when Mr. Allen stops to figure out what effect Tracy is after. In everyday life, we are reluctant to engage in a conversation if we are suspicious of, or even uncertain of, another's intention. Sometimes our assumption turns out to be wrong and has to be revised later, but we can't commit to conversation comfortably without having at least some notion of the effect intended.

Fortunately, most of our everyday talk does not invite suspicion and involves little resistance on the part of a conversational partner. One person isn't trying to influence another's behavior in any way contrary to his or her wishes. In fact, we usually can count on a listener inferring our intended effect easily and correctly. For example, imagine the doorbell rings, you answer it, and there stands your sister Jane's friend. "Is Jane home?" he asks. In this situation, you wouldn't answer, "Yes," and then close the door. You would say, "Come in," or "Wait a

*From Robert Hopper, *Telephone Conversation*. (Bloomington, Ind.: Indiana University Press, 1992), p. 210.

minute, I'll go get her." You would have figured out what effect he wanted his words to have, and he would have counted on your ability to do so.

Inferring Effect

The effect desired in everyday talk or in literature is seldom stated directly. You have to *figure it out* from the words, from the world they refer to, and from their utterance. The process of inferring what the speaker is after is necessarily subjective. In this chapter, our discussions of effect encourage greater interpretive latitude than the considerations of space or time in Chapter 2. Our readings of a text offer only one possible interpretation. We hope you enter into critical dialogue by arguing for alternative soundings of the poem's intended effect. Here is a literary conversation bound to produce some disagreement among performers.

"Two Friends"

by David Ignatow

(David Ignatow, "Two Friends," from Figures of the Human, *copyright © 1964 by David Ignatow. Wesleyan University Press by permission of University Press of New England.)*

I have something to tell you.
I'm listening.
I'm dying.
I'm sorry to hear.
I'm growing old.
It's terrible.
It is, I thought you should know.
Of course and I'm sorry. Keep in touch.
I will and you too.
And let me know what's new.
Certainly, though it can't be much.
And stay well.
And you too.
And go slow.
And you too.

Notice what would happen if you were to begin your rehearsal-analysis of this poem with time or space, as we did in Chapter 2. The poet gives you virtually nothing to go on; no place is specified, no shifts in time occur. Effect, on the other hand, points toward what's most accessible in this conversation—the relationship between *two friends*. We know very little else about these speakers, but we do assume from the poem's title that they are friends.

So far as the title may be trusted, there are two speakers, and assuming each line represents a single speech, we have divided the lines between A and B as follows:

A: I have something to tell you.

B: I'm listening.

A: I'm dying.

B: I'm sorry to hear.

A: I'm growing old.

B: It's terrible.

A: It is, I thought you should know.

B: Of course and I'm sorry. Keep in touch.

A: I will and you too.

B: And let me know what's new.

A: Certainly, though it can't be much.

B: And stay well.

A: And you too.

B: And go slow.

A: And you too.

Furthermore, we have arbitrarily conceived of A as male and B as female. (You may prefer other performance options, but these give us some common reference points for discussion.)

As you play around with "Two Friends," notice that each line or turn in the conversation does not introduce a new effect. One speaker may use several turns at talk to advance a single effect. Some students may find it helpful to think of effect as a speaker's objective or projection, some view of the future that he or she wishes to bring about or to avoid. If we determine that A's intention is to win sympathy from B, his objective informs not only the first line, but several of the lines that follow as well.

We believe A abandons his first objective right after saying, "I thought you should know," and he substitutes a new intention—to bring this conversation to an end. Working with a partner (and we suggest you change partners as you play through alternative readings of this poem), try to perform A's lines so that it is clear he has adopted a new intention at this point.

B's speeches cluster together, too, probably in pursuit of a single objective— to end the conversation as quickly as possible without giving offense to A. Try performing all of B's lines in an attempt to bring about this effect. Alternatively, it may be that B begins the conversation eager to hear what A has to tell her, but at some point in the talk, she loses interest and wants to leave. Decide where and why this change of objective might come and perform her lines accordingly.

Moving from Analysis to Performance

Determining *why* someone says something (the intended effect) should help you decide *how* to perform any given line. Learning to make this jump from why to how is the essential and hard work of rehearsal. When reading literature, a performer can't afford to take in language casually, as one might scan a newspaper column. The kind of engagement performance requires demands hearing the voices and seeing the speakers of language.

As noted in Chapter 1, everyday talk requires more complex performance techniques than literature does, and we can draw on our knowledge of such talk when enacting literature. Your lifetime of experience as a listener and a speaker can show you how to perform a speaker's effect, as well as how to evaluate your success during rehearsal.

Working with a classmate, develop a performance of "Two Friends" beginning with the effects we have indicated for each line:

A: I have something to tell you. (*effect: to get B to listen sympathetically*)

B: I'm listening. (*effect: to make A get to the point*)

A: I'm dying. (*effect: to persuade B to feel sorry for A*)

B: I'm sorry to hear. (*effect: to communicate to A that B is very busy*)

A: I'm growing old. (*effect: to make B feel sorry for A*)

B: It's terrible. (*effect: to make A realize B is busy*)

A: It is, I thought you should know. (*effect: B should feel sorry for A*)

B: Of course and I'm sorry. Keep in touch. (*effect: to make A take his troubles elsewhere*)

A: I will and you too. (*effect: to end on a friendly note*)

B: And let me know what's new. (*effect: to end on a friendly note*)

A: Certainly, though it can't be much. (*effect: to make B feel sorry for A*)

B: And stay well. (*effect: to bring the conversation to an end*)

A: And you too. (*effect: the same*)

B: And go slow. (*effect: the same*)

A: And you too. (*effect: the same*)

In "It's Gun Be Hard to Do," we noted important moments of silence when speakers paused or stammered. These usually indicated that something significant was happening to the speaker, or in the relationship between speaker and listener. No matter how carefully you analyze a speaker's intended effect, your performance will seem mechanical to an audience if you don't give that speaker time to listen and to respond. When working through your rehearsals of "Two Friends," did you find specific moments when the flow of language could be altered to demonstrate your speaker's changing thoughts and feelings?

Remember that every speech in conversation is a response to what has come before. Giving a speaker time to respond is particularly important when a new objective is introduced. In the performance we have just specified of "Two Friends," note, for example, A's fifth line:

A: *I will and you too.* (effect: to end on a friendly note)

Everything A has said up to this time was designed to elicit sympathy from B, but here A is projecting a different effect. Think for a moment of what would have to happen if this were everyday talk. Speaker A would have to determine on the basis of B's "Keep in touch," that he is not getting the effect he seeks, and then he would have to decide on a new effect. We all make such adjustments in everyday talk, and what may take several sentences to describe here actually occurs in a fraction of a second in a character's mental process. But as conversation analysis demonstrates, that fraction does show up in performance.

Read through the following everyday telephone conversation, noting how both speakers wrestle with effect and how their process could be made manifest in performance:

Dawn	Hello?
	(..)
Gordon	Hello is Dawn there
	(..)
Dawn	This is Dawn
	(......)
Gordon	Dawn this is Gordon Turner
	(..............)
Dawn	Yeah?
Gordon	Your old Hilton friend
	(..........)
Dawn	My old who?
Gordon	<u>Hil</u>ton
	(..)
Dawn	Oh? o:h this: a different Dawn.
Gordon	Oh no.

Try to describe what may be going on in each speaker's mind during the pauses in this conversation. Try rehearsing these shifts in response not by monitoring a stop watch, but by *thinking* and *feeling as the speaker would.*

Playing in Everyday Life and in Literature

Characterization or impersonation is a commonplace human activity, begun in childhood and carried on through the myriad roles of most adult lives. As children, we all acted out characters, sometimes using dolls, action figures, or puppets. Sometimes, we made characters with our own bodies, either in solitary play or in the company of other children. When playing a macho intimidator, a child takes on a broad swagger and a bullying tone of voice to create a desired effect. Childhood play-acting draws on voice and dialect, body and movement, costumes and props, plot and theme.

Performance, as we're practicing it here, comes close to what one means in everyday life when trying to model oneself after someone else. When learning to play tennis, for instance, you might try to imitate the groundstroke of a professional player. When retelling a joke, you may try to mimic the vocal pauses and inflections of the person who told it originally. You might even find yourself performing someone else's character unconsciously, as when you see or hear yourself behaving as one of your parents might in a similar situation.

Impersonation is the creative impulse behind characterization. We become characters, mimicking others, for entertainment's sake, of course, but that is not its only value. At a more fundamental level, impersonation is a mode of learning. We learn about others by performing them, by walking and talking, gesturing and moving, thinking and acting as they do. In *The Rebel Angels* by Robertson Davies, Maria Theotoky is one of the novel's two narrators. Here she reflects on her own method of observing *mothers* when she was a girl:

> *Wondering what it was like to be in their skins, it was a short step to doing whatever I could to get into their skins. I used to imitate their walks and postures and their hard, high voices, but most of all their facial expressions. This was not "taking them off" as some of the girls at the convent school "took off" the nuns and the Old Supe; it was "putting them on" like a cloak, to find out what it felt like, as a way of knowing them. When I was fourteen I called it the Theotoky Theory of Exchangeable Personalities, and took huge delight in it. And indeed it taught me a surprising amount; walk like somebody, stand like her, try to discover how she produces her voice, and often astounding things become clear.* *

*From Robertson Davies, *The Rebel Angels* (New York: The Viking Press, 1981), p. 146.

Maria Theotoky goes one step beyond the childhood game of dressing up in a parent's hat and shoes to "get into their skins." She thinks of performance as a kind of investigation that "taught me a surprising amount." By "putting on" characters, rather than "taking them off," she found out what they felt like. This is the kind of performance we're recommending here—characterization as experience and education.

Impersonation, as we're using it, is a method of revealing rather than concealing. By performing a character, we hope to achieve intimacy rather than distance. Ultimately, artistic performance and real-life behavior are impossible to separate because, within both frames, audiences ascribe meaning to the actions and words of others. Effect follows performance.

Learning about a speaker in literature can begin most easily by drawing a demographic profile based on the kinds of questions a census-taker might ask:

1. What is the speaker's name?

2. What is his or her sex?

3. How old is she?

4. Where does he come from (e.g., country, region, neighborhood)?

5. What is the speaker's race and ethnic background?

6. What is her income, means of support, or class?

7. What is his educational background?

8. Is the speaker married? Divorced? Single?

9. Does she have any children? How many? What ages?

10. Does he own a home?

You can extend the list further. Not every question is equally pertinent to all speakers, of course, and not every text answers these questions.

The journey of characterization, both inward and outward, cannot stop with demography, however. Getting to know a speaker means stepping into her shoes, as it were. More intimately, it means stepping inside his skin—taking on the character's body and voice. Defining physical features makes up a second approach to character development. Already, your demographic profile has provided some basic information about embodiment. Age, sex, region, race or ethnicity, education, and class may all have physical manifestations or analogues. Other data may be clearly available from the literary text. Does the author tell you anything about the speaker's body type or appearance, manner of speech or delivery, posture or movement, costuming or affectations? This information may be provided in exposition or may be gleaned from the dialogue or actions of other characters. What isn't clearly stated must be deduced from what you know, or intuited from what you feel.

After demography and physical features, you should investigate a speaker's intelligence and temperament. Intelligence is different from educational level, of course. To ascertain a speaker's intelligence, you must assess his or her cognitive complexity, ability to differentiate, and capacity for good reasoning. Until you can measure a person's general intelligence, it may be impossible to ascribe meaning to what they say. Likewise, temperament is a strong influence on the manner of any speaker's language and behavior. Until you can determine something of the speaker's emotional maturity, psychological stability, and fundamental personality traits (e.g., shy or flamboyant, reticent or bombastic), you may not be able to interpret accurately what they say or do.

A final category of investigation includes motivation and passion. Here we come closest to describing effect from a speaker's point of view. Determining a person's motivations asks you to study his or her desires. What does the speaker want? For some texts, this may reduce to a single desire. More often, however, a complex speaker wants a number of different things, expressing a range of desires, intending a variety of effects. Hence, you may need to trace the changing desires of a speaker from scene to scene, as in, "She seems to want *this* in the opening scene with her mother, but then she seems to want *that* in the next scene with her best friend." Asking what a person wants, as an index to desired effect, can be a helpful analytical question whether you are getting to know a speaker in literature or a person in your life.

Passion points to a speaker's personal *values*. What does he or she care deeply about? Notice that "caring about" and "desiring" are different concepts, though sometimes related or overlapping. A person's values are related to commitment and belief. They draw the line between what actions are permissible for an individual and what are not. Passion is connected to motivation as values are linked with desires. In more concrete terms, motivation asks, "What does a speaker want?" Passion asks, "How badly does he want it? What is she willing to do to get it? How far will the speaker go to get what he or she wants?"

When performing, then, you should aspire to embody the totality of a speaker's being, giving life to his or her unique identity. At the same time, any performer should accept with humility one's own limitations and, hence, the inability to achieve complete at-one-ness with a character. This necessary modesty is akin to the realization you have in any intimate relationship that you can never fully comprehend the life and viewpoint of another. In making the daring leap of embodiment, you can be guided by demographic information provided within the literary text. You should seek to give voice and body to the speaker's defining physical features. You must take into account his intelligence and temperament. You should try to understand her motivation and passion.

Effect and the Authorial Frame

So far, we have noted how intention and effect influence the communication behavior of participants in a conversation. And we have paused to talk about characterization of a literary speaker. Dialogue—whether in everyday life or on the stage—can also have an effect on unintended listeners. When you overhear an animated conversation between two people you don't know, their conversation may have an effect on you, though they did not intend it. You may be entertained or bored, amused or disturbed, approving or disapproving as you listen to them. Their effect on you is simply the product of chance—a combination of what they happened to be talking about and the mood you were in while listening. Similarly, when you read the conversation between mother and daughter in "It's Gun Be Hard to Do," their talk had an effect on you, though neither speaker anticipated any audience beyond themselves.

The speakers in "Two Friends" are equally unaware of outside listeners, but their case is different in one important way from the examples drawn from everyday talk. "Two Friends" is the creation of an author, David Ignatow. The content and order of the poem's speeches may imitate everyday talk, but what the speakers say and how they say it are crafted with a purpose by Ignatow. The poet stages this odd conversation because he, too, wants to create an effect. Ignatow is aware of outside listeners, even if his characters are not. That makes a difference.

Just as you must seek the *why* of motivation behind each character's lines, it is equally important to ask *why* of the author. Why does the writer make particular composition choices? What motivates the author's strategies? In this poem, why does Ignatow believe the talk between two friends should have significance *for us*? What's the point? What effect is he after? And how does he want readers to respond?

When answering these questions, you have to fall back on inference and hunch. As you rehearse "Two Friends," experiment with every possibility you can imagine. Try performing the conversation as an example of how hard it is to talk to even your closest friend about your deepest fears. Then try it as an instance of how foolish one can feel when taking oneself too seriously. Or, trying a third case, imagine the poem as a portrait of the clinging vine. With each different authorial effect, your performance of the poem should change decidedly. The best interpretation is one that fits the most evidence drawn from the language of the poem itself, and one that feels right to you as performer.

QUESTIONS FOR DISCUSSION

As a class, discuss what you believe Ignatow's intended effect on a reader to be. Test your conclusion by questioning specific composition choices.

1. Why did Ignatow provide no details about who these speakers are, or where their conversation takes place, or the time of day?

2. Why does Ignatow leave so many details to the individual performer or reader to supply? How might this openness serve the effect he's after?

3. In determining the effect the author is after, don't forget his title. It is, after all, the only time he addresses you, the reader, directly. Why does he identify the speakers as friends? Is this a straightforward and accurate description, or might it be ironic?

4. In what specific ways does an understanding of the effect the author wants guide your performance choices, including your performance of the poem's title?

We have used "Two Friends" to illustrate how far effect can carry you into a literary text and its performance. We began by looking at individual lines, then at sets of lines grouped around a single projection of effect, and, finally, at the whole conversation as a purposeful composition by the poet. Determining the overall effect of a literary text, as well as the myriad effects intended by each of its speakers, is a complicated, often messy, business. In most instances, you can't begin with a line-by-line analysis until you have read the selection through several times. With each new reading, you're probably making educated guesses, whether consciously or unconsciously, about the identities of speakers and the intentions of their author. An initial gut reaction—"this is *great*"—is a declaration that you grasp something of the effect the author is after. Even when you respond to a poem with "I don't get it," the *it* refers to the author's effect.

Both in silent reading and in public performance, our minds jump continuously from the moment-to-moment effects of speakers to the overall intention of an author. We switch back and forth between effects *in* the text and effects *of* the text. The former is demonstrated by character behaviors; the latter is evident in audience response. In longer works, such as a play or a novel, you may find yourself caught up in the flow of events for awhile and then, at other moments, you'll pull back to take a wider, external view. Something reminds you of what happened a few pages back or in the last scene, and you begin to make connections. Patterns emerge, pointing to the invisible hand of a maker. In short, your engagement with a literary text demands these constant shifts between involvement and detachment, detail and pattern, character and author.

The Single Voice

Dialogue, with its quick back-and-forth talk, seems ideal for demonstrating that speakers intend their talk to produce a specific effect and that listeners, when their turn comes to talk, respond to the effect they think is intended. But in literary texts with only one speaker, it's easy to forget there is still a "you" present, and the speaker is still concerned with producing an effect through performance. In everyday life, solo talk is more common than you might think. Lectures, speeches, telephone sales pitches, and newscasts are all instances of it, and all are designed to produce an effect on the "you" who's listening.

We want to concentrate here on the "you" in single-voiced literature. Or, to put it more accurately, we want to look at the speaker's own conception of the "you" being addressed, and how that conception might influence the speaker's performance. A good place to begin might be with a literary imitation of a speech. Bertolt Brecht's play *The Resistible Rise of Arturo Ui* depicts the career of a Chicago gangster, Arturo Ui. In the following speech, Ui makes an offer of "protection" to the Chicago "Cauliflower Trust."

"The Resistible Rise of Arturo Ui"

by Bertolt Brecht

(Copyright © 1957 by Suhrkamp Verlag, Frankfurt am Main. Translated by Ralph Manheim; translation copyright © 1981 by Stefan S. Brecht. Reprinted from The Resistible Rise of Arturo Ui by Bertolt Brecht, published by Arcade Publishing, Inc., New York.)

In short
Chaos is rampant. Because if everybody
Can do exactly what he pleases, if
Dog can eat dog without a second thought
I call it chaos. Look. Suppose I'm sitting
Peacefully in my vegetable store
For instance, or driving my cauliflower truck
And someone comes barging not so peacefully
Into my store: 'Hands up!' Or with his gun
Punctures my tyres. Under such conditions
Peace is unthinkable. But once I know
The score, once I recognize that men are not
Innocent lambs, then I've got to find a way
To stop these men from smashing up my shop and
Making me, when it suits them, put 'em up
And keep 'em up, when I could use my hands
For better things, for instance, counting pickles.
For such is man. He'll never put aside
His hardware of his own free will, say
For love of virtue, or to earn the praises
Of certain silver tongues at city hall.
If I don't shoot, the other fellow will.
That's logic. Okay. And maybe now you'll ask:

What's to be done? I'll tell you. But first get
This straight: What you've been doing so far is
Disastrous: Sitting idly at your counters
Hoping that everything will be all right
And meanwhile disunited, bickering
Among yourselves, instead of mustering
A strong defense force that would shield you from
The gangsters' depredations. No, I say
This can't go on. The first thing that's needed
Is unity. The second is sacrifices.
What sacrifices? you may ask. Are we
To part with thirty cents on every dollar
For mere protection? No, nothing doing.
Our money is too precious. If protection
Were free of charge, then yes, we'd be all for it.
Well, my dear vegetable dealers, things
Are not so simple. Only death is free:
Everything else costs money. And that includes
Protection, peace and quiet. Life is like
That, and because it never will be any different
The gentlemen and I (there are more outside)
Have resolved to offer you protection . . . But
To show you that we mean to operate
On solid business principles, we've asked
Our partner, Mr. Clark here, the wholesaler
Whom you all know, to come here and address you.

To develop a performance of this speech you could begin by asking what Ui thinks of his audience and what effect he wants his speech to have on them. The latter is easy to figure out: he wants to convince the vegetable dealers to pay him protection money. If you have taken a public speaking course, you'll recognize the pattern behind Ui's remarks, moving from problem to solution. His speech begins by summing up the status quo—chaos, dog-eat-dog, everybody doing exactly what they want to do—and then he gives his listeners a hypothetical example they can all relate to: "Suppose I'm sitting/Peacefully in my vegetable store. . . ." Finally, he points out the failure of the vegetable dealers to solve the problem themselves. The second half of Ui's speech lays out an alternative, namely that the vegetable dealers should pay his gang protection money.

The more subtle issue for your performance is to determine what Ui's speech reveals about his conception of his listeners. They are merchants, and Ui figures nothing scares a merchant more than chaos. Whether armed robbers in the storefront or teenagers loitering in the mall, chaos is always bad for business. Ui believes his listeners think of themselves as hard-headed realists, with a pretty low opinion of their fellow human beings: "If I don't shoot, the other fellow will. That's logic," he asserts, without feeling any need for further proof to convince his listeners. His comment near the end, "The gentlemen and I (there are more outside)/Have resolved to offer you protection," assumes his listeners are a timid lot, easily threatened. Ui also believes that after such veiled threats, these merchants need some reassurance, so he calls on another speaker, someone known and trusted by the merchants, their supplier.

The words Ui speaks are only part of his performance. Your task is to flesh them out with voice and body. Here, too, effect can be a helpful guide. Determining why Ui says what he says should help you select an appropriate tone of voice and physical posture for the character. Try working through Ui's speech, deciding how his posture and tone of voice would change as he moves from the description of chaos, to the reflections on human nature, to the solution he lays out for his listeners, to the mention of other gang members waiting outside, to his introduction of the next speaker. Only through experimentation in rehearsal can you find out which postures and vocal qualities work best.

For Ui's speech, "you" is a group of people within the world of the play, whom we would expect to see listed singly or as a group in the cast of characters at the beginning of the script. If we went to the theatre to see *The Resistible Rise of Arturo Ui,* the person performing Ui's speech might address only the vegetable dealers on the stage. Or he might face forward and include the paying audience as well. This performance choice is so common that audiences accept it with ease. Few audience members would wonder why Ui was talking to them as if they were the vegetable dealers. They accept the role unconsciously.

If performing this speech in class, you would probably pitch it straight to your classmates. And they would not be confused. They would pretend to be vegetable dealers, as you are pretending to be Ui. Some audiences are barely aware of the fact that they, too, are performing, taking on an imaginary role.

Here is another example of a single voice in literature, this one taken from the opening of Virginia Woolf's *A Room of One's Own.* As with Ui's speech, what this lecturer says and how she says it reveal a clear conception of her audience, as well as hinting at her intended effect.

"A Room of One's Own"

by Virginia Woolf

(Virginia Woolf, A Room of One's Own. *London: The Hogarth Press,*
1929, pp. 5–6.)

But, you may say, we asked you to speak about women and fiction—what has that got to do with a room of one's own? I will try to explain. When you asked me to speak about women and fiction I sat down on the banks of a river and began to wonder what the words meant. They might mean simply a few remarks about Fanny Burney; a few more about Jane Austen; a tribute to the Brontes and a sketch of Haworth Parsonage under snow; some witticisms if possible about Miss Mitford; a respectful allusion to George Eliot; a reference to Mrs. Gaskell and one would have done. But at second sight the words seemed not so simple. The title women and fiction might mean, and you may have meant it to mean, women and what they are like; or it might mean women and the fiction that they write; or it might mean women and the fiction that is written about them; or it might mean that somehow all three are inextricably mixed together and you want me to consider them in that light. But when I began to consider the subject in this last way, which seemed the most interesting, I soon saw that it had one fatal drawback. I should never be able to come to a conclusion. I should never be able to fulfill what is, I understand, the first duty of the lecturer—to hand you after an hour's discourse a nugget of pure truth to wrap up between the pages of your notebooks and keep on the mantlepiece for ever. All I could do was to offer you an opinion upon one minor point—a woman must have money and a room of her own if she is to write fiction; and that, as you will see, leaves the great problem of the true nature of woman and the true nature of fiction unsolved. I have shirked the duty of coming to a conclusion upon these two questions— women and fiction remain, so far as I am concerned, unsolved problems. But in order to make some amends I am going to do what I can to show you how I arrived at this opinion about the room and the money. I am going to develop in your presence as fully and freely as I can the train of thought which led me to think this. Perhaps if I lay bare the ideas, the prejudices, that lie behind this statement you will find that they have some bearing upon women and some upon fiction. At any rate, when a subject is highly controversial—and any question about sex is that—one cannot hope to tell the truth. One can only show how one came to hold whatever opinion one does hold. One can only give one's audience the chance of drawing their own conclusions as they observe the limitations, the prejudices, the idiosyncrasies of the speaker.

If you wanted to perform this speaker, once again you would need to take an interest in her audience, in what she thinks of them, and what her intended effect might be. Clearly Ms. Woolf's own thoughts are on her listeners because, from her very first words, she places them centerstage. She begins by performing them, by giving voice and body to a question she thinks they may be asking: "But, you may say, we asked you to speak about women and fiction—what has that got to do with a room of one's own?" Woolf then launches into an analysis of their expectations:

> When you asked me to speak about women and fiction I sat down on the banks of a river and began to wonder what the words meant.

Notice that where Ui conceived of his listeners in contemptible terms, Woolf assumes hers to be both curious and thoughtful. She *respects* them. How might you display this relationship between speaker and audience in Woolf's posture? In her tone of voice? In her pauses and manner of address?

Unlike Ui, Woolf does not want her audience to *do* anything. She claims toward the end that she doesn't even expect them to agree with her. Her sole intended effect is that they should *understand* why she believes a woman cannot write without some money and a room of her own.

One strategy that Woolf employs to achieve her effect in this passage is humor—not of the belly-laugh variety, but something more subtle. Notice, for example, how she gives her listeners a verbal wink and lets them in on her assessment of nineteenth-century women writers:

> *They might mean simply a few remarks about Fanny Burney; a few more about Jane Austen; a tribute to the Brontes and a sketch of Haworth Parsonage under snow; some witticisms if possible about Miss Mitford; a respectful allusion to George Eliot; a reference to Mrs. Gaskell and one would have done.*

Your performance of "and one would have done" needs to express her literary judgment by comic understatement. Her humor is all wrapped up in a relationship with this audience on this occasion.

When rehearsing passages like this, you need to break down the whole into smaller parts. Consider the following:

> *But at second sight the words seemed not so simple. The title women and fiction might mean, and you may have meant it to mean, women and what they are like; or it might mean women and the fiction that they write; or it might mean women and the fiction that is written about them; or it might mean that somehow all three are inextricably mixed together and you want me to consider them in that light.*

If the audience is bored by your performance, no effect will be achieved but boredom. To hold audience attention, you might choose to build these clauses so that each option increases in intensity. Such a performance could imply that each possibility is more intriguing, interesting, and important than the last.

> *But when I began to consider the subject in this last way, which seemed the most interesting, I soon saw that it had one fatal drawback. I should never be able to come to a conclusion. I should never be able to fulfill what is, I understand, the first duty of the lecturer—to hand you after an hour's discourse a nugget of pure truth to wrap up between the pages of your notebooks and keep on the mantlepiece for ever.*

Notice in this section how prominent the I/you relationship becomes. Is the speaker after the same effect as in the previous passage? How might posture and tone of voice mark a difference? Assume that the last sentence is intended to be humorous. Is the speaker poking fun at her listeners, or does she share the joke with them? Try to perform the last sentence both ways and note what different performative behaviors they call for.

> *All I could do was to offer you an opinion upon one minor point—a woman must have money and a room of her own if she is to write fiction; and that, as you will see, leaves the great problem of the true nature of woman and the true nature of fiction unsolved. I have shirked the duty of coming to a conclusion upon these two questions—women and fiction remain, so far as I am concerned, unsolved problems.*

Here Woolf continues to underscore her relationship with the listeners. She refers to herself three times and to them twice. But now the emphasis seems to be on lowering the listeners' expectations. She can give them no grand truth to set on the mantlepiece. Instead, her lecture makes only "one minor point." What performance strategies of voice and body could help you make this shift?

> *But in order to make some amends I am going to do what I can to show you how I arrived at this opinion about the room and the money. I am going to develop in your presence as fully and freely as I can the train of thought which led me to think this. Perhaps if I lay bare the ideas, the prejudices, that lie behind this statement you will find that they have some bearing upon women and some upon fiction. At any rate, when a subject is highly controversial—and any question about sex is that—one cannot hope to tell the truth. One can only show how one came to hold whatever opinion one does hold. One can only give one's audience the chance of drawing their own conclusions as they observe the limitations, the prejudices, the idiosyncrasies of the speaker.*

Perhaps the most obvious difference between the effects intended in this passage and the previous one is that this one raises, rather than lowers, audience expectations. Woolf now takes pains to insist that her "minor point" may not be so minor after all. Woolf has carefully delineated the connections among speaker ("I"), audience ("you"), and topic ("women and fiction").

Finally, if you were to perform this passage in class, you would probably address classmates directly, even though they are no more the audience specified in the text than you are its speaker. Your direct address would require your listeners to perform or to pretend to be the audience of young women who asked Virginia Woolf to talk to them about women and fiction.*

Building a performance on effect focuses your attention on the relationship between a speaker and a listener within the text. Speakers always cast their lis-

---

*A Room of One's Own is based on two papers read to the Arts Society at Newnham and the Odtaa at Girton in October, 1928.

teners in specific roles—as adversaries or allies, confidantes or critics, insiders or outsiders. One major task of performance is to make this casting clear and to assist an audience in taking on their parts.

Performing Listeners

"What the author does is to make his reader very much as he makes his characters."
Henry James

"Yes, Dan'l Webster's dead—or at least, they buried him" is the first sentence of Stephen Vincent Benét's "The Devil and Daniel Webster." If you were performing this story, your very first word, "Yes," casts your audience in a specific role. They must pretend they just asked you the question, "Is Webster dead?"

Here is the rest of Benét's opening paragraph. As you read it, try to determine the performance expectations the speaker makes of his audience:

> But every time there's a thunderstorm around Marshfield, they say you can hear his rolling voice in the hollows of the sky. And they say that if you go to his grave and speak loud and clear, "Dan'l Webster—Dan'l Webster!" the ground'll begin to shiver and the trees begin to shake. And after a while you'll hear a deep voice saying, "Neighbor, how stands the Union?" Then you better answer the Union stands as she stood, rock-bottomed and copper-sheathed, one and indivisible, or he's liable to rear right out of the ground. At least, that's what I was told when I was a youngster.

QUESTIONS FOR DISCUSSION

1. Notice that the speaker refers to "Marshfield" as if it were a familiar place to the listener. If you were audience for this performance, what specific expectations does the text make of you? Are you cast as a citizen of Marshfield or as an outsider?

2. Besides the location of Marshfield, what other factual information does the speaker assume the listener knows? To play this audience role effectively, what gaps in your personal knowledge would need to be filled in?

3. The speaker says "Dan'l" instead of "Daniel" and uses some other archaic vocabulary. How might such pronunciations influence your performance as audience?

When engaged in everyday conversation, a speaker usually addresses you as yourself. In the case of literary language, on the other hand, performance demands as much role-playing from the listener as from the performer.

Read through the following poem and pay special attention to the performance demands made of the *listener.*

"Where Are the Waters of Childhood?"

by Mark Strand

(From Selected Poems by Mark Strand, Copyright © 1979, 1980 by Mark Strand. Reprinted by permission of Alfred A. Knopf, Inc.)

See where the windows are boarded up,
where the gray siding shines in the sun and salt air
and the asphalt shingles on the roof have peeled or fallen off,
where tiers of oxeye daisies float on a sea of grass?
That's the place to begin.

Enter the kingdom of rot,
smell the damp plaster, step over the shattered glass,
   the pockets of dust,
the rags, the soiled remains of a mattress,
look at the rusted stove and sink, at the rectangular stain
on the wall where Winslow Homer's *Gulf Stream* hung.

Go to the room where your father and mother
would let themselves go in the drift and pitch of love,
and hear, if you can, the creak of their bed,
then go to the place where you hid.

Go to your room, to all the rooms whose cold, damp air you
   breathed,
to all the unwanted places where summer, fall, winter, spring,
seem the same unwanted season, where the trees you knew have
   died
and other trees have risen. Visit that other place
you barely recall, that other house half hidden.

See the two dogs burst into sight. When you leave,
they will cease, snuffed out in the glare of an earlier light.
Visit the neighbors down the block; he waters his lawn,
she sits on her porch, but not for long.
When you look again they are gone.

Keep going back, back to the field, flat and sealed in mist.
On the other side, a man and a woman are waiting;

they have come back, your mother before she was gray,
your father before he was white.

Now look at the North West Arm, how it glows a deep cerulean
   blue.
See the light on the grass, the one leaf burning, the cloud
that flares. You're almost there, in a moment your parents
will disappear, leaving you under the light of a vanished star,
under the dark of a star newly born. Now is the time.

Now you invent the boat of your flesh and set it upon the waters
and drift in the gradual swell, in the laboring salt.
Now you look down. The waters of childhood are there.

The speaker of this poem *commands* listeners to see, to enter, to smell, to look
at, to go to. You must pretend that the images of the speaker's past—the house,
the dogs, the neighbors—are the images of your own past, that the speaker's
parents are "your mother and father," the room "your room." Performance is always a collaborative achievement between speaker and listener. Or, to put it another way, literature is achieved through an ensemble performance where both
speaker and listener must play their parts.

QUESTIONS FOR DISCUSSION

1. If you were in the audience to hear this poem in performance, what
   might induce you to comply with the speaker's commands? What attitudes of voice and body on the speaker's part could help reduce resistance and encourage your playing along?

2. How many different things does the speaker ask you to do? Where
   does each mental activity begin and end?

3. You are asked to create places and actions out of your imagination.
   In the third stanza, the speaker asks you not only to go to "your
   room," but to "all the rooms" where you experienced or felt a particular way. Can you describe, in your own words, what Strand's
   speaker is talking about here? Are there actual "rooms," places,
   houses in your own past that fit the speaker's description?

4. Would it be possible to perform the "you" of this poem as the speaker
   talking to him or herself? What performance behavior would signal
   to the audience that you were talking to yourself and not to them? If

someone in your class performed it this way, how would your role as listener change?

Preparing to Perform the Listener

If the performance of literature is a collaborative enterprise, then the person standing in front of an audience cannot be held solely responsible for its success or failure. Performance occurs in a common space shared by both performer and audience, by speaker and listener. If it is a public performance, and you as listener don't know the literature, your responsibility may be less than if you have been expected to read the work previously. In the latter case, you have an opportunity (indeed, an obligation) to prepare yourself for the audience's role. This can be accomplished first by narrowing the gap between what you know and what the listener in the text is expected to know. When Ui says to the cauliflower salesmen, "Chaos is rampant," he assumes they know what both words mean. Your responsibility, before listening to any text in performance, is to look up unfamiliar words. When Woolf says to her listeners,

> [A lecture on "Women and Fiction"] might mean simply a few remarks about Fanny Burney; a few more about Jane Austen; a tribute to the Brontes and a sketch of Haworth Parsonage under snow; some witticisms if possible about Miss Mitford; a respectful allusion to George Eliot; a reference to Mrs. Gaskell . . . ,

she assumes you know who these people are. If you don't, some simple research is required. Nobody can make you do this, of course, unless your instructor gives a quiz. It's a matter of taking responsibility for your half of the performance collaboration.

Knowing the dictionary definition of words is only a starting point for audience preparation. The more creative and harder work comes when trying to take on the perspective of a listener projected inside the text. Can you adopt that listener's knowledge and attitudes? Can you become a citizen of her region or a member of his club? Can you hear the dialect and embody the physical presence of the listener? Ultimately, everything that we recommend to performers about the embodiment of a speaker applies to audiences, as well.

To help an audience enter the shared space of literature, you may want to consider introductory remarks before certain performances. For instance, if you were performing the Woolf lecture, you might want to point out a connection between the Bronte sisters and the reference to Haworth Parsonage.

EXERCISE: BECOMING RESOURCEFUL

One of the most obvious but troublesome aspects of performing the listener is the need to "know" basic information the speaker assumes you know. Sooner or later, a conscientious listener is forced to do some research. At first, this process may be tedious. But with practice, you will learn where to go to find out the kinds of information required to perform the listeners of literature. Listed below are a sampling of expectations demanded of listeners by the speakers of poems or stories in this book. Divide them up among class members, and ask each student to report back *the process* of seeking answers. (You might choose to compile these resources as a class for future reference work in your own library.) There are some obvious places to start, such as an unabridged dictionary, the *Oxford Companion to American Literature,* and the *MLA Bibliography,* but don't forget that most wonderful of research resources, the reference librarian.

1. p. 6   Where is Llano?

2. p. 7   What story do the characters Tilly and Spike come from?

3. p. 9   Who are Sappho and Seuss?

4. p. 10   Give a plot synopsis of *Electra.*

5. p. 11   Who is Richard Schechner?

6. p. 13   Who is Eudora Welty?

7. p. 43   What do the letters IGA stand for?

8. p. 54   Who is Garcia Lorca, and what does he have in common with Walt Whitman?

9. p. 54   Who is Charon?

10. p. 54   Where is Lethe, and what is unusual about it?

11. p. 80   Name all the famous people who lived at Haworth Parsonage.

12. p. 85   Describe what Homer's *Gulf Stream* looks like.

Talking to Oneself

A special instance of the single voice in literature is any text in which the speaker addresses himself or herself. This is not an unusual circumstance, whether it takes the form of private reflection, confessional poem, dramatic soliloquy, diary, or journal. Even in such a case, the speaker (or writer) intends a certain effect.

Many people keep journals or diaries as records of their internal dialogues. Confined to her bed, Alice James, the invalid sister of novelist Henry and psychologist William, recorded her thoughts and feelings in a now famous diary. Assuming that she wrote primarily for herself, can you determine the intended effect in each of the following excerpts? How would you build a performance to make that effect clear for an audience?

The Diary of Alice James

by Alice James

(Excerpts from The Diary of Alice James, *edited by Leon Edel. First published in 1934 by Dodd, Mead & Co. Inc.*)

September 27, 1890: . . . These doctors tell you that you will die, or *recover!* But you *don't* recover. I have been at these alterations since I was nineteen and I am neither dead nor recovered—as I am now forty-two there has surely been time for either process. I suppose one has a greater sense of intellectual degradation after an interview with a doctor than from any human experience. . . .

May 31, 1891: To him who waits, all things come! My aspirations may have been eccentric, but I cannot complain now, that they have not been brilliantly fulfilled. Ever since I have been ill, I have longed and longed for some palpable disease, no matter how conventionally dreadful a label it might have, but I was always driven back to stagger alone under the monstrous mass of subjective sensations, which that sympathetic being "the medical man" had no higher inspiration than to assure me I was personally responsible for, washing his hands of me with a graceful complacency under my very nose. Dr. Torry was the only man who ever treated me like a rational being, who did not assume, because I was a victim to so many pains, that I was, of necessity, an arrested mental development too.

Notwithstanding all the happiness and comfort here, I have been going downhill at a steady trot; so they sent for Sir Andrew Clark four days ago; and the blessed being has endowed me not only with cardiac complications, but says that a lump that I have had in one of my breasts for three months, which has given me a great deal of pain, is a tumour, that nothing can be done for me but to alleviate pain, that it is only a question of time, etc. This with a delicate embroidery of "the most distressing case of nervous hyperaesthesia: added to a spinal neurosis that has taken me off my legs for seven years; with attacks of rheumatic gout in my stomach for the last twenty" ought to satisfy the most inflated pathologic vanity. It is decidedly indecent to catalogue oneself in this way, but I put it down in a scientific spirit, to show that though I have no productive worth, I have a certain value as an indestructible quantity.

March 4, 1892: I am being ground slowly on the grim grindstone of physical pain, and on two nights I had almost asked for K.'s lethal dose, but one steps hesitatingly along such unaccustomed ways and endures from second to second; and I feel sure that it can't be possible but what the bewildered little hammer that keeps me going will very shortly see the decency of ending his distracted career; however this may be, physical pain however great ends in itself and falls away like dry husks from the mind, whilst moral discords and nervous horrors sear the soul. These last, Katharine has completely under the control of her rhythmic hand, so I go no longer in dread. Oh the wonderful moment when I felt myself floated for the first time into the deep sea of divine *cessation*, and saw all the dear old mysteries and miracles vanish into vapour! That first experience doesn't repeat itself, fortunately, for it might become a seduction. . . .

AuTHoRiAl EffECT REvisiTED

In May Swenson's poem "Bleeding," the poet provides the reader with a narrator, in addition to two speaking characters. As you work through this poem, analyze what effect you think the narrator is after, as well as what effects the two characters pursue. Assume that the effect the author is after is the same as the narrator's. Describe the difference between the effects the Cut and the Knife pursue, and contrast both of those with the effect the author is after.

"BLEEdiNG"

by May Swenson

("Bleeding," by May Swenson, copyright © 1970. Used with permission of the literary estate of May Swenson.)

Stop bleeding   said the knife.
I would if I   could said the cut.
Stop bleeding   you make me messy with this blood.
I'm sorry said   the cut.
Stop or I will   sink in farther said the knife.
Don't said the   cut.
The knife did   not say it couldn't help it but it sank in farther.
If only you   didn't bleed said the knife I wouldn't have to do this.
I know said   the cut I bleed too easily I hate that I can't
help it I   wish I were a knife like you and didn't have to bleed.
Meanwhile   stop bleeding will you said the knife.
Yes you   are a mess and sinking in farther said the cut I will
have to   stop.
Have you   stopped by now said the knife.
I've almost   stopped I think.
Why must you   bleed in the first place said the knife.
For the reason   maybe that you must do what you must do said the
                                                                        cut.

I can't stand   bleeding said the knife and sank in farther.
I hate it too   said the cut I know it isn't you it's me

you're lucky   to be a knife you ought to be glad about that.
Too many cuts   around said the knife they're messy I don't know
how they stand   themselves.
They don't said   the cut.
You're bleeding   again.
No I've stopped   said the cut. See you're coming out now the
blood is drying   it will rub off you'll be shiny again and clean.
If only cuts   wouldn't bleed so much said the knife coming out a
                little.

But then knives   might become dull said the cut.
Aren't you bleeding   a little said the knife.
I hope not said the   cut.
I feel you are just   a little.
Maybe just a little   but I can stop now.
I feel a little   wetness still said the knife sinking in
a little but then   coming out a little.
Just a little maybe   just enough said the cut.
That's enough now   stop now do you feel better now said the knife.
I feel I have to   bleed to feel I think said the cut.
I don't I don't have   to feel said the knife drying now becoming
                shiny.

After a public performance of this poem by the poet, an audience member asked what it was about, and May Swenson answered, "Power." Assuming this is the subject matter of "Bleeding," how does this assumption help you determine effect? Who has the power—the Knife? or the Cut? What do you think the Knife and the Cut could represent outside the poem, in your own world? What impact does the poem's typographical presentation make on the reader, and who decides to cut the lines in a neat curve all the way down from top to bottom? The Knife? The Cut? The poet? How might you represent that feature of print in the space and time dimensions of performance?

"The Tale of Peter Rabbit," a familiar story by Beatrix Potter, begins with Mrs. Rabbit warning her children: "Now my dears, . . . you may go into the fields or down the lane, but don't go into Mr. McGregor's garden: your Father had an accident there; he was put in a pie by Mrs. McGregor."

It doesn't take Sherlock Holmes to decipher the effect that Mrs. Rabbit intends to create on her children, namely, to frighten them enough that they won't go into Mr. McGregor's garden. How you choose to perform that line depends in part on your knowledge of how a mother in everyday life might try to get her children to obey rules for their own safety. But notice how Mrs. Rabbit's speech to her children is framed:

> *Once upon a time there were four little Rabbits, and their names were—*
> *Flopsy, Mopsy, Cotton-tail, and Peter. They lived with their Mother in a*

> sand-bank, underneath the roots of a very big fir-tree. "Now my dears,"
> said old Mrs. Rabbit one morning, "you may go into the fields or down the
> lane, but don't go into Mr. McGregor's garden: your Father had an acci-
> dent there; he was put in a pie by Mrs. McGregor."

Important as it is that you should perform Mrs. Rabbit's warning to her children believably, it's even more important that her speech should further the intention of the narrator, who may or may not be interested in warning the reader to stay out of any gardens. The narrator wants to establish several effects at the outset of her story. She wants the reader to know (1) that the garden is dangerous; (2) that Peter has been warned not to go there; and (3) that something interesting is about to happen in the story.

To make matters more complicated, you have to ask in the performance of any story whether a narrator's intention is the same as the author's. Usually they are. For example, there appears to be no significant difference between what the narrator is after in "The Tale of Peter Rabbit" and the effect desired by the author. We could even name the narrator Beatrix Potter and not seriously mislead the reader. However, we have already witnessed several instances where the author's intention is clearly different from the speaker's. In such a case, the performer is accountable for the widest frame, that of the author.

In *Huckleberry Finn*, Huck encounters men hunting for runaway slaves. They ask him if he knows where any are hiding. Of course, Huck's companion on the raft is Jim, a runaway slave. Understand that Huck had been reared to accept slavery, had never questioned its morality, and believed it was wrong to hide slaves. Nevertheless, his love for Jim keeps Huck from betraying him. Huck, the innocent narrator, thinks he has done wrong and says,

> They went off and I got aboard the raft, feeling bad and low, because I
> knowed very well I had done wrong, and I see it warn't no use for me to
> try to learn to do right; a body that don't get started right when he's little
> ain't got no show—when the pinch comes there ain't nothing to back him
> up and keep him to his word, and so he gets beat.

For Huck, these words represent a confession. But for the author, Mark Twain, the same words intend an opposite effect. He wants his readers to admire Huck's natural morality.

Performance adds yet another frame to literature's nest of intentions. Just as Huck and Twain have their individual aims, so do you as their performer. In many cases, the effect you want to create in an audience is the same as what you believe the author's to be. But not always. There are times when you may choose to resist authorial or narrative intentions.

Here's an excerpt from Cotton Mather's essay "The Wonders of the Invisible World," written in the seventeenth century to justify witchcraft trials then taking place in Salem, Massachusetts:

> *An army of devils is horribly broke in upon the place which is the center,*
> *and after a sort, the first-born of our English settlements [Salem]: and the*
> *houses of the good people there are filled with the doleful shrieks of their*
> *children and servants, tormented by invisible hands, with tortures alto-*
> *gether preternatural. . . . These our poor afflicted neighbors, quickly after*
> *they become infected and infested with these demons, arrive to a capacity*
> *of discerning those which they conceive the shapes of their troublers; and*
> *notwithstanding the great and just suspicion that the demons might impose*
> *the shapes of innocent persons in their spectral exhibitions upon the suf-*
> *ferers (which may perhaps prove no small part of the witch-plot in the*
> *issue), yet many of the persons thus represented, being examined, several*
> *of them have been convicted of a very damnable witchcraft. . . .*

Regardless of one's view of the supernatural, it's hardly likely that any contemporary performer would share Mather's clear intention to provoke his audience to burn supposed witches. In fact, a performer today might choose a style that would parody the speaker, creating an opposite effect to Mather's original intention. (In Chapter 7, we talk further about performances that resist their texts.)

Multiple Effects: "Medicine Woman"

Effect can be followed like a trace chemical through the body of any literary work, revealing an author's vision, articulating a speaker's viewpoint, motivating a character's action, provoking a listener's response, and enticing the reader's collaboration. Here is a new poem for analysis. Read it slowly. Hear its voices. Delineate the multiple effects registering on different characters.

"Medicine Woman"
—for Dovie

by Cheryl Savageau

(*"Medicine Woman" from Cheryl Savageau's* Dirt Road Home. *Curbstone Press,*
1995. Copyright © 1995 by Cheryl Savageau. Reprinted with permission of
Curbstone Press. Distributed by Consortium.)

medicine woman they call me
as if I should like it
like the kids in school
who called me little white dove
from some stupid song
about one more Indian woman

jumping to her death
how come you have an animal name?
they asked me, how come?
and I went home to ask my father
how come, Dad, how come
I have an animal name?

now white women come into my shop
and ask me to bless their houses
(what's wrong with them, I want to ask)
name their grandchildren
(do I know your daughters?)
blow some smoke around
say some words, do
whatever it is you do
we want someone spiritual—
you're Indian, right?

right. my tongue is held
by their gray hair
they are grandmothers
deserving of respect
and so I speak
as gently as I can
you'd let me, a stranger,
come into your home, I ask
let me touch
your new grandchild
let me name the baby
anything
that comes into my head?
I am not believing this
but they are smiling
and tell me again
we want someone spiritual to do it

I write to my father
how come you never
told me who we are, where
we came from?

Women keep coming into my shop
putting stones in my hands
Can you feel that? they ask

Of course I can feel it
I'm not dead, but that
is not the right answer

My father writes back
the garden is doing good
the corn is up
there's lots of butterflies
all I know is
we come from the stars.

Part of the complexity of this poem is that its single speaker quotes so many other speakers. Her solo voice becomes a virtual choir of the voices of others. The very first words of the poem, "medicine woman," are quoted speech; it's the name "*they* call me." That name reminds the speaker of an earlier name, "little white dove," that the kids in school used to call her, another form of quotation. And even "little white dove" is an allusion drawn "from some stupid song." Later in the first stanza, she quotes two actual conversations:

how come you have an animal name?
they asked me, how come?
and I went home to ask my father
how come, Dad, how come
I have an animal name?

In the second stanza, the speaker's voice doubles itself into public and private utterance. The two parenthetical questions are interior for the speaker's own musing, what she would *like* to say to the white women who come into her shop but does not say.

(what's wrong with them, I want to ask)
(do I know your daughters?)

Any analysis of this poem for performance would have to begin by sorting out the multiple voices of its single speaker. They provide cues for performance behaviors *because* they point to the effects hoped for by both speaker and poet.

Right from the start, the reader meets a woman living in a double-bind. What's most apparent in her poignant words is the call for recognition of her individual and authentic identity. She resents being categorized, marginalized, by others. "Medicine woman," her current status, and "little white dove," her childhood name, offend and discomfort her equally. But these names are not mere words, without ethical and political consequences. The *effect* of these names, especially "medicine woman," is to make "white women come into my shop and ask me to bless their houses, name their grandchildren, blow some smoke around, say some words." The script spinning out from the name "medicine woman" is as logical as it is unfair. The last two lines of the second stanza point to the blind assumptions of the white women who frequent the speaker's shop:

> we want someone spiritual—
> you're Indian, right?

The double-bind of the speaker's life becomes evident when you stand back from the poem and listen to what is *not* spoken. She is dependent for her livelihood on the very people who demean her. Her identity—at least her economic self—depends on those who rob her of identity, a paradox of repression.

The third stanza lays out a classic case of co-dependency between "medicine woman" and "white women." She gives native respect to the grandmothers whose unbelievable requests make her hold her tongue. The multiple effects of this conflict are that the white women receive what they cannot understand and do not deserve, while the "medicine woman" gives what she would not lose.

In the fourth stanza, the speaker writes to her father, asking the age-old questions: Who are we? Where did we come from? In the sixth stanza, he writes back, "All I know is we come from the stars"—an answer tucked in sequence with other natural observations about the garden, the corn crop, and an abundance of butterflies. Perhaps it is ironic that the speaker who knows who she is *not*—namely, the person whom others think her to be—should have to ask her father who she is. That the poet gives him the last word may suggest his answer is satisfying, or at least as close to the truth as the speaker is likely to come.

Notice that the conversation of this poem is spoken in confidence to the reader. We become privy to the silent thoughts, discreet judgments, and razor-sharp humor of a woman whose outward speech and appearance are enigmatic. As a result, her words provoke a response from us that's quite different from their effect on the "white women" inside the world of the poem. This distinction is key to the overall effect intended by the poet.

Cheryl Savageau places us, her readers, in a double-bind of our own. She invites us to empathize and identify with the "medicine woman" while, at the same time, indicting us for marginalizing her. This push and pull of multiple effects bonds together the poet, the poem's speaker, the unnamed characters of her world, and us, the readers. We are co-dependent, all of us, in the collaborative achievement of meaning.

QUESTIONS FOR DISCUSSION

To explore the *effects* of a poem demands asking the question *why.*

1. Why does the poem begin with names? What's the effect on the speaker? What's the effect on the reader?

2. Why, if naming is so important, do we never learn the speaker's name? What's the effect of this omission?

3. In the first stanza, she asks her father, "How come I have an animal name?" She ends the poem by asking her father, "How come you never told me who we are, where we came from?" Why doesn't she tell us her father's answer to the first question? And why does she tell us the answer to the second?

4. Annoyed at the grandmothers, she says, "My tongue is held by their gray hair. They are grandmothers deserving of respect. And so I speak as gently as I can." In what ways does this respect influence the reader's perceptions of the "medicine woman"?

5. If someone in class were to perform "Medicine Woman" addressing the audience directly, this performer would be asking you to play the listener in the poem.

    a. Who is the listener in the poem?

    b. Do you share the values that the speaker assumes her listeners hold?

    c. If so, what challenges do you face in embracing the listener's role?

    d. If not, what challenges do you confront?

    e. How is your sympathy aroused by the speaker's resentment of the names "medicine woman" and "little white dove"?

    f. How does the speaker paint the "white women" throughout the poem?

6. In Virginia Woolf's *A Room of One's Own*, the speaker used humor to achieve her effect. This speaker also uses humor. Where does it occur? What are its effects?

7. Throughout this poem, the speaker asks an implicit question: Who am I? But the poet asks a different question of the reader: Who are *you*? That is, are you the "white women" or the kids at school? Who are you in relation to this speaker? As a class, discuss the effects intended by the poem's speaker and its author. Are these effects different, as in several other cases we have read in this chapter? Are they the same? How do you know?

8. When performing "Medicine Woman," you would have to perform at least two voices other than the main speaker's—the white grandmothers and the speaker's father. How does the poem's intended effect shape these two voices?

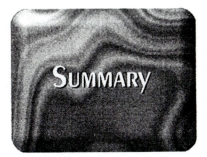

SUMMARY

In this chapter, we have complicated our understanding of how literature works. Within the space and time worlds of language, there exist multiple levels of effect. All literary speakers—named and unnamed, characters and narrators—intend effects that usually must be inferred from their speech situation. Sometimes such intentions are observable within the fictive world by noting their effects on other inhabitants, but we have considered literary examples in which a speaker addresses himself or herself, rather than another person. Even then, language continues to display effect. Many works are meant to be overheard by the reader, who stands unobserved by anyone inside the fictive world. Outside the frame of any speaker's consciousness exists yet another dimension of semantic control, as defined by an author's effect. And we have added a final frame in the actions of a performer giving voice and body to all the other frames. If wheels within wheels, frames within frames, are beginning to spin dizzyingly in your mind, perhaps it's time we focused on sense—the subject of Chapter 4.

Chapter Four

Performing to Make Sense

"If there's no meaning in it," said the King, "that saves us a world of trouble, you know, as we needn't try to find any."
Lewis Carroll, *Through the Looking-Glass*

Faced with the challenges of creating a world through language and determining the dynamics of effect for every utterance spoken, making "sense" out of literature may seem comparatively easy. Most of us labor under the illusion that "sense" is the *first* thing we make when reading. However, you can't make reliable sense of what any speaker says until you've situated the utterance in a concrete world and within a specific relationship. This is not to say that making sense takes care of itself. As a performer, you must work out strategies for communicating meaning. If your audience doesn't "get it," all is lost. Conversely, when your audience does "get it," they can help achieve fullness in the collaboration of a literary experience.

What's the Role of Sense-Making?

At the beginning of a movie, an audience may not be able to make immediate sense of what the characters are doing or saying. Steven Spielberg, whose films are hardly obscure, frequently confronts his audiences with an initial series of scenes that don't make sense. "Close Encounters of the Third Kind" is typical. You jump from (1) the Sonoran Desert where a group of officials find World War II airplanes, to (2) an airport control tower where an incoming plane has a close encounter with a UFO, to (3) the Gobi Desert where scientists come upon a ship, to (4) a home in Muncie, Indiana where every electrical appliance switches on at the same time. None of these scenes makes sense by itself. You may not even be able to make an educated guess what the characters are talking about (for example, the old man who keeps muttering in Spanish, "The sun came out and sang last night"). Oddly, audience members thoroughly enjoy the movie long before they are able to make sense of what they are watching.

Some literary authors have gone so far as to insist that making sense is only a minor concern in their enterprise. T. S. Eliot compared "meaning" to the meat a burglar throws to a guard dog so he can go about his business unimpeded. When a friend of the French poet Mallarmé expressed puzzlement that he could not write a good poem despite having so many good ideas, Mallarmé responded, "That is because poems are made out of *words*, not ideas."

It's hard to generalize about the role of sense-making in our enjoyment of the verbal arts. In everyday interactions, we know that almost every single word has many possible meanings. Most of these are provided in a dictionary, although only the context tells us which one is right. The word "note," for example, means one thing to a musician, another thing to a lover, and a third thing to a student writing a term paper.

All the dimensions of world that we have discussed (space, time, speakers, action) and effect (the nesting of intentions for multiple audiences) are sometimes lumped together under the single term *context*. Speakers and listeners can make sense of one another's words only by considering their context. What is true of individual words is applicable, as well, to sentences and longer verbal sequences.

If we shift this analysis from everyday interactions to literature, however, we encounter a paradox. The reader must have some context to make sense of the words on the page. At the same time, he or she can grasp the context only by making sense of those same words. When reading a story, you can enter its world only by interpreting sentences, but sentences can make sense only after you've entered the story's world. It would appear that sense and context are linked together so inextricably that one can "get it" only by getting both at the same time.

Personal Significance

Even when context is carefully delineated, the sense of words tends to expand and contract for each reader. Even for a single person, the same story may make sense in a different way with each new encounter. This is so because a poem, play, or story permits many possible interpretations, and you can make many different senses out of a single work of verbal art. Those who argue that rap lyrics represent a threat to society and should be censored are making different sense than other listeners who find the same lyrics merely entertaining. Both interpretations differ from that of rap fans who find the words profoundly expressive. Our point is that a given set of lyrics, the words themselves, don't change. Individuals make very different sense of the same language in part because they bring such different assumptions and values *to* their listening.

Often, you can read a story or view a performance on two or more levels at the same time, making multiple senses of the words simultaneously. In fact, one of the enduring appeals of literature for many people is that any story can be read as being about *them and their world*, while clearly acknowledging that it is primarily about others in a different world. Literary theorists struggle to distinguish between the literal or objective meanings of words and the personal or subjective interpretations ascribed by each reader. This differentiation is sometimes marked by the words "sense" and "significance." *Sense* is what the author intends the words to mean, whereas *significance* is what an individual reader makes of them.

Significance is probably what motivates you to select a particular piece of literature to perform. The poem, story, or play means something to you personally. It speaks to you in some special way, perhaps resonating with your own experience. Your rehearsal process becomes a laboratory for exploring personal significance. To realize vividly the place, time, speaker, and effect of a literary text requires that you put so much of yourself into the language that you may begin to feel indistinguishable from its world. When this melding occurs between self and text, a poem begins to make *perfect sense*. Human beings long for the kind of personal significance that art affords. The intimate connection between yourself and another, which is available through performance, is one of the fundamental attractions of this art form.

Social Significance

The *significance* of literature extends beyond the personal realm to encompass public, social, and political dimensions, as well. If you turn back to the poem "At the I.G.A.," we can illustrate the point. Some readers identify personally with the woman living in the trailer. Others are more interested in the economic conditions of the woman's life and in the societal values that constrain it. Still others find the poem's greatest significance to be its statement about *class* in North America, or its social construction of *gender*. While each interpretation emerges from an individual's viewpoint, many of these readings move well beyond the personal.

Finding significance in literature is a matter of discovering *correspondences* between the world of the text and your own personal experience or some social reality. Throughout this book we have been exploring the similarities between everyday and literary language. Maybe the only important distinction is that we read literature hoping to find many kinds of significance in it. One theorist argues that what makes an experience aesthetic is the presence of a "heightened perceptual interest in making sense."*

The performance of literature has an obvious advantage over print on the page, because you can make sense happen with your body and voice, as well as through words. The telephone has a similar advantage over a letter when it comes to making sense, because speakers and listeners can rely on inflection and pause as guides to meaning.

How Vocal Performance Makes Sense

If you review the conversation transcriptions of "It's Gun Be Hard to Do" and *'Night Mother* in Chapter 1, you'll be reminded of how every performance marker helps to make sense of the language being spoken. Our analysis of those

*Richard Lind, "The Aesthetic Essence of Art," *Journal of Aesthetics and Art Criticism*, 50, No. 2 (Spring 1992), p. 123.

two interactions demonstrated that meaning was often tied more closely to vocal features of performance than to the dictionary definitions of words.

Research indicates that, in our everyday interactions, most of us hear only a fraction of what others say to us. Some tests of interactive listening suggest that we process as little as fifteen percent of what we hear. One way that speakers manage to communicate despite this startling inefficiency is to emphasize *key words* through the vocal variables of force, pitch, and volume. This is as true in the performance of literature as in everyday life. It is possible to communicate by eliminating everything but key words, as we do in a telegram. Read, for instance, the following poem:

"Biography"

by Imamu Amiri Baraka

(*In* Anthology of American Literature II: Realism to the Present, *3rd edition, edited by George McMichael. New York: Macmillan, 1985.*)

Hangs
whipped
blood
stripped
meat pulled
clothes ripped
slobber
feet dangled
pointing
noised
noise
churns
face
black sky
and moon
leather night
red
bleeds
drips
ground
sucks
blood
hangs
life wetting
sticky
mud

laughs
bonnets
wolfmoon
crazyteeth
hangs

hangs

grandaddy
grandaddy, they tore

his
neck

In everyday talk, key words make sense in context. With this poem, how-ever, key words must create their own context, and you must make sense of these key words by supplying a frame of reference. As you imagine a situation in which the words can make sense, you must begin to guess missing words, filling in the blanks of the poet's sparse language. With a minimalist poem like "Biography," the performer plays a very active role in sense-making. If several members of your class were to rehearse and perform this poem without con-sulting one another, you'd likely see a wide range of interpretations, and that variety would speak to the active collaboration of each sense-making performer. Or if each of you were to try writing out the poem in prose paragraphs, sup-plying the missing words you believe should surround these key words, no two texts would be exactly alike. As long as all of your versions agreed on *what's going on* in the poem, they would make the same sense of the situation. On the other hand, if some versions diverged in the interpretation of key words, they would make a whole new sense of the poem. Compare the following attempts to fill in the blanks for just the first four lines of "Biography":

> *The man hangs. He has already been whipped, and blood has striped the body.*

> *The sausage hangs. The butcher has just whipped its ingredients, and there is fresh blood on the striped label.*

Which performer has the *right* situation, context, or world in mind? If you continue both these prose passages through the next four lines, is one easier to fill in than the other? Can you think of other situations that might make sense of the words in this poem? When faced with two or more contexts that make very different sense of the same words, how do you decide which one to perform?

Most poems provide fuller language worlds than the one we just looked at and, in such cases, *you* must decide which key words to emphasize to make sense for your audience. One approach to making this determination is to differentiate between *new ideas* and *echo ideas*. The first introduction of a new word, image, or idea usually demands greater emphasis than its repetition, whether in the same or similar form. Try reading the following sentences aloud:

1. I hear jazz.

2. I hear great jazz.

3. I hear great modern jazz.

Depending on the context, any word in the first sentence might be the key to making sense since they are all *new* ideas. In the second sentence, "great" receives stress because all the other words *echo* ideas already introduced. Likewise, in the third sentence, only "modern" needs special emphasis. Again, you could return to any of the transcripts of everyday conversation discussed in earlier chapters to find easy analogues to the concept of new and echo ideas.

When performing the language of life *and* literature, you make sense by stressing key words and, as it were, throwing others away. Key words are those that can do the most work in making sense within the context of an utterance. Writers have long been aware of this convention and often deliberately feature key words in their literary constructions. Here are two selections, one written in the earliest days of modern English, and the other in 1992. Develop a performance of their sense by relying primarily on vocal stress.

From "The Merchant of Venice"

by William Shakespeare

Bassanio: Sweet Portia,
          If you did know to whom I gave the ring,
          If you did know for whom I gave the ring,
          And would conceive for what I gave the ring,
          And how unwillingly I left the ring,
          When naught would be accepted but the ring,
          You would abate the strength of your displeasure.

Portia: If you had known the virtue of the ring,
          Or half her worthiness that gave the ring,
          Or your own honor to contain the ring,
          You would not then have parted with the ring.

(V, i, 192–200.)

"Like Most Revelations"

by Richard Howard

It is the movement that incites the form,
discovered as a downward rapture—yes,
it is the movement that delights the form,
sustained by its own velocity. And yet

it is the movement that delays the form
while darkness slows and encumbers; in fact
it is the movement that betrays the form,
baffled in such toils of ease, until

it is the movement that deceives the form,
beguiling our attention—we supposed
it is the movement that achieves the form.
Were we mistaken? What does it matter if

it is the movement that negates the form?
Even though we give (give up) ourselves
to this mortal process of continuing,
it is the movement that creates the form.

To see how natural it is to stress new ideas and "throw away" echoes, read aloud the following sentences, and note your natural vocal emphasis:

It is the movement that incites the form.
It is the movement that delights the form.
It is the movement that delays the form.
It is the movement that betrays the form.
It is the movement that deceives the form.
It is the movement that achieves the form.
It is the movement that negates the form.
It is the movement that creates the form.

To start a rehearsal process with vocal stressing is to work with very small units (individual words) and only one performance tool (your voice). If this approach works for you, it should soon suggest other dimensions of the literature to explore and other performance choices to consider. Don't resist these, but let stressing lead you where it will in an effort to make sense happen for yourself and your audience.

While rehearsing the lines from "The Merchant of Venice," though you began by working out a conventionally stressed performance of its key words, you might well move to a consideration of the *effect* these words are intended to have. Bassanio, you might conclude, wants forgiveness, whereas Portia wants to inflict guilt. The new and echo ideas in these two speeches are exaggerated so far beyond what you would expect in ordinary conversation that they draw attention to themselves right from the start. If Bassanio seeks forgiveness, you could explore the rhetorical strategy of his trying to charm Portia through his semantic playfulness. In working out Portia's response, which rises to the challenge of Bassanio's verbal game and ups the ante, you could tie the sense of her words to the effect you believe she intends. Of course, your performance of both Bassanio's and Portia's language is linked to their space-and-time world, as well as to their effects and sense.

If you begin rehearsing Howard's poem by working out its patterns of verbal stress, you won't get too far before needing to consider what those abstract terms "movement" and "form" might be referring to. The poet's reluctance to specify invites you, the performer, to find references or applications that are most significant for you. For one performer, "movement" and "form" may refer to dance. For another, to music. For still another, to the acts that shape our lives. In the natural shift from matters of stress to questions of subject, a performer of this poem moves from sense to significance, whether personal, social, or political.

Sense and Irony

One of the most dramatic ways that you can make sense of literary language for an audience is through the orchestration of tone of voice. In fact, tone of voice is capable of reversing the literal sense of words to create an entirely different, even opposite meaning. In the middle of printing a paper for a class assignment, your printer malfunctions and you say, "Oh, that's just great!" Of course, you mean just the opposite. If someone happens to be listening at the time, they'll know what you really meant from your tone of voice, not your words.

When the literal sense of language is subverted by tone of voice, the result is irony. In everyday life, irony is the basis for teasing or pulling someone's leg. It's a vocal wink. But irony can serve more serious ends, too.

You might say to a friend, "Jane can't help us because she's just too tired," and a literal interpretation makes easy sense of the sentence. However, if you were to imitate and exaggerate Jane's voice when saying "she's just too tired," you'd go beyond stating a fact and would be implying a negative judgment through an ironic tone of voice. In everyday language, there are so many vocal strategies for signaling irony—from mock innocence to heavy sarcasm—that a complete list would be very long.

Sometimes the literal sense of a literary text sounds so outrageous that the words convey irony without any need for vocal underscoring. Jonathan Swift, writing in the early eighteenth century, had become so incensed at the British treatment of the Irish people that he offered "A Modest Proposal" that English landlords should consider solving the Irish problem by eating the children of their tenants:

> *A Child will make two Dishes at an Entertainment for Friends: and when the Family dines alone, the fore or hind Quarter will make a reasonable Dish; and seasoned with a little Pepper or Salt, will be very good Boiled in the fourth Day, especially in* Winter. . . . *I GRANT this Food will be some-what dear, and therefor very* proper for Landlords; *who, as they have already devoured most of the Parents, seem to have the best Title to the Children.*

Critic Wayne Booth would call this kind of talk "stable irony," since the speaker's tongue is planted firmly in his cheek from beginning to end. When communicating irony that's this obvious, it's usually best to perform it straight, as if a speaker sincerely intended the literal meaning, knowing that your audience will get the point without vocal assistance. As always, your best cues to satisfactory performance choices are the strategies used by a writer within the text. Most literary examples of irony are more subtle than this, however, and their authors count on a reader to hear the necessary tone of voice and put the proper spin on literal sense.

EXERCISE & DISCUSSION

Determining when a writer or speaker is being ironic and when not shifts our analysis from sense to effect. One of the most famous examples of irony in American literature is Edwin Arlington Robinson's "Miniver Cheevy." As you read through this poem, can you find specific places where the speaker clues the performer in to irony, offering a verbal wink?

"Miniver Cheevy"

by Edwin Arlington Robinson

Miniver Cheevy, child of scorn,
    Grew lean while he assailed the seasons;
He wept that he was ever born,
    And he had reasons.

Miniver loved the days of old
  When swords were bright and steeds were prancing;
The vision of a warrior bold
  Would set him dancing.

Miniver sighed for what was not,
  And dreamed, and rested from his labors;
He dreamed of Thebes and Camelot,
  And Priam's neighbors.

Miniver mourned the ripe renown
  That made so many a name so fragrant;
He mourned Romance, now on the town,
  and Art, a vagrant.

Miniver loved the Medici,
  Albeit he had never seen one;
He would have sinned incessantly
  Could he have been one.

Miniver cursed the commonplace
  And eyed a khaki suit with loathing;
He missed the mediaeval grace
  of iron clothing.

Miniver scorned the gold he sought,
  But sore annoyed was he without it;
Miniver thought, and thought, and thought,
  and thought about it.

Miniver Cheevy, born too late,
  Scratched his head and kept on thinking;
Miniver coughed, and called it fate,
  And kept on drinking.

In the first stanza, the speaker reports that Miniver wept and assures us that "he had reasons." Can you come up with two different performance strategies, one communicating that the reasons should be taken seriously, and a second that says those "reasons" are pretty silly ones?

1. Where in the text do you get the first convincing clue that this speaker is making fun of Miniver?

2. Be sure to research all the allusions and idioms of the poem to understand the levels of its irony.

3. How does the expression "on the town" expose the speaker's irony?

4. What is a "khaki suit," and with what does Miniver contrast it?

5. What overall strategy would you adopt in performing this poem? Is the irony obvious enough that you could perform it straight? Are there places where you might use imitation, exaggeration, or sneering?

6. In "Miniver Cheevy," we can assume that the author agrees with the speaker's viewpoint. But irony can be more subtle when the *author* pokes fun at the *speaker.*

"Nostalgia"

by Billy Collins

(From Georgia Review, *edited by Stanley Lindberg.*
University of Georgia, Athens, GA 30602.)

Remember the 1340's? We were doing a dance called the Catapult.
You always wore brown, the color craze of the decade,
and I was draped in a cape with pomegranates in needlework.
Everyone would pause for beer and onions in the afternoon.
And at night we would play a game called "Find the Cow."
Announcements were hand-lettered then, not like today.

Where has the summer of 1572 gone? Brocade and sonnet
marathons were the rage. We used to dress up in the flags
of rival baronies and conquer one another in cold stone rooms.
Out on the dance floor we were doing the Struggle.
Alone in her room your sister would practice the Daphne for hours.
We borrowed the jargon of farriers for our slang.
These days words seem transparent, a code everyone has broken.

The 1790's will never come again. Childhood was big.
People would take walks to the very tops of hills
and write everything down in their journals without speaking.
Our collars were very high and our hats were very soft.

We would surprise each other with alphabets made of twigs.
It was a great time to be alive, or even dead.

I am also fond of the period between 1815 and 1821.
Europe was trembling but we were having our portraits done.
1901 is a year I would love to return to, if only briefly,
time enough to wind up a music box and do a few dance steps.
Or take me back to 1922, 1941, or 1957, or at least
let me recapture the mood of last month when we picked
berries and glided through afternoons in a canoe.

Even this morning would be an improvement on the present.
I was in the garden, then, surrounded by the hum of bees
and the Latin names of flowers, watching the early light
flash off the slanted windows of the greenhouse
and gild the needles on the limbs of dark hemlocks.

As usual, I was thinking about the past
whose moments were stones on the bottom of a stream
and my memory was the water rushing over them.
I was even thinking a little about the future, that place
where people are doing a dance we cannot imagine,
a dance whose name we can only guess.

Like "Miniver Cheevy," this poem pokes fun at a human tendency to look at the past through rose-tinted glasses. Here, however, it's as if Miniver were the one speaking instead of the subject being talked about. The challenge for a performer is to convey an ironic effect when the actual person speaking isn't being ironic at all. One strategy might be to exaggerate the speaker's nostalgia.

1. Of the options you can think of to display irony, which might serve best to help an audience see this speaker as a figure of fun?

2. Go through the poem to find particular items from the past that the speaker yearns for, but you don't find particularly appealing. Can you come up with a strategy to get the audience to adopt your attitude toward these things, rather than the speaker's?

Sense in the Form of Argument

In all the poems looked at so far, we've begun with the smallest unit of literary and everyday talk, the word. But you may find it more productive to start with a larger concern, the *argument* of language as developed throughout your text. By "argument" we don't mean some kind of disagreement but, rather, any unit that constitutes a whole thought, idea, or topic. Beginning your rehearsal with the argument of a poem is not just an analytical exercise but a process of thinking and doing together, moving between the intellect and the body.

Return for a moment to Richard Howard's "Like Most Revelations" to isolate the different arguments in that poem. As we did when concentrating on the elements of time and space in the worlds of literature, we recommend laying out this poem solely along the lines of its arguments or ideas. No two performers see these in exactly the same way, but one possible division could look like this:

"Like Most Revelations"

1. It is the movement that incites the form, discovered as a downward rapture—

2. yes, it is the movement that delights the form, sustained by its own velocity.

3. And yet it is the movement that delays the form while darkness slows and encumbers;

4. in fact it is the movement that betrays the form, baffled in such toils of ease,

5. until it is the movement that deceives the form, beguiling our attention—

6. we supposed it is the movement that achieves the form.

7. Were we mistaken?

8. What does it matter if it is the movement that negates the form?

9. Even though we give (give up) ourselves to this mortal process of continuing,

10. it is the movement that creates the form.

Most of our performance recommendations in this chapter have called on the voice to help make sense. But thoughts, ideas, and topics in literature affect your entire body. In the early stages of rehearsal, you need to find ways of getting as much physical involvement with the language as possible by actually moving from one place to another with each change of argument.

Performing sense through movement is an exercise in analogous thinking. On the one hand, there are the thoughts of the poem, story, or play and, on the other, your options for stance and movement. If these two phenomena seem unrelated, just recall the metaphors of everyday speech when one refers to "the movement of thought," "arriving at a conclusion," or "going off on a tangent."

To work out movement for Howard's "Like Most Revelations," the first step (there's no escaping this connection) is to think of each thought in terms of a particular movement. Keep in mind that the best movement is based on correspondences that *you* make. For purposes of illustration, however, we'll return to our ten-point division of the poem's arguments.

If #1 is the starting point of the poem's sense-making, #2 is a *continuation* or *furthering* of that initial proposition. If you were to step toward the audience as you speak #1, our physical analogy would dictate that any movement selected while performing #2 should be in the same direction.

But #3 asserts a new and more antagonistic relationship between movement and form: "And *yet* / it is the movement that delays the form / while darkness slows and encumbers. . . . " Not only do the words "And yet" check the prior direction, but so does the key word "delays." Here the speaker realizes an opposition between movement and form. You might mark this change in direction by stopping, by backing up, or even by taking a "delayed" third step, among other possibilities.

Both #4 and #5 are continuations of the intellectual and physical change signaled by #3: "in fact / it is the movement that betrays the form, / baffled in such toils of ease, until / it is the movement that deceives the form, / beguiling our attention." These two sections could be rehearsed as steps backward or sideways. Following our idea of analogy or correspondence, they could not be performed by standing still since they are continuations of the new direction introduced in #3.

Look closely at the next thought in the poem, #6: "we supposed / it is the movement that achieves the form." This is not so much a continuation of the notion of conflict between movement and form as it is a recalling of the poem's first argument. Analogous physical movement might be to retrace your first steps, or to stand back and look at the place where they occurred, as though remembering them.

At #7, "Were we mistaken?" the argument of the poem comes to an abrupt halt. A strict analogy dictates that you do likewise.

But just as #6 was a reconsideration of the positive relationship between form and movement enunciated at the start of the poem, #8 is a reconsideration of the notion that movement and form are antagonistic: "What does it matter if / it is the movement that negates the form?" If you executed #6 as a retracing of the first two steps of the performance, analogy would suggest that #8 should be a retracing of the blocking for #3, #4, and #5.

The last two thoughts of the poem represent the speaker's conclusion. In spite of what has been revealed about the antagonism between movement and form, "we give (give up) ourselves to this mortal process of continuing." This then would seem to be a return to the direction taken at the outset, and your movement should end with a reaffirmation of the poem's original direction.

Like an actor running through blocking for the first time or a dancer walking through choreography, rehearsing such blocking as we've recommended may seem awkward. Every step you take feels artificial at first, and your focus is more on the question "where do I go next?" than "how is the poem making sense at this moment?" Awkwardness persists until you begin to connect the movement of your body with the sense in your mind, until thinking and doing become one.

As you rehearse any piece of literature in this manner, you should keep adjusting your movement whenever new, more subtle correspondences occur to you. Add movement to your original plan, or cut it back severely to mere shifts of posture or bodily attitude.

EXERCISE & DISCUSSION

Divide the next poem into its individual ideas or topics, noting how these relate to each other. Try to devise a choreography that reflects your understanding of the poem's changing arguments.

"THE HOUSE ON THE HILL"

by Edwin Arlington Robinson

> They are all gone away,
>   The House is shut and still,
> There is nothing more to say.
>
> Through broken walls and gray
>   The winds blow bleak and shrill:
> They are all gone away.
>
> Nor is there one to-day
>   To speak them good or ill:
> There is nothing more to say.

Why is it then we stray
  Around the sunken sill?
They are all gone away,

And our poor fancy-play
  For them is wasted skill:
There is nothing more to say.

There is ruin and decay
  In the House on the Hill:
They are all gone away,
There is nothing more to say.

When planning movement for this poem, be sure to answer the following questions:

1. Does my movement reflect where this poem is going from one idea to the next?

2. Is there a clear analogy between how separate arguments connect with each other and how my movement flows?

3. Is there any evidence in the poem that the sense of its language may also be personally significant?

4. A number of lines are repeated in this poem. What are your physical and vocal options for representing the sense and significance of these repetitions?

How Characters Make Sense of Each Other

In literature with multiple speakers, characters must make sense of one another's language inside their own world, just as we, outside the text, try to make sense of the text as a whole. Let's look at a complete play as an example of conversation in the service of a literary story. "Your Lover Just Called," by John Updike, was adapted by its author from a short story of the same name originally published in *The New Yorker*. Updike rewrote the story as a playlet for an evening of fifteen-minute plays at the Blackburn Theatre, in Gloucester, Massachusetts, on April 10, 1989.

Your Lover Just Called
A Playlet

by John Updike

(John Updike, Odd Jobs: Essays & Criticism (New York: Alfred A. Knopf, 1991), 26–30. Reprinted by permission of Alfred A. Knopf, Inc.)

DRAMATIS PERSONAE: *Richard and Joan Maple, in their thirties*

SCENE 1: *An upstairs hall, Friday morning, ten o'clock*

SCENE 2: *Same place, next day, same time*

(Stage set: A table with a telephone on it. Chair. Door left leads to bedroom.)

PHONE: *(Rings. Rings twice. Thrice.)*

RICHARD: *(sniffling, coughing, in pajamas, emerges from bedroom door)*: Hello? *(Listens, then sings musically)* Hello hello? *(Hangs up. Stands there puzzled.)*

JOAN: *(coming upstairs, carrying a blanket, a jar of vitamin C, a glass of apple juice, a book)*: Richard, you *must* stay in bed if you want to get well enough to entertain Mack tonight.

RICHARD: Your lover just called.

JOAN: What did he say?

RICHARD: Nothing. He hung up. He was amazed to find me home on a Friday.

JOAN: Go back to bed. Here's an extra blanket, some chewable vitamin C, a glass of apple juice, and that book you wanted from the library. It took me the *longest* time to find it. I didn't know whether to look under "L" for "Laclos," "d" for "de," or "C" for "Choderlos."

RICHARD: *(taking book)*: Great. *(Reads title)* Les Liaisons dangereuses.

JOAN: How do I know it wasn't *your* lover?

RICHARD: If it was my lover, why would she hang up, since I answered?

JOAN: Maybe she heard me coming up the stairs. Maybe she doesn't love you any more.

RICHARD: *(after blowing his nose)*: This is a ridiculous conversation.

JOAN: You started it.

RICHARD: Well, what would *you* think, if you were me and answered the phone on a weekday and the person hung up? He clearly expected you to be home alone like you always are.

JOAN: Well, if you'll go back to bed and fall asleep I'll call him back and explain what happened.

RICHARD: You think *I'll* think you're kidding but I know that's really what *would* happen.

JOAN: Oh, come on, Dick. Who would it be? Freddy Vetter?

RICHARD: Or Harry Saxton. Or somebody I don't know at all. Some old college sweetheart who's moved to West Gloucester. Or maybe the milkman. I can hear you and him talking while I'm shaving sometimes.

JOAN: We're surrounded by hungry children. He's sixty years old and has hair coming out of his ears.

RICHARD: Like your father. You *like* older men. There was that section man in Chaucer. You and he were always going out for coffee together after the lecture.

JOAN: Yes, and he gave me a C for the course. C for coffee.

RICHARD: Don't try to change the subject. You've been acting awfully happy lately. There's a little smile comes into your face when you think I'm not looking. See, there it is!

JOAN: I'm smiling because you're so ridiculous. I have no lover. I have nowhere to put him. My days are consumed by devotion to the needs of my husband and his numerous children.

RICHARD: Oh, so I'm the one made you have the children? While you were hankering after a career in fashion or in the exciting world of business. You could have been the first woman to crack the wheat-futures cycle. Or maybe aeronautics: the first woman to design a nose cone. Joan Maple, girl agronomist. Joan Maple, lady geopolitician. But for that patriarchal brute she mistakenly married, this clear-eyed female citizen of our milder, gentler republic—

JOAN: Dick, have you taken your temperature? I haven't heard you rave like this for years.

RICHARD: I haven't been wounded like this for years. I hated that *click.* That nasty little I-know-your-wife-better-than-you-do *click.*

JOAN: It was some child, playing with the phone. Really, if we're going to have Mack for dinner tonight, you better convalesce now.

RICHARD: It is Mack, isn't it? That son of a bitch. His divorce isn't even finalized and he's calling my wife on the phone. And then proposes to gorge himself at my groaning board.

JOAN: The board won't be the only thing groaning. You're giving me a headache.

RICHARD: Sure. First I foist off more children on you than you can count, then I give you a menstrual headache.

JOAN: Darling. If you'll get into bed with your apple juice, I'll bring you cinnamon toast cut into strips the way your mother used to make it.

RICHARD: You're lovely. (*Kisses her brow, takes blanket, pills, and juice, and goes into bedroom. She turns to head downstairs.*)

PHONE: (*Rings.*)

JOAN: Hello . . . yes . . . no . . . no . . . sorry.

RICHARD: (*shouting from behind door*): What was it?

JOAN: Somebody wanting to sell us the *World Book Encyclopedia.*

RICHARD's *voice, after pause, with obscure satisfaction:* A likely story.

(*Blackout to indicate lapse of time. Next morning.*)

PHONE: (*Rings.*)

JOAN: (*entering from downstairs in tennis dress*): Hello . . . oh, pity . . . don't worry about it . . . I'll be there.

RICHARD: (*coming out of bedroom still in pajamas*): Who was that?

JOAN: Nancy Vetter. Francine has had to take little Robbie to the orthodontist this morning because Harry's plane got fogged in in Denver. So our tennis won't be until eleven.

RICHARD: Mmh (*the noise indicating slight surprise: not* Hmm *or* Humph). One good thing about a hangover, it makes a cold feel trivial.

JOAN: I don't know why you drank so much. Or why Mack stayed until one in the morning.

RICHARD: It's obvious why. He had to stay to make sure there were no hard feelings.

JOAN: Why would there be? Just because you were sneaking around outside your own kitchen windows and saw him giving me a friendly peck?

RICHARD: Friendly peck! That kiss was so long I thought one of you might pass out from oxygen deprivation!

JOAN: Don't try to be funny about it. It was shockingly sneaky of you, and we were both embarrassed on your behalf.

RICHARD: *You* were embarrassed! You send me out for cigarettes in the dark of the night, and stumbling back through my own backyard what do I see all lit up in the kitchen but you two making like a blue movie!

JOAN: You could have coughed. Or rattled the screen door or something.

RICHARD: I was paralyzed with horror. My first primal scene. My own wife doing a very credible impersonation of a female spider having her abdomen tickled. Where did you learn to flirt your head like that? It was better than finger puppets.

JOAN: Really, Richard, how you go on. We were hardly doing anything. Mack always kisses me in the kitchen. It's a habit, it means nothing. You know for yourself how in love with Eleanor he is.

RICHARD: So much he's divorcing her. His devotion borders on the quixotic.

JOAN: The divorce is her idea, you know that. He's a lost soul. I feel sorry for him.

RICHARD: Yes, I saw that you do. You were like the Red Cross at Verdun.

JOAN: What I'd like to know is, why are you so pleased?

RICHARD: Pleased? I'm annihilated.

JOAN: You're delighted. You should see your smile.

RICHARD: You're so incredibly unapologetic about it, I guess I keep thinking you're being ironical.

PHONE: *(Rings.)*

JOAN: Hello? *Hello? (Hangs up, stares at him.)* So. She thought I'd be playing tennis by now.

RICHARD: Who's she?

JOAN: You tell me. Your lover. Your loveress.

RICHARD: Honey, quit bluffing. It was clearly yours, and something in your voice warned him off.

JOAN: *(with sudden furious energy):* Go to her! Go to her like a man and stop trying to maneuver me into something I don't understand! I have no lover. I let Mack kiss me because he's lonely and drunk! Stop trying to make me more interesting than I am! All I am is a beat-up housewife who wants to go play tennis with some other beat-up victims of a male-dominated society!

RICHARD: *(studying her as if for the first time):* Really?

JOAN: *(panting):* Really.

RICHARD: You think I want to make you more interesting than you are?

JOAN: Of course. You're bored. You left me and Mack alone last night deliberately. It was very uncharacteristic of you, to volunteer to go out for cigarettes with your cold.

RICHARD: My cold. I feel rotten, come to think of it.

JOAN: You want me to be like that woman in the book, in the movie. The Marquis de Whatever. Glenn Close. All full of wicked schemes and secrets.

RICHARD: *(putting hand to forehead)*: I think I do have a fever now.

JOAN: When I'm really, sad to say, that other woman. Poor Madame Something. Too good to live.

RICHARD: You are? You're Michelle Pfeiffer?

JOAN: Exactly. Without you, I'd just go back to the convent and curl up and die.

RICHARD: Feel. *(Puts her hand to his forehead.)*

JOAN: A *teeny* bit warm.

RICHARD: Would you . . . ?

JOAN: *(sharply, on her mettle)*: Would I what?

RICHARD: If I went back to bed would you come tuck me in before you go off to tennis?

JOAN: I'll tuck you in. No toast, though.

RICHARD: No nice sliced cinnamon toast. It's sad, to think of you without a lover.

JOAN: I'm sorry. I'm sorry to disappoint you.

RICHARD: You don't, entirely. I find you pretty interesting anyway. *(They move toward the door and through it. From behind the door)* You're interesting here, and here, and here.

JOAN's *voice:* I said I'd just tuck you in.

(Silence. Empty stage.)

PHONE: *(Rings. Twice. Thrice. Four times. Stops. Then a little questioning pring, as when someone in passing bumps the table. Then, perhaps, more rings, as many as the audience can stand, unanswered.)*

The structure of this short play is built on a pair of matching scenes occurring one day apart between husband and wife, Richard and Joan. Action begins by a telephone ringing three times, Richard answering it, and then hanging up. When, a moment later, he teases Joan by saying, "Your lover just called," she answers with nonchalance: "What did he say?" The conversation deteriorates quickly, however, with his sniping suspicions that she really does have a lover. He even makes some guesses who that lover might be. Joan, for her part, becomes frustrated with their emerging script. She insists on defining her character very differently from her husband's casting. Husband and wife are making different sense of the episode. The scene closes with a second phone call.

The next morning begins with the phone ringing a third time. The couple launches into a new script of accusations and recriminations centering on their behavior the night before when Mack came over for dinner. Richard charges Joan with carrying on clandestine sexual relations based on a kiss he saw with her and Mack in the kitchen. Joan counters by accusing Richard of spying. The scene ends with her in a state of utter frustration and him becoming inexplicably pleased. The curtain comes down while the audience hears the phone ringing again and again.

Looking at the evidence presented in these two short scenes, we may conclude that Richard and Joan have been married for a long time and that their current relationship is marked by mutual dissatisfaction. Their story, enacted in dramatic dialogue, plays itself out through theatrical metaphors. Richard tries to make sense of what's going on by becoming a playwright, as it were, imagining an extramarital affair between his wife and some unknown lover, although he has no real evidence of this. Initially, Richard's improvised scenario seems playful but, very quickly, it takes on serious overtones and yields harmful consequences. Notice that the couple's argument about Richard's accusation hinges on plausibility rather than fact—a theatrical rather than legal criterion of judgment. Extending the metaphor further, Richard's efforts to discover the identity of Joan's lover become a kind of casting call. He auditions Freddy Vetter, Harry Saxton, and "that section man in Chaucer," with Joan rejecting each possibility as implausible, as not making sense.

When the conversation turns personal and nasty (see Richard's long line beginning, "Oh, so I'm the one made you have the children?"), he tries revising the script by recasting Joan in a series of imaginary roles. The first scene ends with Richard's fictive judgment: "A likely story."

In the second scene, husband and wife engage in a debate of theatre criticism, another form of sense-making. Each offers his or her interpretation of the scene enacted the night before between Joan and Mack. Joan was onstage, of course, and represents the critical kiss as merely "a friendly peck." Richard, who saw the scene from his audience position outside their kitchen window, depicts it differently: "That kiss was so long I thought one of you might pass out from oxygen deprivation!"

Richard claims, "I was paralyzed with horror. My first primal scene. My own wife doing a very credible impersonation of a female spider having her abdomen tickled. Where did you learn to flirt your head like that? It was better than finger puppets." Notice that his diatribe is replete with performance criticism.

Joan offers a different interpretation, suggesting that what seemed a "horror" to Richard was actually an old and familiar script: "We were hardly doing anything. Mack always kisses me in the kitchen. It's a habit, it means nothing."

As the tension heightens, Richard's and Joan's drama takes on a sharper edge. She accuses him of trying to rewrite her to make her more "interesting." At one point she says, "You want me to be like that woman in the book, in the movie. The Marquis de Whatever. Glenn Close. All full of wicked schemes and secrets." Joan draws on an intertextual argument, citing the film version of *Dangerous Liaisons* starring Glenn Close and Michelle Pfeiffer. Rather than rejecting the comparison as out-of-hand, she claims that Richard has miscast her. She sees herself as playing the role of Michelle Pfeiffer instead of Glenn Close.

The play's ending is a particularly pathetic portrait of their relationship. We see Richard trying to rewrite Joan's role two more times, casting her first as his mother (slicing the cinnamon toast just so) and then as his lover: "You're interesting here, and here, and here." Joan's voice can be heard offstage correcting the play's blocking: "I said I'd just tuck you in."

Try performing the play yourself, either in its entirety or by dividing it into shorter scenes and assigning them to different partners. In rehearsal, search for clues to both characters' demographic profiles, their physical features, their signs of intelligence and temperament, and especially their psychological motivations and emotional passions (as discussed in Chapter 3). Use every bit of information provided by the play to guide you in developing plausible characterizations. Then, work for a performance that features not just two individual people but, more importantly, the tensions apparent at and below the surface of their *relationship*. Lead your audience to make sense of the play by *showing* how Joan and Richard make sense (or don't make sense) of each other.

SENSE, GESTURE, ANd STANCE

One way of focusing rehearsal of any work of literature is to concentrate on the connections between sense and both gesture and stance. By "gesture," we mean the specific movement of any part of a performer's body—arms, hands, or facial expression. By "stance," we mean posture or bearing—the way the body is held.

Watch closely when two people are talking, and you can begin to isolate the great contribution of stance and gesture to the performance of everyday language. And don't think that stance comes into play only if you are standing. A person's body communicates when sitting, lounging, crossing legs, turning away, inching to the edge of a chair, leaning back, slouching, and the scores of other attitudes one could strike during a conversation. All of these postures can play their roles in communicating sense and significance to a listener or viewer.

Gestures are the salt and pepper of everyday talk. Language would lose much of its taste without them. The range of gestures is so various, and they can serve so many communicative functions, that scholars of nonverbal communication have been forced to categorize them. Thus, using one set of labels,* *dietic* gestures

---

*Terms taken from Fernando Poyatos, "New Research Perspectives in Cross Cultural Psychology Through Nonverbal Communication Studies," in *Cross-Cultural Perspectives in Nonverbal Communication*, edited by Poyatos (Lewiston, NY: C. J. Hogrefe, 1987).

are those that "truly point to the location of a person, object, or place." *Pictographs* draw a picture on the air. *Kinetographs* imitate a sound, such as rapping fingers on a table to suggest a galloping horse; *identifiers* are our own unique ways of gesturing; *externalizers* reveal what we feel inside; and the list goes on.

What is relevant for us is not the classifications themselves but their demonstration that gesture is critically important to everyday communication. Gesture and stance are absent only in the most extreme circumstances, and their absence severely impedes sense-making. (They even operate during telephone conversations.) Every one of us talks with friends by tossing off "pictographs" and "dietics." Our "identifiers" mark our own individual styles of gesture and stance. When playing cards, we have to suppress "externalizers" lest they give away our hand. What we don't do in everyday conversation is think consciously about this natural behavior. Rather, we concentrate simultaneously on the sense we want to convey while focusing on the person to whom we are speaking.

In the performance of literature, the words are already given on the page, and you must work with them to find a voice and body that make sense. Ideally, appropriate nonverbal strategies arise spontaneously during rehearsal. Realistically, though, you're likely to hit places in the text that call for deliberate decision-making in regard to gesture and stance. Improvisation, or trial and error, is the best method for making such choices. Remember, during the actual performance no gesture or stance can work if it is so under-rehearsed that you are paying more attention to your body than to the sense of the language being expressed.

The purpose of a rehearsal that concentrates on gesture and stance is not so much to come up with final answers to how and where your body will be involved as it is to free your body for greater access to the poem's language world throughout an entire rehearsal process.

Making Sense Inside and Out

Since Roman times, teachers have been developing different procedures for building performances out of literary texts. Numerous as these are, most can be classified as one of two types: (1) an approach that moves from the inner mental and emotional states of a performer outward toward vocal and physical behaviors perceptible to an audience (expression); and (2) an approach that starts with vocal and physical behaviors and then moves toward the performer's inner state (elocution).

Throughout our chapters on world, effect, and now sense, we have been recommending performance procedures derived from both these traditions. Thus, when we advised you to choreograph shifts in a poem's argument, we were, like the elocutionists, starting with physical behavior and hoping for a deeper realization of the connectedness between ideas. On the other hand, when we asked you to begin with the effect a speaker wanted, or with some personal significance the literature held for you, we were starting with an inner state and proceeding toward its manifestation in outward behavior.

Perhaps it would have been neater or easier if we had treated these two approaches separately, instead of switching from one to the other. You might have discovered early on whether you work best from outside in, as the elocutionists recommend, or else from inside out, like the expressionists. Truth to tell, none of us is purely one kind of performer or the other. The direction of one's process depends on many variables, including the nature of the literary text and all that an individual performer brings to it.

Wherever you begin as a performer, you must follow through to the other side. You can feel about a poem interiorly all you want, but unless those feelings produce vocal and physical behaviors, the literature cannot make sense to an audience. Conversely, you can design the most elaborate choreography or compose the most sophisticated vocal stressing, but if they don't stir your consciousness to an authentic experience of the literature, you produce only a wooden or artificial performance.

The great lesson for the performer in everyday conversation is that mind and body are a unity. In lively, unselfconscious talk, whether in the company of friend or foe, we don't think or feel first and then perform second. Nor do we speak first and then think later. We do both acts simultaneously. What may be two acts in theory become one in practice.

Making Sense Happen through Images and Figurative Language

The kinds of language that demonstrate most forcefully the unity between thought and behavior, feeling and form, are imagery and figurative words. Both are drawn from everyday speech and can be appropriated for the artistic purpose of a literary author. Images are mental pictures, sounds, tastes, smells, or touches. They conjure a real world in the imagination, and they affect a reader's body profoundly. Kids count on this happening when they dare one another to imagine sliding down a banister and then suddenly change the mental picture into a razor blade. Most audiences have a similar reaction to the following poem by Canadian writer Margaret Atwood:

"Power Politics"

by Margaret Atwood

(From Power Politics, *Margaret Atwood. Copyright © House of Anansi Press, 1971.)*

you fit into me
like a hook into an eye

a fish hook
an open eye

Images in literature, like those in everyday talk, require that a performer not only imagine them, but also make sense of them. Such double involvement—first creating the image and then making sense happen—constitutes the mental activity that figurative language demands. Poems abound in figurative language, as do our everyday conversations. "*Death.* (.) *offends me*," says the daughter in "It's Gun Be Hard to Do." This is such an unusual way of putting the sentiment that her mother has to repeat it in her own performance: "It *offends* you:."

Whole books are devoted to naming and classifying the dozens of kinds of figurative words (sometimes called *tropes*). We use them all in everyday conversation, usually without knowing their technical names. Generally speaking, we may define figurative language as words or phrases having significance beyond their literal meaning, or words that make sense happen by speaking on two or more levels simultaneously.

Metaphors and *similes* are figures of comparison that identify two unlike things, either through assertion (metaphor) or analogy (simile). When declaring the metaphor "he is an oak," one identifies a human being with a tree to point to certain qualities, probably strength or sturdiness. When suggesting the simile "her eyes are like diamonds," one identifies a human being with a gem, suggesting such features as sparkle, dazzle, elegance, or, perhaps, hardness.

Synecdoche and *metonomy* are figures of contiguity that substitute one thing for another, either in part (synecdoche) or whole (metonomy). If one says, "the price of admission is two bucks a head," one uses a synecdoche, allowing one part of the human body, the head, to substitute for the whole person. If one says, "the ship floats upon the deep," metonomy substitutes "deep" for "ocean."

Other familiar figures of speech include *personification* (assigning human qualities to animals or inanimate objects), *hyperbole* (purposeful exaggeration), and *onomatopoeia* (words whose sound resembles their meaning, as in "buzz").

When we ask why a poet would want to make sense happen by putting something in an unusual or arresting way, startling the reader and causing one to pause, we are asking the familiar question of intended effect. What is the poet after? What's important here is not your ability to label a figurative word, or even to recognize figurative language, but to experience the unique sense such words make possible.

Read the following work, paying particular attention to the sense made by the speaker's thought, images, and figurative language. Then rehearse options for giving voice and body to this speaker.

"Giant Snail"

by Elizabeth Bishop

(From The Complete Poems 1927–1979 *by Elizabeth Bishop. Copyright © 1979, 1983, by Alice Helen Methfessel. Reprinted by permission of Farrar, Straus & Giroux, Inc.)*

The rain has stopped. The waterfall will roar like that all night. I have come out to take a walk and feed. My body—foot, that is—is wet and cold and covered with sharp gravel. It is white, the size of a dinner plate. I have set myself a goal, a certain rock, but it may well be dawn before I get there. Although I move ghostlike and my floating edges barely graze the ground, I am heavy, heavy, heavy. My white muscles are already tired. I give the impression of mysterious ease, but it is only with the greatest effort of my will that I can rise above the smallest stones and sticks. And I must not let myself be distracted by those rough spears of grass. Don't touch them. Draw back. Withdrawal is always best.

The rain has stopped. The waterfall makes such a noise! (And what if I fall over it?) The mountains of black rock give off such clouds of steam! Shiny streamers are hanging down their sides. When this occurs, we have a saying that the Snail Gods have come down in haste. I could never descend such steep escarpments, much less dream of climbing them.

That toad was too big, too, like me. His eyes beseeched my love. Our proportions horrify our neighbors.

Rest a minute; relax. Flattened to the ground, my body is like a pallid, decomposing leaf. What's that tapping on my shell? Nothing. Let's go on.

My sides move in rhythmic waves, just off the ground, from front to back, the wake of a ship, wax-white water, or a slowly melting floe. I am cold, cold, cold as ice. My blind, white bull's head was a Cretan scare-head; degenerate, my four horns that can't attack. The sides of my mouth are now my hands. They press the earth and suck it hard. Ah, but I know my shell is beautiful, and high, and glazed, and shining. I know it well, although I have not seen it. Its curled white lip is of the finest enamel. Inside, it is as smooth as silk, and I fill it to perfection.

My wide wake shines, now it is growing dark. I leave a lovely opalescent ribbon: I know this.

But O! I am too big. I feel it. Pity me.

If and when I reach the rock, I shall go into a certain crack there for the night. The waterfall below will vibrate through my shell and body all night long. In that steady pulsing I can rest. All night I shall be like a sleeping ear.

EXERCISE & DISCUSSION

1. Find an example of metaphor in this poem, and explain its contribution to sense and effect.

2. Find an example of simile, and explain its significance.

3. Find an example of *allusion* to another literary work, and speculate on its value in this poem.

4. Describe how visual and tactile images contribute to this poem.

5. Throughout the poem, Bishop personifies the giant snail. If she is using the snail to talk about a person, do you identify in any way with that person? Do you know someone else who might? If you can, are you finding the poem's sense or its significance?

6. Demonstrate physically places in the poem where its sense motivates changes of stance, gesture, or other movement.

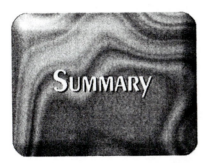

SUMMARY

One meaning of the word "perform" is "to carry out or bring about." In this chapter, we have indicated some of the ways that performers, starting with words on the page, can carry out or bring about the sense of literary language—both for the speakers inside the literary world and for an audience. We have suggested technical features of performance—voice, movement, gesture, and stance—that can help make sense. A series of good rehearsals of a single poem should reveal quickly that we have only hinted at the real complexity of our subject with these suggestions. Be assured that no matter how subtle the sense of words on the page may be, including the reversals of irony or the jazziness of figurative language, there is always a performance correspondence to express them. And it doesn't matter ultimately whether you work from the outside in, or from the inside out. Eventually, you must find the resonance between inner and outer forms where the poem's world can take on reality, its speaker an identity, and where you and your audience can *make sense happen*. Rehearsal should provide the laboratory for your discovery of connectedness among language, sensation, mind, and body.

Chapter Five

Performing Poetic Language

In Chapters 2, 3, and 4, we discussed three dimensions of language as they function in everyday discourse and in literature—world, effect, and sense. The fourth dimension, genre, becomes the focus of our next two chapters. Simply put, genre is a classification or category of talk. It's a recognizable script for human speech or behavior. Perhaps an anecdote can open the door to this subject most agreeably.

> An American friend of mine, invited out to tea in London and alarmed at the prospect of having to participate in a performance with which he was only vaguely familiar, asked an English lady friend for guidance.
> "Isn't there some kind of tea ritual?"
> "Heavens no!"
> "But don't you stand in front of a low table, and the lady of the house sits behind it, and there's lots of silver, and porcelain cups, and a special cake knife, and sugar tongs? And you're expected to talk about the weather, and how the garden is growing, and doesn't she ask you whether you take milk or lemon with your tea?"
> "Well, of course," came the reply, "but there's no ritual!"
> —from Adrain Bailey, The Cooking of the British Isles

Most of us speak everyday language and perform social acts without conscious awareness that we're conforming to a ritual. Not until we confront an unfamiliar speaking situation, such as English high tea, do we realize anew that different kinds of speaking situations demand different kinds of language performance. Faced with a first date, a first job interview, or a first performance in class, one begins to worry about behaving appropriately.

We learn how to handle new situations by classifying them into general categories—a job interview, a date, a classroom performance, or an English high tea. Even though each particular instance may be unique, we comprehend it in terms of membership in some group. Another word for such a group or category is *genre*, a term some scholars of everyday language define as a "system of appropriateness behavior."* The "American friend" above asks about the genre of a tea party in order to behave appropriately. To do well on a job interview, you may take a course that teaches behavior appropriate to that genre of conversation.

In this chapter and in Chapter 6, we examine two traditional genres of literature—poems and stories. We focus on what should be of particular interest to performers. Like the everyday language scholars, we treat genres as guides to appropriate behavior. We begin with the performance behavior appropriate to poetry.

*Elizabeth Traugott, "Generative Semantics and the Concept of Literary Discourse," *Journal of Literary Semantics* 3 (1973), quoted in Mary Louise Pratt, *Toward a Speech Act Theory of Literary Discourse* (Bloomington, Ind.: Indiana University Press, 1977), p. 86.

Poetry and Everyday Language

When a reporter once asked Dixieland great Louis Armstrong to define "jazz," he laughed and said, "Man, if you've got to define it, you'll never know what it is." Like Armstrong, you already know what poetry is and can distinguish a poem from a story or a play, in most cases simply by looking at its layout on the page. Although this genre may seem to put as much distance as possible between itself and the language of everyday life, poetry is deeply rooted in natural talk. Robert Frost* remarked on the intimate connection between poetic composition and everyday conversation:

> *Someone had complained that a little thing of mine was "too near the level of talk." I didn't see why it shouldn't be. So I resolved to go ahead and see what would happen if I went a little nearer with it. It wasn't all obstinancy. It was inspiration. In that criticism I suddenly saw something I had been on the track of ever since I had tasted success in words with a friend I used to sit late with in old high school days. Why was a friend so much more effective than a piece of paper in drawing the living sentences out of me? I thought it might come to my having to remember exactly the shape my sentences took under provocation or under social excitement. How would a piece of paper ever get the best out of me? I was afraid I hadn't imagination enough to be really literary. And I hadn't. I have just barely enough to imitate spoken sentences. I can't keep up any interest in sentences that don't SHAPE on some speaking tone of voice. I'm what you would call reproductive.*
>
> —Robert Frost, Letter to Lewis N. Chase, 1917

Frost's insight—that poetry is not fundamentally different from everyday speech—begs the question, which *aspects* of everyday speech are fundamentally poetic. To answer that, we introduce the transcripts of two actual telephone conversations. The first involves three college students engaged in a boasting contest about the brands of cars businessmen drive. As with previous conversation transcripts, read it through once for its world, effect, and sense. Then go back and try to replicate the sound markings on the transcription, attempting to give voice and body to the original participants. Find partners and work on this exercise together. Time permitting, you might switch roles so that everyone can experience the perspectives of its participants, Sam, Jon, and Lil. It will probably take several rehearsals to make this conversation play naturally in performance—the laugh particles present a special challenge—but your effort will pay off.

*Quoted in Elaine Barry, *Robert Frost on Writing* (New Brunswick, N.J.: Rutgers Univiversity Press, 1973), p. 70.

Cars Businessmen Drive*

Sam: What if you wan'd to be a businessman and wanda wear je:ans.
                      And then you wouldn't fit into the category.
                      of I E: (.) the businessman =

Jon: =Yes but what cars businessmen dri:ve.

5   They drive Cougars and Mercedeses they don't drive uh
                      nineteen eighty one uh (.) Chevrole:ts (..)Gray Malibu:s and
                      ⌈and u::h and Pontiacs that don't work

Sam: ⌊ih hih ⌈hih heh heh heh

Lil: ⌊hhuh

10   Sam: hih ⌈hih hih hih   ⌈hah hah
                        ⌊and need radiators it – ⌊Nineteen fifty Datsun⌈s
                      that need new brake dances=

Jon: ⌈hhh hu:h hu:h hh hh huh huh

Sam: ⌊hih hihuh Well hey ma:n that's a part a gittin (........)

15   that's right there hey (..) majority people in this world
                      not driving Bee Em Dubyuhs
                      (........)

Sam: And they gonn say (tell) I'm working directly with the people

Lil: Ri:⌈ght.

20   Jon: ⌊ehhh hunuh

Sam: Support the p⌈eople

Lil: ⌊ih hih hih=

Sam: =Drivin the car – ⌈like the people.

Lil: ⌊Relating to the people

25   Lil: ⌈hih heh heh

Jon: ⌊ehhu huh hhh huh huh huh huh huh
                      (....)

*This example, taken from University of Texas Conversation Library [A30], was published by Robert Hopper, "Speech Errors and the Poetics of Conversation," *Text and Performance Quarterly* 12(1992): 113–124. Used with permission.

	Sam:	=I would– I wouldn't want my <u>fe</u>llow consti<u>t</u>uents
	Jon:	↑Hhh⌈<u>h</u>ah hah hah
30	Sam:	⌊to <u>fee</u>l <u>out</u> of pl<u>a</u>ce. When <u>I</u> dri<u>:</u>ve <u>up</u>
		(........) in what <u>East Austin.</u>
	Lil:	Eh⌈h<u>eh</u> h<u>a</u>h hah
	Sam:	⌊in muh– <u>P</u>er se? (...) <u> Be</u>nz.
	Sam:	And what they gonn say this uppity mobile <u>p</u>erson.
35		wonta wonsta come t<u>e</u>l l me wh<u>a</u>t– wh<u>a</u>t could he tell me, he–
		loo– l<u>oo</u>k at him, he– (...) shit he alr<u>ea</u>dy up in the hierarchy
		so sh<u>i</u>t (....) why should I l<u>i</u>sten to <u>hi</u>m he duh– you know
		he can't help me
		(....)
40	Sam:	<u>Bu</u>t (.) if I dri:ve up (....) in ma: (.........) s::::<u>i</u>xtee:n ninetee:n.
		⌈get out and p<u>u</u>sh: so⌈<u>h</u>elp me:
	Lil:	⌊heh hih heh hih ⌊hih
	Lil:	⌈ihh ih<u>e</u>h heh <u>h</u>eh h<u>a</u>h hah hah huh
	Jon:	⌊ih ih ih ih ih ih
45	Sam:	everyb<u>o</u>dy else in the n<u>ei</u>ghborhoo:d car.
	Lil:	heh heh⌈heh heh ehh–
	Jon:	⌊<u>u</u>hh ↑hah hy<u>u</u>h
	Sam:	This d<u>u</u>de will probly call wel↑hey this is a individual
		probly who, you know (..) who's gonna share something
50		of common <u>i</u>nterest with me

Now let's go back and notice some of the poetic features operating in this everyday talk. Sam's first two lines begin like a rap lyric—highly rhythmical, repeating the "w" sound twice in each phrase. At another level, he introduces the businessman theme that runs throughout the entire dialogue.

By line 4, when Jon comes in, "businessman" has been repeated three times. In line 5, then, he introduces a set of related images, the cars themselves, that are used to classify two different kinds of businessmen.

What follows for fifty lines is an inventory of cars (Cougar, Mercedes, Chevrolet, Malibu, Pontiac, Datsun, BMW), car parts (radiators, brakes), and car symbols (old, broken, expensive, uppity).

The co-mingling of car imagery with the idea of "constituencies" permits Jon and Sam to talk in a highly symbolic way about a number of difficult subjects: how does the businessman identify with "the people"? What are the ethical obligations of business practice? What are the symbols of personal success? The poetic density and verbal complexity of this telephone conversation is belied by the easygoing give-and-take of the participants. Nevertheless, their interaction displays many features we commonly associate with the best verse compositions.

Professor Robert Hopper has reconfigured these lines into a two-speaker poem, illustrating its verse structure:

CARS BUSINESSMEN DRIVE

Sam: What if you wan'd to be a businessman and wanda wear jeans.
And then you wouldn't fit into the category
of i e, the businessman.

Jon: Yes but what cars do businessmen drive?
They drive Cougars and Mercedeses
they don't drive uh, nineteen-eighty-one Chevrolets,

Gray Malibus and uh and Pontiacs
that don't work and need radiators,
nineteen-fifty Datsuns that need new brake (dances).

Sam: Well hey man just a part a gittn, that's right there hey
majority people in this world
not driving Bee Em Dubyuhs.

And they gonn say I'm working directly with the people
support the people
drivin the car- like the people.

I would- I wouldn't want my fellow constituents
to feel out of place when I drive up
in what East Austin, in my Per se Benz.

And what they gonn say this uppity mobile person.
wonta wonsta come tell me what-
what could he tell me.

Look at him, he- shit, he already up in the hierarchy
so shit, why should I listen to him
he doesn't—you know he can't help me.

But, if I drive up, in my
sixteen nineteen get out and push, so help me
everybody else in the neighborhood car
this dude will probly call well hey
this is a individual probly who, you know,
who's gonna share somethin of common interest with me.

Professor Hopper demonstrates another instance of poetic structure in everyday talk in the following telephone transcription. When caller Rick asks Pam, "Have you had dinner yet," she makes a verbal mistake, substituting the verb "ate" for "eaten." She immediately corrects herself, but Rick picks up the unintended humor of the slip. The two of them are off to the races in a self-conscious play on errors in verb usage. First we'll print the transcription of the actual conversation and then a version simplified into stanzas:

Rick and Pam*

Rick:	Have you had dinner yet?
	(....)
Pam:	No I haven't.
Pam:	Have you.
Rick:	I'm so h(h)ungr(h)y,
Pam:	Are you starving?
Rick:	Ye:s
	(....)
Pam:	Have you *ate* today?
	(....)
Pam:	*Eaten*
Rick:	*heh* heh heh huh
Pam:	heh hueh I said *eated* hhh=
Rick:	=No I-I-I already *eated* *hhh*ih
Pam:	You already *eated*?
Rick:	Yes
Pam:	What did you eat at, *hh* hih=
Rick:	But I'm going to go-I'm gonna go (.) ran now
Pam:	You gonna go *ran*
Rick:	I'm gonna go ran,

*This example, taken from the University of Texas Conversation Library (D8), was published by Robert Hopper in his article "Speech Errors and the Poetics of Conversation," *Text and Performance Quarterly* 12 (1992): 113–124. Used with permission.

Pam:	nh *ha ha ha* ha
Rick:	-hh
Pam:	F___ you, *hhh ha ha ha* ha He's gonna go *ran* now yhuh hih
	huh huh *hh* Leave me alo:ne.
Rick:	and the- and then- and then I'm gonna and then I'm gonna
	*go:*n to a movie *hhh hh*
Pam:	Gonna *gone* to a movie?
Rick:	Gonna gone to a mov (h)ie.
Pam:	ehhih hih hnh hnh hnh *Are* you gonna
	gone to a movie?
Rick:	Yeah.
	(..)
Rick:	You wann *comed*? (.) no(h),
Pam:	I wanna *came*.
Rick:	*hhh* Wanna c*(h)*ome,
Pam:	hnh huh You wanna came hnh hnh hnh hnh hnh (....) *hhh* heh
	Leave me alone.

As you rehearse, notice how differently these speakers talk from the mothers and daughters we asked you to perform in Chapter 1. Listen especially to the playfulness of their conversation. The mothers and daughters in the earlier cases were most interested in the outcome of their talks. For them, conversation was a means of getting something they wanted. Here the speakers seem to be in a different genre, focusing on *how* they are using language, tossing it back and forth as in a game. Their playfulness, their awareness of what they are doing in language, and their enjoyment of "getting it right" are all behaviors appropriate to the performance of poetry.

Now here's the same conversation rewritten into verse form, maximizing its self-conscious banter:

Rick and Pam

Pam:	Have you ate today? eated
Rick:	No I already eated.
Pam:	You ready eated?

Rick: Yes.

Pam: Who did you eat at?

Rick: But I'm going to go ran now.

Pam: Y'gonna go ran?

Rick: I'm gonna go ran.

Pam: F___ you, gonna go ran now.
         LEAVE ME ALONE

Rick: And then I'm gonna gone to a movie.

Pam: Gonna gone to a movie?

Rick: Gonna gone to a movie.

Pam: And you gonna gone to a movie?

Rick: Yeah, you wanna comed? No.

Pam: I wanna came.

Rick: Wanna comed?

Pam: You wanna came?
         LEAVE ME ALONE.

Inside the Poetic Sensibility

"You're a poet and you don't know it" goes the hackneyed rejoinder when someone breaks into unintended rhyme in everyday speech. Then comes the second
part, teasing the speaker, "But your feet show it, they're Longfellows," itself
demonstrating poetic structure and allusion. We may define poetry simply as
patterned speech and, as such, recognize that it bears a close kinship to all other
kinds of patterned talk.

Human beings speak in highly patterned utterances, on occasion, all the way
from the crib to the deathbed. A baby's first syllables—goo, goo, gaa, gaa—come
out in a chain of repeated sounds, displaying patterns of alliteration and assonance. When a great aunt, now ninety-two years old, gets out of bed each morning, wracked by the pain of arthritis, she allows herself the strongest expletive
of a circumspect life—"oh boy, oh boy, oh boy"—formulating by repetition the
excruciation of a condition that will not go away.

The infant experiences her earliest form of play in the form of verbal patterning, as in "This little piggie went to market. This little piggie stayed home."
Even so simple a game displays poetic features in its five lines of identical

syntax. "This little piggie" demands interactive performance by literally tickling a response from the infant.

When baby becomes toddler, poetic play turns into a verbal duet between parent and child: "Patty cake, patty cake." Patterned speech, in this instance, expresses the body's rhythms and, at the same time, assists in developing coordination.

Poetic speech arises from the total involvement of mind and body in language. There is something dance-like and musical about poetry, just as there is something poetic about the physical interplay of everyday talk. According to conversation analyst Deborah Tannen,

> . . . rhythm is as basic to conversation as it is to musical performance. . . . Finding a way into a conversation is like joining a line of dancers. It is not enough to know where other dancers have been; one must also know where they are headed: To bring one's feet into coordination with theirs, one must grasp the pattern in order to foresee where their feet will come down next. The sharedness, or lack of sharedness, of rhythm, is crucial for conversational outcome.*

If you have ever tried to join a lively conversation between two friends, you've probably experienced what Tannen is describing. Because they are already *into* the conversation, they've established a rhythm or beat that you have to pick up. A poem works the same way, wanting to get everyone *involved*—poet, performer, and audience together. In fact, poetry is so physical that critic Richard Stern maintains it mimics the body's own organic rhythms:

> Poetry, rhythmic speech, is, in my view, connected with the body's rhythms. In moments of deep emotion the autonomic nervous system takes over, the pulse of the hematic system dominates the body's rhythms, and there ensues a sense of unreality. The techniques of poetry mimic and express such states.**

All of us display this poetic sensibility—a tendency toward highly patterned speech—in moods of playfulness, moments of exhilaration, times of sorrow, and fits of anger. We may mark social affiliation with *rap*, religious worship with *psalms*, private spirituality with a sacred *mantra*, and public ceremony with poetic proclamation. From silly rhymes to solemn rituals, we invoke poetry as an expression of personal emotions and an assurance of collective values.

Our speech can be patterned in so many different ways: by simple repetition of words, by duplication of sounds, by clustering of images, or by metrical

---

*Deborah Tannen, *Talking Voices: Repetition, Dialogue, and Imagery* (Cambridge, England: Cambridge University Press, 1989), p. 18.

**Richard Stern, *One Person and Another: On Writers and Writing* (Dallas: Basketville Publishers, 1993), p. 51.

rhythm, to name only a few. Patterning itself becomes a mode of expression going well beyond the simple sense of words. At the most fundamental level, a poetic sensibility appears to be part and parcel of our physical being in the world.

The writer A. R. Ammons had this connection between language and body in mind when he compared poetry to taking a walk:

> *How does a poem resemble a walk? First, each makes use of the whole body, involvement is total, both mind and body. You can't take a walk without feet and legs, without a circulatory system, a guidance and coordinating system, without eyes, ears, desire, will, need: the total person. This observation is important not only for what it includes but for what it rules out: as with a walk, a poem is not simply a mental activity; it has body, rhythm, feeling, sound, and mind, conscious and subconscious. The pace at which a poet walks (and thinks), his natural breath-length, the line he pursues, whether forthright and straight or weaving and meditative, his whole "air," whether of aimlessness or purpose—all these things and many more figure into the "physiology" of the poem he writes.*

Remember, our poetic sensibility—this penchant for patterned speech—is not a feature of print on the page. We recognize it first and foremost in performance. It is as commonplace as the farmer in the dell or London Bridge is falling down, and as profound as the Lord is my Shepherd or dust to dust and ashes to ashes. Intricate patterning is coded into the neurons and synapses of our brains, the joints and sinews of our skeletons, and, most importantly, the rhythms and expressions of our speech. As we've observed from the beginning of this book, the threshold between language spoken in life and that used in literature can be crossed in either direction with one small step.

Patterns in Poetic Speech

We have said that poetry is, essentially, patterned speech that demands involvement. Prosody—the study of how poems are patterned—is a complex and extensive subject deserving its own full course. Scholars have devoted entire careers to detailing the poetic patterning preferred in one literary era or another, or fashioned by a single group of poets.** Our purpose is to demonstrate the poetic sensibility operating in both literary *and* everyday uses of language.

---

*A. R. Ammons, "A Poem Is a Walk," in *Claims for Poetry*, edited by Donald Hall (Ann Arbor: University of Michigan Press, 1982), p. 5.

**Your college library is stocked with classic volumes on prosody, including the works of Paul Fussell, Harvey Gross, Joseph Malof, T. S. Osmond, George Puttenham, Karl Shapiro, John Thompson, and George Saintsbury.

One strong evidence of the poetic impulse in everyday talk may be found in our speech errors. The separate research projects of conversation analysts Robert Hopper and Gail Jefferson* show that we possess a natural or automatic tendency toward patterned or repeated sounds. Speech errors seem to be the result of our voice speaking on its own, as though it were drawn to poetic patterning even when our conscious thought is not.

Here are several examples, taken from actual conversation transcripts. Christine says, "He was standing in the shower of the tower. Hah, I mean shadow." She hears her own mistake (saying "shower" instead of "shadow") and corrects it; yet, her error follows its own poetic logic, preferring "shower" to "shadow" in spite of the sense. A football announcer reports, "Foreman stopped at the forty, thirty yard line." Again, his mistake (saying "forty" instead of "thirty") is not a failure of eyesight but a natural predilection for sound associations.

Our everyday talk displays other kinds of sound patterns beside speech errors. Gail Jefferson collected the following instances from various football broadcasts. Notice how, in each case, the very sound of a player's name sets in motion an expectation of some poetic resonance.

- Bill Knox *knocked* the ball loose . . .

- Kenny Stabler has really *stabilized* the club.

- Chester Markol *checks* in . . .

- I guess Plunkett's biggest *plus* as a quarterback is . . .

- Eischeid has really been *shining* here in the second half.

- A nineteen yard touchdown run by Gregg Pruitt. So the Browns are really *proving* tough today.

It's doubtful that all of the sound patterns in these excerpts were intentional on the part of their broadcasters. Some surely came automatically, from a natural impulse toward poetic repetition.

Another excellent laboratory for studying everyday poetic language is the grade school playground. There, children compose or memorize poetry and perform physical involvement with its patterned utterance.

> Quick! quick!
> The cat's been sick.

---

*All examples of speech errors that we cite come from Robert Hopper's "Speech Errors and Poetics of Conversation," *Text and Performance Quarterly* 12 (1992): 113–124, or from Gail Jefferson's lecture "On the Poetics of Ordinary Talk."

Where? where?
  Under the chair.

Hasten! hasten!
  Fetch the basin.

Alack! alack!
  It is too late.

The carpet's in
  An awful state.

No! no!
  It's all in vain.
For she has licked it
  Up again.*

Much playground poetry is accompanied by physical activities such as jumping rope, skipping, swinging, or playing hopscotch. The words themselves, as well as the patterns of their speaking, become a literal game.

When poets try to replicate the patterned speech we hear in everyday talk, they rely on certain strategies of involvement. We can inventory these as patterns involving the eye, patterns involving the ear, patterns involving the mind, and patterns involving the whole.

PATTERNS INVOLVING THE EYE

A reader first encounters a poem by looking at its print layout on the page. Involvement begins with the eye. Even before you sound out the poem's language, you see its visual imprint in the form of *lines* and *stanzas*. As you glance at the page, you take note of stanza breaks and line endings. These become visual guides to the back and forth balancing act of reading a poem.

Everyday speech has no exact equivalent to the visible lines of a poem. Conversation is punctuated by turn-taking, one speaker after another, and many turns of talk constitute the visual layout of a play. A prose story is printed in sentences and paragraphs. But the line is a defining characteristic of the poetic genre. In fact, that ragged right margin is the first clue that we are reading poetry and not prose. For some poets, the length of a line is determined by breath. That

*An English rhyme from *I Saw Esau: The Schoolchild's Pocket Book,* edited by Iona and Peter Opie, illustrated by Maurice Sendak (Cambridge, Mass.: Candlewick Press), 1992.

is, each line ending marks a place where a performer would stop to inhale. For others, it represents a rhythmic or musical unit. In any case, your performance of a poem will need to take line endings into account. This is part of the appropriateness behavior of the genre.

Nineteenth-century performers used a rehearsal exercise to test and strengthen the line as a meaningful unit of poetry. They would read the poem first as a series of lines, clearly pausing at the end of each, as if there were a period there. Then they would read the poem again, dividing it into sentences and ignoring line endings where there were no periods. We can illustrate the helpfulness of this "line/sentence" exercise with the opening four lines of Robert Browning's "My Last Duchess":

> *That's my last Duchess painted on the wall,*
> *Looking as if she were alive. I call*
> *That piece a wonder, now: Fra Pandolf's hands*
> *Worked busily a day, and there she stands.*

Try performing this text by emphasizing each line as a separate entity, placing a period at the end of each one. Pay no attention to any element except the line endings.

Then perform the passage again, not as lines but as sentences, as you would say them in everyday conversation. Try to make these sentences sound as natural as possible. It may be helpful to lay the text out as if it were prose:

> *That's my last duchess painted on the wall, looking as if she were alive. I*
> *call that piece a wonder, now: Fra Pandolf's hands worked busily a day,*
> *and there she stands.*

In aiming for naturalness, you should depend on your intuitive understanding of how everyday talk sounds—the same intuition that guided your understanding of talk between Rick and Pam, or among Sam, Lil, and John in the telephone conversations discussed earlier. In these sentences by Browning, you may find it hard to sound natural when saying a phrase such as "busily a day." Don't hesitate with this exercise to paraphrase your own words, perhaps "busily every day," or "Pandolf worked at the painting every day. . . ." Then go back and replace your words with Browning's originals.

You should now have two very different performances of the same words. They have different music and make different sense. Neither one alone can serve the poem as well as a sensible blend of the two, balancing sense and structure to achieve a feeling of patterned speech.

Here's a poem that invites your involvement by its strategic division into lines. It's a playful portrait of "Watermelons."

"WATERMELONS"

by Charles Simic

(From Return to a Place Lit by a Glass of Milk. *New York: George Braziller,
1974. Reprinted by permission of George Braziller.)*

> Green Buddhas
> On the fruit stand.
> We eat the smile
> And spit out the teeth.

It's easy enough to *see* line endings on the page, but it may not always be apparent how they should relate to the performance of a poem. We begin with the assumption that line endings are not arbitrary. Even during silent reading, there is a split-second pause while your eye moves left and down to the next line. This pause, however brief, is apt to emphasize either the word preceding or following it. Sometimes a line break comes at the end of a phrase, where you would tend to pause anyway. Other times the break comes at a place where you would not pause *unless* the poet wanted you to emphasize a particular word, mood, or image.

As always, the performer must ask *why.* Why does the poet break off the line at this particular moment and not another? In each of the following, can you figure out why the line breaks come where they do? Try to answer in terms of how line endings could affect your perfomance:

> Will we walk all night through solitary streets? The trees add
> shade to shade, lights out in the houses, we'll both be lonely.

> Will we stroll dreaming of the lost America of love past blue
> automobiles in driveways, home to our silent cottage?

> Ah, dear father, graybeard, lonely old courage-teacher, what
> America did you have when Charon quit poling his ferry and you
> got out on a smoking bank and stood watching the boat disappear
> on the black waters of Lethe?

From "A Supermarket in California" by Allen Ginsberg (see p. 53)

> At any moment he could put his fist
> right through that window. And on your side:
> you could grab hold of something like
> this letter opener, or even now you could try

very slowly to slide the revolver
out of the drawer in the desk
where you're sitting, . . .

From "The Sudden Appearance of a Monster at the Window"
by Lawrence Raab (see p. 50)

It was all the clods at once become
precious; it was the barn, and the shed,
and the windmill, my hands, the crack
Arlie made in the axehandle: oh, let me stay
here humbly, forgotten, to rejoice in it all;

From "Earth Dweller" by William Stafford (see p. 154)

    Merely to mark a line ending with a mechanical pause, without making sense of it, without integrating it into a deliberate effect, will only result in an awkward performance. In rehearsal, you should work to make a poem's line endings as natural and organic as breathing, marking the subtle interior movement of the poem's speaker.

    Few poets have experimented with the layout of lines as creatively as e. e. cummings. He saw a poem's appearance on the page as a valuable guide to its performance. Here is one of his most famous experiments:

"In Just-"

by e. e. cummings

in Just-
spring   when the world is mud-
luscious the little
lame balloonman

whistles   far   and wee

and eddieandbill come
running from marbles and
piracies and it's
spring

when the world is puddle-wonderful

the queer
old balloonman whistles
far   and   wee
and bettyandisabel come dancing

from hop-scotch and jump-rope and

it's
spring
and
    the

        goat-footed

balloonMan   whistles
far
and
wee

As you work through this poem, try to come up with a reason for every line break. What is the difference in the meaning of "Just in spring," and "in just spring"? Why does cummings end not only the first line with "Just" but capitalize the word, as well? Why does he make you pause between "Just" and "Spring"? Is the description "mud/luscious" more sensuous if you perform the line break? What gets emphasized when you hesitate between "little" and "lame"? Each time the speaker says "it's spring," cummings makes you hesitate between the two words. What clues does this provide to the speaker's emotions? When the poet lays out the fifth line as "whistles   far   and wee," how should these spaces affect the tempo of the line? What should the tempo of the last three lines be? What does "wee" mean in this context?

PATTERNS INVOLVING THE EAR

We may meet a poem initially as print on the page, but *sound* instills the vital signs of its real life. A poem has a rhythmic heartbeat pulsing regularly or irregularly beneath its patterned speech, and a musical signature inscribed in the associated sounds of its verbal utterance.

Most poems contain a rhythmic beat, although some instances are obvious and others more subtle. Listen to the regular pattern of four beats in the first, third, and fifth lines, and three beats in the second, fourth, and sixth in these lines from Edgar Allan Poe's "Annabel Lee":

> It was many and many a year ago
>   In a kingdom by the sea,
> That a maiden there lived whom you may know
>   By the name of Annabel Lee;
> And this maiden she lived with no other thought
>   Than to love and be loved by me.

Or hear the four-beat line of e. e. cummings's "Anyone Lived in a Pretty How Town":

> anyone lived in a pretty how town
> (with up so floating many bells down)

Contemporary rap is an excellent example of the poetic beat because its performers are challenged to stretch certain words and hurry others to keep to the rhythm of the line.

In the silent scanning of a poem on the page, rhythm is sometimes difficult to detect, but in oral performance it is often the first thing we notice. Rhythm is a physical phenomenon that gets listeners and speakers moving together, whether it be in conversation or in poetry. Because rhythm is such a powerful involvement strategy, you need to sensitize yourself to its sources in poetry.

English is called a "stressed language." Given any word with two or more syllables, one of them must be performed with more energy than the others. We say "per FORM ance," not "PER FOR MANCE," "re pe TI tion," not "RE PE TI TION." In the everyday conversation between Rick and Pam, a strong rhythmic quality emerges from the stressing patterns of the two speakers.

As a performer of literature, your task is to sound the rhythm of a poem, inviting an audience's involvement in it, without letting that rhythm predominate over all other elements of the experience. Strong rhythm must be balanced against the poem's sense, all the dimensions of its language world, and the intended effects of its speaker or author. This balancing act calls on your analytical skills, as well as your intuitive knowledge derived from everyday interactions.

Here's an example from Shakespeare's *Macbeth* (I, vii, 35–39). If a performer were to stress every second syllable with an absolutely regular beat, the lines would sound like this:

> [Was the hope drunk]
> whereIN you DRESSED yourSELF? hath IT slept SINCE?
> and WAKES it NOW, to LOOK so GREEN and PALE
> at WHAT it DID so FREELy? FROM this TIME
> such I acCOUNT thy LOVE . . .

Although this reading does highlight the underlying rhythm of Shakespeare's blank verse, no one would normally consider performing the lines as we've marked them. An audience would get the rhythm all right, but they'd miss the plain sense. Who, in everyday talk, would say, "hath IT slept SINCE?" or "FROM this TIME such I acCOUNT thy LOVE"? More naturally, one would sound these words something like, "hath it SLEPT SINCE?" and "from THIS TIME SUCH i acCOUNT thy LOVE."

Now read the full passage aloud:

> Was the HOPE DRUNK
> whereIN you DRESSED yourSELF? hath it SLEPT SINCE?
> and WAKES it NOW, to LOOK so GREEN and PALE
> at WHAT it DID so FREEly? from THIS TIME
>
> SUCH i acCOUNT thy LOVE . . .

In this last version, we try to balance the complementary appeals of rhythm and sense. Deciding how best to do that—and you may quibble with some of our stresses—requires your experience of everyday language and talk.

With some poems, the steady beat of a strong rhythm enhances both the sense and emotion of a speaker. For instance, Coleridge's "The Rime of the Ancient Mariner" describes what it was like to be adrift in the Pacific Ocean with all the mariner's shipmates dead:

> Alone, alone, all, all alone,
> Alone on a wide wide sea!
> And never a saint took pity on
> My soul in agony.

No matter how much you stress the rhythm under these words, it only swells their meaning and emotion.

In the twentieth century, many English-language poets have tried to write verse in language that *sounds* as close as possible to everyday speech. This is not to say, however, that they abandon rhythm or that their poems display no patterns of vocal stress. As we have seen with conversation transcripts, rhythm is a natural strategy for involvement. Everything depends on the effect a speaker intends. Ultimately, only the performer can determine what effect a poem is after.

"Root Cellar"

by Theodore Roethke

> Nothing would sleep in that cellar, dank as a ditch,
> Bulbs broke out of boxes hunting for chinks in the dark,
> Shoots dangled and drooped,

Lolling obscenely from mildewed crates,
Hung down long yellow evil necks, like tropical snakes.
And what a congress of stinks!—
Roots ripe as old bait,
Pulpy stems, rank, silo-rich,
Leaf-mold, manure, lime, piled against slippery planks.
Nothing would give up life:
Even the dirt kept breathing a small breath.

The stressing of this language is quite complicated, but if you perform the poem aloud several times, you should be able to hear a rhythmic pattern (falling from accented to unaccented syllables) recurring despite interruptions:

NOthing would SLEEP in that
DANK as a
BROKE out of
HUNTing for CHINKS in the
DANGled and
LOLLing ob
TROpical
CONGress of
RIPE as old
NOTHing would
EVen the
BREATHing a

Why do you think Roethke keeps interrupting the pattern of stresses established in the first half of the first line? Perhaps, as in everyday conversation, to underscore his intended meaning or effect. His subject is the refusal of living things to stay put, the irrepressibility of a life force. Perform just the first two lines, concentrating only on what happens to the rhythm as the bulbs come to life:

Nothing would sleep in that cellar, dank as a ditch,
Bulbs broke out of boxes hunting for chinks in the dark,

Now perform the next three lines, letting Roethke's reptilian images guide the rhythm of your speech, especially the slithering slowness of the last line:

Shoots dangled and drooped,
Lolling obscenely from mildewed crates,
Hung down long yellow evil necks, like tropical snakes.

In the next four lines, imagery changes from what you can see to what you can smell. Try to perform them so that rhythm enhances the images:

And what a congress of stinks!—
Roots ripe as old bait,
Pulpy stems, rank, silo-rich,
Leaf-mold, manure, lime, piled against slippery planks.

Finally, the last two lines not only revert to the rhythm that started the poem, but they actually repeat the same words.

Nothing would give up life:
Even the dirt kept breathing a small breath.

As poetry moves closer to the rhythms of everyday talk, it depends more on a performer's ear and knowledge of such talk. As poets rely less on meter (a regular pattern of stressed syllables) and more on the cadences of conversation, the naturalness of everyday speech becomes your most reliable guide. Disagreements among performers as to a particular poem's sound patterns may point to their different interpretations of what the text is after. As we've found with the discovery of every other literary element, the rhythm of a poem becomes manifest in the experimentations of rehearsal. The best performance of rhythm is that which embodies a speaker's state of mind, demonstrates the world in which utterance occurs, makes sense of the speaker's words, and realizes the effect the poet (and, ultimately, you) are after.

After stressing, probably the most obvious source of rhythm in a poem is the repetition of end-sounds in different words, known as *rhyme*. Not every poet employs rhyme, although for centuries it was a staple of English-language verse. And, as we have already observed in the examples collected by Jefferson, rhyme is commonplace in everyday speech. We may think of rhyme occurring only at the ends of lines, but many poets slip it inside lines, too. As with all sound patterns, a rhyme, once recognized by the ear, pulls the reader backward into the poem through repetition.

Eighteenth-century readers loved rhyming verses, favoring sound replication at the ends of regularly metered lines. They even fashioned a poetic structure (the heroic couplet) to highlight both meter and rhyme. Alexander Pope, in his rhyming "Essay on Criticism" (1711), made fun of this convention of his own time in a section on "Sound and Sense":

But most by Numbers judge a Poet's song,
And smooth or rough, with them, is right or wrong;
In the bright Muse tho' thousand charms conspire,
Her Voice is all these tuneful fools admire.

To experience the rhythmic power of rhyme alone, read *out loud* the following lines from Ogden Nash's "Parsley for Vice-President!"

I'd like to be able to say a good word for parsley, but I can't,
And after all what can you find to say for something that even the
    dictionary dismisses as a biennial umbelliferous plant?
I will not venture to deny that it is umbelliferous,
I will only add that it is of a nasty green color, and faintly
    odoriferous.

Rhyme and stress are complementary patterns in the overall design of a poem, and they usually provide acoustic support for the visual layout of lines and stanzas.

Couple regularly occurring stress with rhyme, and you get a rhythm so dominant that nobody could miss it:

> whose WOODS these ARE i THINK i KNOW
> his HOUSE is IN the VILlage THOUGH
> he WILL not SEE me STOPping HERE
> to WATCH his WOODS fill UP with SNOW
> From "Stopping By Woods on a Snowy Evening" by Robert Frost

The following poem uses both rhyme and regularly occurring stress to communicate the poet's rhythm. Try to work up a performance that features both sense and rhythm.

"The Amish"

by John Updike
(In Telephone Poles and Other Poems. New York: Alfred A. Knopf, 1969.
Reprinted by permission of Alfred A. Knopf, Inc.)

The Amish are a surly sect.
They paint their bulging barns with hex
Designs, pronounce a dialect
Of Deutsch, inbreed, and wink at sex.

They have no use for buttons, tea,
Life insurance, cigarettes,
Churches, liquor, Sea & Ski,
Public power, or regrets.

Believing motors undivine,
They bob behind buggied horse
From Paradise to Brandywine,
From Bird-in-Hand to Intercourse.

They think the Devil drives a car
And wish Jehovah would revoke
The licensed fools who travel far
To gaze upon these simple folk.

Patterns of repeated sound can include single consonants or vowels, as well as replicating larger units in rhyme. Repeated consonant sounds are instances of *alliteration;* repeated vowel sounds are called *assonance.* Both alliteration and assonance are acoustic patterns appealing to the ear; hence, don't be fooled by spelling. (Remember: English is not a phonetic language.)

You can hear alliteration clearly in the opening line of John Keats' poem "To Autumn":

Season of mists and mellow fruitfulness

Most obvious are the repeated "m" sounds in "mists" and "mellow." But the line doubles back on itself in other alliterative patterns, too. The initial "s" of "season" is repeated in "mists" and "fruitfulness." (Notice that the second "s" in "season" is *not* part of the alliterative pattern because it sounds as a "z.")

John Milton begins a poem composed in 1652 with this line:

When I consider how my light is spent

The short "e" sound of the opening preposition is repeated in the final verb "spent." The long "i" of the first pronoun is repeated twice in the possessive pronoun and in the noun "light." Notice how, when reading the line aloud, this simple sound pattern slows your pace. That's quite intentional.

These three patterns—alliteration, assonance, and rhyme—can carry you a long way toward identifying sound repetition in poems, although other jazzy strategies are available to poets, as well. In combination with stressing, they constitute the musical rhythm of a poem and invite a reader's involvement through appeals to the ear.

PATTERNS INVOLVING THE MIND

In moving from patterns that appeal to the eye and the ear to patterns involving the mind, we shift from physical collaboration with the poet to mental creation. Imagery and figurative language are once removed from the sensations of sound and sight. They exist at a level of abstraction where meaning can be made. Return to Chapter 4, pages 126–129, for a review of images and figurative language.

Here are some passages containing figurative language (for example, metaphor, simile, synecdoche, metonomy, personification, and hyperbole) from poems we have looked at in this chapter. In each case, try to calculate what new or more vivid meaning results from the trope, and how it contributes to the effect the poet wants to achieve.

1. We eat the smile
    And spit out the teeth (p. 145)

2. Believing motors undivine,
    They bob behind a buggied horse
    From Paradise to Brandywine,
    From Bird-in-Hand to Intercourse. (p. 152)

3. And what a congress of stinks!—(p. 150)

4. when the world is puddle-wonderful (p. 146)

PATTERNS INVOLVING THE WHOLE

We have spent a good deal of time on individual poetic features involving the eye, the ear, and the imagination. But poems also depend on a reader's ability to connect parts into a whole. Finding coherence is another kind of involvement, and the ways of going about this process are countless. In the happiest instances, a poem's wholeness presents itself to you effortlessly—sometimes on your first reading, sometimes later in the rehearsal process. Like strands of gold thread woven into a tapestry, recurring images emerge, themes form around these images, and the poem's ending connects integrally with its beginning.

But be warned. No two people are likely to make the exact same connections when reading a poem. One of the rewards of performance is to demonstrate for others the wholeness you perceive in a poem, and to do so in such a way that they see it too. After reading the following poem, we hope you see the connections we describe. But, as importantly, we hope you find themes, patterns, and connections that we have not.

"Earth Dweller"

by William Stafford

(Copyright © 1977, The Estate of William Stafford. Originally appeared in Stories That Could Be True. *New York: Harper & Row, 1977. Used by permission.)*

> It was all the clods at once become
> precious; it was the barn, and the shed,
> and the windmill, my hands, the crack
> Arlie made in the axe handle: oh, let me stay
> here humbly, forgotten, to rejoice in it all;

let the sun casually rise and set.
If I have not found the right place,
teach me; for, somewhere inside, the clods are
vaulted mansions, lines through the barn sing
for the saints forever, the shed and the windmill
rear so glorious the sun shudders like a gong.

Now I know why people worship, carry around
magic emblems, wake up talking dreams
they teach to their children: the world speaks.
The world speaks everything to us.
It is our only friend.

To analyze the patterning of this poem, you might start by observing its sixteen lines divided into two stanzas—pointing roughly toward the conventional
sonnet, but not quite. Then you might listen for stress or try to read for meter,
discovering a basic rhythm lurking beneath each line. The poem does not em-
ploy end rhyme, but, like Roethke's "Root Cellar," individual sounds are repeated closely enough together to make us aware of them. But we do find clear
patterns among the many items the poem lists. The coherence of this poem
comes from the way two patterns of images interact.

The first group of images includes ordinary things, apparent to anyone
equipped with the five basic senses: clods, barn, shed, windmill, hands, axehandle, sun, and people. ("Clods," "shed," and "windmill" are even repeated.)
These are common items associated with a farm. A second pattern of images is
interwoven with the first. It consists of items not necessarily available to the five
senses. This group includes vaulted mansions, saints, magic emblems, worship,
and dreams. Bringing these two different patterns together seems to be the chief
undertaking of the poem. The reader is encouraged to find magic in what's
earthly, to discover the spiritual in the ordinary. This is an important *effect* the
poet is after, his organizing principle.

For other poems, coherence may not be found on the tangible surface of imagery but may be hidden in the inner life of the speaker. Especially with lyric
poetry, the speaker's experience may build to a moment of insight, the sudden
realization of meaning that James Joyce called an "epiphany." Charlotte Lee, author of one of the most successful textbooks on performing literature, refers to
these moments as "fulcrums" or "points of balance"* in a poem. They are not
necessarily emotional climaxes but are turning points, where the speaker's realization causes everything that follows to move in a different, sometimes opposite, direction.

*For a fuller discussion of this unifying pattern, consult Lee's discussion of "Balance and Proportion" in any
edition of *Oral Interpretation* (Boston: Houghton Mifflin).

Try to locate the turning point in the following poem.

"The Elder Sister"

by Sharon Olds

(From The Dead and the Living, *by Sharon Olds. Copyright © 1983 by Sharon Olds. Reprinted by permission of Alfred A. Knopf, Inc.)*

When I look at my elder sister now
I think how she had to go first, down through the
birth canal, to force her way
head-first through the tiny channel,
the pressure of Mother's muscles on her brain,
the tight walls scraping her skin.
Her face is still narrow from it, the long
hollow cheeks of a Crusader on a tomb,
and her inky eyes have the look of someone who has
been in prison a long time and
knows they can send her back. I look at her
body and think how her breasts were first to
rise, slowly, like swans on a pond.
By the time mine came along, they were just
two more birds in the flock, and when the hair
rose on the white mound of her flesh, like
threads of water out of the ground, it was the
first time, but when mine came
they knew about it. I used to think
only in terms of her harshness, sitting and
pissing on me in bed, but now I
see I had her before me always
like a shield. I look at her wrinkles, her clenched
jaws, her frown-lines—I see they are
the dents on my shield, the blows that did not reach me.
She protected me, not as a mother
protects a child, with love, but as a
hostage protects the one who makes her
escape as I made my escape, with my sister's
body held in front of me.

There is an intellectual Catch-22 when finding the patterns that hold a poem together. The connections you discover actually come out of you; they are "subjective." But they have to *seem* to you to be inherent in the text, if they are to hold the poem together as a single experience. Remember that your under-

standing of a poem's coherence may not be the same as another reader's interpretation. No two performances produce quite the same poem. This doesn't
mean that one is right and the other wrong. More likely, it means that two performers have found different connections unifying the poem, and their performances may convince us that both are inherent in the text.

Analyzing a Poem

Here is a work by A. E. Housman (1859–1936), a British poet. Originally published with the title "Terence, This Is Stupid Stuff," Housman re-titled the poem
"Epilogue" for a volume of his collected works. As you can see, it is a poem *about*
poetry, and specifically about the collaborative relationship between poet and
reader. You need to read it several times before feeling comfortable analyzing its
poetic features. At first, it's best to follow the language as a straightforward conversation between two friends, probably set in a pub. (We've added line numbers to make later discussion easier.)

"Epilogue"

by A. E. Housman

1	"Terence, this is stupid stuff:
2	You eat your victuals fast enough;
3	There can't be much amiss, 'tis clear,
4	To see the rate you drink your beer.
5	But oh, good Lord, the verse you make,
6	It gives a chap the belly-ache.
7	The cow, the old cow, she is dead;
8	It sleeps well, the horned head:
9	We poor lads, 'tis our turn now
10	To hear such tunes as killed the cow.
11	Pretty friendship 'tis to rhyme
12	Your friends to death before their time.
13	Moping, melancholy, mad:
14	Come, pipe a tune to dance to, lad."
15	Why, if 'tis dancing you would be,
16	There's brisker pipes than poetry.
17	Say, for what were hop-yards meant,
18	Or why was Burton built on Trent?
19	Oh many a peer of England brews
20	Livelier liquor than the Muse,

21   And malt does more than Milton can
22   To justify God's ways to man.
23   Ale, man, ale's the stuff to drink
24   For fellows whom it hurts to think:
25   Look into the pewter pot
26   To see the world as the world's not.
27   And faith, 'tis pleasant till 'tis past:
28   The mischief is that 'twill not last.
29   Oh I have been to Ludlow fair
30   And left my necktie God knows where,
31   And carried half-way home, or near,
32   Pints and quarts of Ludlow beer:
33   Then the world seemed none so bad,
34   And I myself a sterling lad;
35   And down in lovely muck I've lain,
36   Happy till I woke again.
37   Then I saw the morning sky:
38   Heigho, the tale was all a lie;
39   The world, it was the old world yet,
40   I was I, my things were wet,
41   And nothing now remained to do
42   But begin the game anew.

43   Therefore, since the world has still
44   Much good, but much less good than ill,
45   And while the sun and moon endure
46   Luck's a chance, but trouble's sure,
47   I'd face it as a wise man would,
48   And train for ill and not for good.
49   'Tis true, the stuff I bring for sale
50   Is not so brisk a brew as ale:
51   Out of a stem that scored the hand
52   I wrung it in a weary land.
53   But take it: if the smack is sour,
54   The better for the embittered hour;
55   It should do good to heart and head
56   When your soul is in my soul's stead;
57   And I will friend you, if I may,
58   In the dark and cloudy day.

59   There was a king reigned in the East:
60   There, when kings will sit to feast,
61   They get their fill before they think
62   With poisoned meat and poisoned drink.

63	He gathered all that springs to birth
64	From the many-venomed earth;
65	First a little, thence to more,
66	He sampled all her killing store;
67	And easy, smiling, seasoned sound,
68	Sate the king when healths went round.
69	They put arsenic in his meat
70	And stared aghast to watch him eat;
71	They poured strychnine in his cup
72	And shook to see him drink it up:
73	They shook, they stared as white's their shirt:
74	Them it was their poison hurt.
75	—I told the tale that I heard told.
76	Mithridates, he died old.

This is a long and complex poem, so let's start by trying to make out something of its world. Like all poems printed on the page, it involves us first by appealing to the eye. The piece contains seventy-six lines, divided into four unequal stanzas. That information is vital to the discovery of the poem's coherence and overall argument.

The poem's initial involvement of the reader's ear is in the opening line, a quotation from an unnamed speaker: "Terence, this is stupid stuff." From this line alone, we may deduce several things. First, the person being addressed is named Terence. The speaker and the listener have a close enough relationship to call each other by their first names. The casual level of talk suggests an informal setting. Even with these clues, the reader still doesn't know what *this* stupid stuff is.

In lines 2 to 4, the speaker tries to diagnose Terence's problem, saying in effect, "You seem to be eating your food just fine, and there can't be too much wrong with your constitution judging by how much beer you're able to consume." In lines 5 and 6, we finally begin to figure out what's eating the speaker: "But oh, good Lord, the verse you make. It gives a chap the belly-ache." Apparently, Terence is a poet, and his unnamed friend—the speaker of the first stanza—doesn't care much for his poetry.

The next two lines seem to come out of nowhere and show no immediate connection to what's gone before:

> The cow, the old cow, she is dead;
> It sleeps well, the horned head:

By listening to what the speaker says just before and right after these two lines, we may conclude that they represent a quotation from one of Terence's poems. If so, the speaker would deliver them in a sarcastic voice. Then, immediately after his mock-performance, the speaker pulls in a larger circle of critics ("we poor lads") and says, in effect, "It's nice of you to lay such depressing poetry on your pals. Why can't you write something more upbeat?"

In the second stanza, Terence begins his answer. We know that the speaker has changed from several signs. The first stanza was within quotation marks; the second is not. The first stanza set out a verbal challenge; the second answers it. The style of the first was belly-aching; the style of the second is analytical. There seems to be a purposeful ambiguity after the first stanza as Terence addresses both his unnamed critic *and* us, his unacknowledged audience.

Terence begins by picking up the exact words and images used by his critical friend. Throughout this stanza, Terence argues that, if you need to be made happy, why not try ale instead of poetry. He invokes a long list of images associated with beer—from brewing to consuming.

It's not until the third stanza, beginning "therefore," that Terence makes an outright defense of his poetry. And he does so by contrasting its benefits to those of beer. Even though its "smack is sour," Terence recommends poetry as more beneficial than beer. He argues that a poem is good for you, because it can prepare you to endure hardships. He implies that poetry should be ingested more as a medicine than a libation, and a specific kind of medicine at that—a preventive antidote to life's troubles.

In the final stanza, Terence tells a story illustrating his argument. This story is not about poetry but about poison. It represents an allusion to the ancient legend of Mithridates. It seems that in this king's era courtiers often poisoned their monarchs. But Mithridates outsmarted his would-be assassins by eating small doses of natural poisons; he gradually built up greater and greater tolerance. Then, when others tried to kill him by putting arsenic in his meat and pouring strychnine in his drink, he got the last laugh. His routine of taking increasing doses of poison had given him immunity. Terence concludes the story with the kicker: "Mithridates, he died old."

Taken together, Terence's three stanzas develop a unified argument back to his unnamed critic, as well as articulating an unusual poetic theory. In contrast to drinking ale, which only provides a temporary relief from life's troubles, you should take daily doses of poetry. It is much more effective at immunizing you against hardship and treachery. And, by implication, Terence is offering his own poems—the very ones that make his friends melancholy—as a supply of beneficial poisons.

If you're comfortable with this reading of the poem, let's go back and look more closely at how it's patterned. First, and most obviously, it is structured as a drama, a conversation. Terence's unnamed friend speaks the first 14 lines (the first stanza), and Terence responds for the next 62 lines (stanzas two, three, and four). Inside the overall drama are various other literary genres. Lines 29 through 42 comprise a songlike story ("Oh I have been to Ludlow Fair"). In fact, you could easily compose a melody for those fourteen lines to the tune of a beer-drinking song. The drama also contains several aphorisms that sound like toasts among drinking buddies (for examples, lines 23–24 and 25–26). Then the entire final stanza makes up its own stand-alone story, the tale of Mithridates.

Looking (and listening) more closely at the poem's structure, notice how it's written in rhyming couplets—two-line units with full end rhyme. This is an absolutely regular pattern repeated thirty-eight times. The pattern of stresses is also clear—four per line—except for unusual instances when the meter is broken for a purpose. In lines 7 and 8, for instance, the difference represents a quotation from a poem by Terence.

In addition to rhyme and meter, the poem is chock-full of alliteration and assonance. If you look at lines 13 and 14, you'll hear the clever use to which a sound pattern can be put:

> *Moping, melancholy, mad:*
> *Come, pipe a tune to dance to, lad.*

The "m" sounds in the first line, as well as its deviant stress pattern, are a literal downer. They sound moping, melancholy, and mad. By contrast, the consonants of the next line are undeniably perky. They almost sound like a drum beating.

Not only is this poem structured by genres of everyday talk (conversation, aphorism, song, and story), and patterned by sound repetitions (stress, rhyme, alliteration, and assonance), but it displays clusters of images, as well. Two primary patterns are images associated with beer and images associated with poetry.

The patterning of this poem is part and parcel of its sense. Terence recommends poems to his friend as little doses of poison that, if taken regularly, can make one immune to the more lethal dangers of life. By extension, we can imagine Housman himself making the same argument. Indeed, his rhyming couplets help his thematic poison go down for the reader. Sounding almost like playground rhymes, he sugar-coats his poison with easygoing prosody. As readers, we ingest his point of view before realizing it.

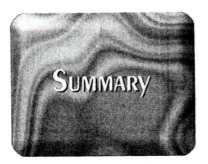

SUMMARY

Our thesis in this chapter has been that poetry *is* performance. Poetic language springs from the body's need and desire to express itself in patterns. Rhythmic speech seeks total involvement from performer and audience. Strategies for involvement may appeal to the eye—lines and stanzas. They certainly appeal to the ear—stress, rhyme, alliteration, and assonance. Involvement of the imagination is encouraged by sense imagery and figurative language. The patterning of poetic speech may be decorative and pleasurable, but it is never extraneous. Patterns of involvement define the genre.

We have mentioned rap lyrics as one instance of poetry's resurgence in popular culture. Another example is the increasing popularity of Poetry Slams, like the open-mike night at a comedy club. These are amateur competitions usually conducted in a bar, in which poets recite their works to the raucous assessment of a charged audience.

The profession of poetry comes and goes in popularity; the expression of poetry is with us always. Patterned speech reaches down to touch deep places of personal intimacy and cultural cohesion. It springs forth in moments of fun or playfulness, sorrow or hurt, rejoicing or celebration, anger or despair. It is the vehicle of religious praise and the medium of philosophical reflection. It is the feather to tickle a baby's toes and the sacred relic to test a convert's vows.

Octavio Paz, Nobel prize-winning poet of Mexico, says,

> *Poetry existed before writing. Essentially, it is a verbal art, that enters us not only through our eyes and understanding but through our ears as well. Poetry is something spoken and heard. . . . We are different from other animals because we can talk and the supreme form of language is poetry.* *

When performing poems, work for a full involvement of sound and sense, pattern and theme. Remember that a poem is rhythmic *speech*; what's most important is to convey the person speaking and to understand the effect he or she wants to achieve in a listener. Recall the fun of playground rhymes, the naturalness of poetic speech "errors," and the earnestness of Housman's philosophy. Trust the patterns themselves. Embody the language; let it inhabit you.

We want to end this chapter on poetry with a question. Earlier, we stipulated that poetry is orally and visually patterned language. But this is not the only way to define the genre. Return to "Admission of Failure" on page 64. We found this selection in *Best Poems of 1992*, edited by Charles Simic, who is a respected contemporary critic and winner of the Pulitzer Prize for Poetry. You can safely assume he knows what poetry is, but if "Admission of Failure" is poetry, his definition of the genre is markedly different from ours. Can you decide what definition of poetry would admit "Admission of Failure" to this genre instead of, say, narrative prose, the subject of our next chapter?

---

*Octavio Paz, in *Writers at Work: The Paris Review Interviews*, Ninth Series, edited by George Plimpton (New York: Penguin Books, 1992), p. 107.

Chapter Six

Performing Narrative

Narratives in Life and Literature

"Story" has been with us from the beginning of this book. Starting with the conversations we analyzed in the first chapter, implicit in the discussions of world, effect, and sense, and throughout our analysis of poetic language, many of the texts we have considered from life or literature have included stories. In this chapter, we focus more specifically on story as a thing in itself.

Everyday talk is full of stories. Here are just a few examples of how commonplace interactions can lead into stories:

"Did you hear what happened to Chris Monday night?"

"I talked to a guy who took this class last term, and he told me the final was a killer."

"My folks split up when I was eight."

"She was just walking down the hall toward me, like everything was normal, but she had this really funny look in her eye."

From church pulpit to political platform, from dinner table to bedroom, from back alley to Main Street, we experience our world through stories. These take the form of intimate conversation or party-stopping *tour de force*. They tell secrets or teach lessons. They elicit laughter and tears, compassion and anger. When parents ask a child, "How was school today?" they're inviting a story. When children ask their parents, "Where do babies come from?" they're looking for a story to satisfy curiosity and assist understanding. Religious leaders teach their most sacred truths through stories. Persons accused of crimes rely on narratives to establish their alibis. Indeed, our entire criminal justice system works by comparing competing stories to determine a defendant's guilt or innocence.

Stories or narratives provide a fundamental way of knowing the world. Young children turn naturally to stories, more than to rational propositions, to make sense out of perplexity. James Moffett puts the matter succinctly:

> *Whereas adults differentiate their thought with specialized kinds of discourse, generalization, and theory, children must, for a long time, make narrative do for all. They utter themselves almost entirely through stories—real and invented—and they apprehend what others say through story.* *

*James Moffett, *Teaching the Universe of Discourse* (Boston: Houghton Mifflin, 1982), p. 49.

Choose an incident from your own memories of childhood, something that happened to you. It could be something funny, or something sad—a story that, on recollection, makes you want to cry or laugh or get angry. Search among your memories for a story that has become part of your family's collective mythology. Perhaps it's an incident that your mother or father, sister or brother, aunt, uncle, or cousin might repeat at a family gathering when conversation turns to childhood memories.

Prepare to tell this story to your class by rehearsing it aloud. Do not write it down on paper. Just go over the incident in your memory to select the most telling details. Then practice actually performing the story, keeping the whole tale to no more than a few minutes. You needn't memorize the language you want to use. It doesn't matter if the words come out the same way with every rehearsal. Simply look at your classmates and tell them your childhood story.

After each performance the class should discuss the following questions:

1. What *happened* in this story, and how did the incident *affect* the child at the time it took place?

2. What seems to be the *attitude* of the storyteller toward the incident now? How does she or he feel about it now? How might you account for the differences of perception between childhood experience and adult storytelling?

3. What is it about the story that has caused the storyteller to remember it?

If time permits, try a variation on this exercise. Retell the same story, but tell it from the perspective of another participant in the incident. For example, if the story involves something you did with your cousin, retell it from the cousin's point of view. Think how she or he might feel toward the incident. In performance, actually try to become the other participant, using the other's language and situating the story in the other's body. After this second version, invite the class to discuss differences in the two versions.

Stories and Storytellers

The distinctive quality about story or narrative as a genre of talk is the presence of a storyteller or narrator, a speaker who organizes events in a meaningful sequence and tells them to a listener. All of us tell stories, and all of us listen to them. Storytelling is a fine art, published in the form of novels or short stories or even poems, but it is also one of the communication arts of everyday living. You probably know at least one individual whom others urge to tell stories because she is so good at it. You also may know someone who's infamous for his boring stories. Not only are you an experienced narrator and consumer of stories, you are also a confident critic, constantly separating the good from the bad in everyday interactions.

We are apt to be unaware of how much storytelling we engage in every day because the form of these stories is so much more varied than their counterparts in literature. In the typical short story or novel, one person tells the story, and everything that occurs in the telling relates directly to the tale. By contrast, the performance of story in everyday life is a messy affair. For instance, if you meet two friends who want to tell you what happened to them last night, both probably narrate the event, tossing the story back and forth as they tell it.

In this chapter, we study narrators in the act of telling stories and work for a better understanding of how they do it.

Narrative *Is* Performance

By definition, storytelling is performance, whether it occurs on the theatrical stage, on the cinematic screen, in the pages of a book, or through the conversations of everyday life. From ancient times to the present, narrative performance has provided one of the enduring pleasures of human experience because it is such a familiar, homespun, art. Stories are made accessible by their telling.

The American novelist John Updike, lecturing in Sweden, underscored the performative nature of narrative in his description of an "author":

> The very first people whom we consider authors—the minds and voices behind the tribal epics, the Bible and Homer, the Vedas and the sagas—were, it would seem, public performers, for whom publication took the form of recitation, of incantation, of (we might say) lecturing. The circumstances wherein these primal literary works were promulgated are not perfectly clear, nor are all examples of oral literature identical in purpose and texture; but we could risk generalizing that the bard's function was, in the Horatian formulation, to entertain and to instruct, and that the instruction concerned the great matter of tribal identity. The poet and his songs served as a memory bank, supplying the outlines of the determinative tribal

struggles and instances of warrior valor. Who we are, who our heroic fathers were, how we got where we are, why we believe what we believe and act the way we do—the bard illuminates these essential questions, as the firelight flickers and the mead flows and the listeners in their hearts renew their pact with the past. The author is delivering not his own words but his own version of a story told to him, a story handed down in an evolving form and, at a certain point, fixed into print by the written version of a scribe. The author is not only himself but his predecessors, and simultaneously he is part of the living tribal fabric, the part that voices what all know, or should know, and need to hear again. *

The success of any story depends on the skill of the narrator and the appeal of the story. It may be a fictional occurrence created out of the narrator's imagination, or it may be an experience from the actual world. No matter. A story is made up solely of words. In the performance of these words, however, both teller and listener can affirm legend, construe history, share secrets, imagine fantasy, or construct reality.

When discussing speakers in Chapter 2 on *world*, we suggested that one of the most important considerations for any performer is to determine the relationship between a speaker and a listener. An old philosophical conundrum asks whether a tree falling in the woods with no one there to hear it makes any noise. There can be no arguing the point when it comes to narrative. If no one is there to hear it, a story ceases to exist. A story cannot come into being apart from a pact of cooperation between teller and audience.

A Teller, a Listener, and the Tale Told

A story can't happen unless someone wants to tell it and someone else is willing to hear it. Listen to this contemporary Scottish tale told in the form of a dialogue.

"An Old Story"

by James Kelman

(Reprinted by permission of Farrar, Straus & Giroux, Inc.: "An Old Story" from Greyhound for Breakfast *by James Kelman. Copyright © 1987 by James Kelman.)*

She'd been going about in this depressed state for ages so I should've known something was up. But I didnt. You dont always see what's in front

*John Updike, from a speech "Should Writers Give Lectures?" delivered at the Gothenburg Book Fair, in Gothenburg, Sweden, on August 20, 1987; published in *Odd Jobs: Essays and Criticism* (New York: Alfred A. Knopf, 1991), p. 137.

of your nose. I've been sitting about the house that long. You wind up in a daze. You dont see things properly, even with the weans, the weans especially. There again but she's no a wean. No now. She's a young woman. Ach, I dont want to tell this story.

But you cant say that. Obviously the story has to get told.

Mm, aye, I know what you mean.

Fine then.

Mmm.

Okay, so about your story . . .

Aye.

It concerns a lassie, right? And she's in this depressed state, because of her boyfriend probably—eh?

I dont want to tell it.

But you've got to tell it. You've got to tell it. Unless . . . if it's no really a story at all.

Oh aye christ it's a story, dont worry about that.

This short-short story is about telling and listening and a tale told or, in this case, not told. "An Old Story" concerns the nature of collaboration, the mutual accountability felt between teller and listener in any narrative performance.

The first speaker sets the stage for his story in the opening sentence. Such narrative elements as character, place, time, and event are all stated or suggested. In the second sentence, the narrator situates himself in relation to this subject: "But I didnt [know something was up]." At the end of the paragraph, after rationalizing his lack of perception, the narrator reneges on his part of the storytelling bargain: "Ach, I dont want to tell this story."

His listener becomes the story's second speaker when he complains, "But you cant say that. Obviously the story has to get told." Why does he say "obviously"? He may mean: It's obvious you must tell the story *because* you've started it, and it would be unfair to begin a collaboration and then quit on it. Or: it's obvious you *want* or *need* to tell the story, despite your denial.

The first speaker acknowledges the obvious by saying, "Mm, aye, I know what you mean," although we, as readers, are not so clear what the speaker may know or mean.

The listener inside the story settles back and says, "Fine then," as if to indicate, "Begin your story. I'm ready."

The narrator seems to be thinking about it—either the story itself or the decision whether or not to tell it—when he hums a noncommittal reply: "Mmm."

The listener prompts him, almost as if feeding the narrator a cue line: "Okay, so about your story . . . "

The narrator replies, "Aye."

And the listener once again tries to jump start the storyteller by reminding him, "It concerns a lassie, right? And she's in this depressed state, because of her boyfriend probably—eh?" This last suggestion goes beyond the information provided initially by the narrator. The listener is taking an active hand in shaping the tale.

Now the original narrator seems to have made up his mind: "I dont want to tell it."

And the listener confronts him with the terms of their narrative pact: "But you've got to tell it. You've got to tell it. Unless . . . if it's no really a story at all." In this last sentence, the listener throws down the gauntlet, as it were. Perhaps the narrator didn't have a story to tell in the first place, in which case it was deceitful to have begun.

Finally, protecting his reputation, the narrator vows, "Oh aye christ it's a story, dont worry about that."

Our narrative, the one entitled "An Old Story" by James Kelman, is about two characters who enact the drama of an incomplete storytelling. The tale within our narrative, the one about a lassie in a depressed state, never gets told. Nonetheless, even in as short a space as this half-page narrative, we're confronted with the relationship between two characters in crisis. There is always a narrative pact between a speaker and a listener. To break it risks breaching the relationship itself.

Here are some additional questions to consider as you discuss this story and what it can teach us about narrative performance:

1. The author James Kelman, winner of Great Britain's 1994 Booker Prize, lives and writes in Glasgow, Scotland. By what signs within the language of the story can you identify these two characters as being Scottish? How significant is the *placement* of the story to its meaning? What difference might this make to the story's performance?

2. From what you *know* of the story's two characters, what additionally might you *speculate* about them? Are they close friends? Have they often exchanged personal narratives in the past? Where do you think this conversation occurs? In one of their homes? In a pub? On a bus? What difference would it make to your performance?

3. How should the story's final line be spoken? With what attitude? If the narrative were to continue, what do you think would happen next?

4. Can you find instances in the conversations in Chapter 1 and the Appendix when a storyteller withdraws from a narrative pact, cutting short his or her tale before the listener was ready to conclude? Can you find examples in which the listener might call a halt to storytelling before the narrator is finished?

5. How much can you make of James Kelman's title for this story?

6. In our discussion of "An Old Story," we referred to both the narrator and the listener as "he." Was this gender assignment justified by the text?

Understanding Listeners

"An Old Story" can teach an important lesson to those of us interested in the performance of narrative. When you listen to the performances of classmates, you can influence the success of their stories because, as audience, you are part of the storytelling. Helping a performer to bring a story off may require little more than patience. As with many songs and movies, a verbal story usually asks for careful attention from the audience to arouse interest.

On the other hand, your role as listener within a literary text always requires role-playing. Recall our earlier discussion in Chapter 3 on effect. There, we analyzed several instances of how speakers cast listeners in roles.

"An Old Story," brief as it is, manages to shape your role as the reader. The teller begins, "She'd been going around in this depressed state," and you are immediately aware that because you don't know who "she" is, you aren't the listener being addressed. To enter the telling as an active collaborator, you must listen carefully for clues to the identity of "she" and other parts of the teller's unfamiliar world.

In the same paragraph, the teller says, "You don't see things properly even with the weans, the weans especially." If you don't know what "weans" are, you must take on a homework assignment to become a good listener to this story. Using a dictionary is part of taking the listener's role seriously and conscientiously.

There are reasonable limits to what a performer can expect of an audience, and these vary according to the situation. If listeners have not read the story prior to its performance, they can hardly be expected to look everything up. The performer has to give the audience some help with knowledge that can't be figured out from the context. This is usually done in the form of an introduction.

In "An Old Story," the tale fails to happen because the storyteller loses his commitment to it. As a performer of a story, your commitment to its telling is crucial. Unless you want to bring it off, it is doomed to fail. Whether you stop, like the teller of "An Old Story," or plow through to the end by just going through the motions, the result is still a failed story. Every suggestion we make in this chapter is calculated to let a story have its way with your listeners.

The Worlds of Storytelling

The presence of a storyteller is the easiest way to identify the genre of narrative, and because this is so, we want to devote the rest of the chapter to the unique challenges of performing narrators. Like all speakers, narrators have their own world. Your ability to perform the narrator depends on your understanding of how his or her world relates to all other worlds in the act of storytelling.

THE NARRATOR'S WORLD

In the narrator's world, he or she is telling a story to a listener. That world is the place and time where the telling happens. In "It's Gun Be Hard to Do," when the mother tells the daughter about Barry, the narrative world is on the telephone sometime after she has talked to Barry. In 'Night, Mother, the mother tells her daughter about Agnes in the kitchen after going to the fair. Usually, however, a narrator wants the listener to ignore the world of story*telling* and imagine, instead, the world of the story itself.

THE CHARACTER'S WORLD

A *character* is any participant in the events of the story, and the character's world is the place where the story happens. Within this world, characters frequently become speakers with their own listeners—listeners who are probably different from those in the narrator's world.

The fact that these worlds are different should influence how you behave when performing a story. For example, the next story, "David and Goliath," includes the following shift from the narrator's world to that of a character:

> Then one day Jesse said to his son David, "Take your brothers an ephah of this parched grain and these two loaves of bread, and run with them to the camp."

The speaker of the first nine words is the narrator. If you were performing this narrator, you would probably be looking at your listeners. But when you got to the words in quotation, you would be performing Jesse, a character *in* the story, and in that character's world there is only one listener, David. The audience should be able to tell from what you do in performance when you are the storyteller talking to them, and when you are Jesse talking to David.

THE AUTHOR'S WORLD

Let's assume that you successfully communicate to your listeners when you are the narrator speaking to the listeners and when you are Jesse speaking to David—to be more accurate, when you are performing the narrator and when you are performing the narrator performing Jesse. For this to happen, a good deal of pretending has to take place. After all, you aren't the narrator, you are only pretending to be. And your classmates aren't the listeners the narrator thinks he is talking to, they are only pretending to be.

Just as there is a storyteller behind the character Jesse, there is an author behind that storyteller. The author writes in yet another world, this one invisible since the author never speaks except through the narrator. We can only infer the author's world from his or her creation of the narrator's and characters' worlds.

Often the narrator seems so close to what we imagine the author to be like, there is no performative reason to distinguish between the narrator's world and that of the author. In "David and Goliath," the difference between author and narrator is insignificant. In many stories, however, the distinction between author and narrator is profound. In these, the storyteller is clearly marked as separate from the author. Edgar Allan Poe's horror stories are sometimes told by a narrator on the brink of insanity. Though we suspect the voice telling the story of "The Tell-Tale Heart" or "The Pit and the Pendulum" is insane, the author, who creates our experience of listening to a mad narrator, is not insane. Such storytellers are *unreliable narrators*, and the challenge of performing them lies in showing to the audience the narrator as you believe the author wants us to see him, rather than as he sees himself.

THE PERFORMER'S WORLD

Finally, there is the world of your performance, in which you pretend to be an author-shaped narrator, who in turn occasionally pretends to be various characters. You make these transformations for your audience, who pretend they are the listeners to whom the shaped narrator is speaking.

While this may sound complicated, it's actually a commonplace interaction you handle any time somebody tells you a story. The key to narrative performance is to be aware of the connectedness among these various worlds but to pay particular attention to the world of the storyteller. After all, it is the narrator who selects details, who decides what to put in the story and what to leave out, who determines how to sequence the reporting of events, and whose tone of voice insinuates itself into every single word. In everyday life, we remind each other of this narrative power when we say, "Consider the source."

The Narrator and the Story

Point of view describes the way a narrator looks at the events and characters in the story. You may identify any narrator's *point of view* by looking at several constraints on his or her perception. First, the storyteller stands in some *physical relation* to the action. Where is the person located within the event? How close to the central action—two feet removed? twenty yards away? on a rooftop across the street? in an oncoming car? in a rearview mirror? Physical relationship to the action may be a critical constraint on a person's perceptions. For this reason, witnesses of a crime are often cross-examined in detail when testifying in court as to their location and angle of vision. Second, a narrator's point of view is limited by *psychological* constraints, including unconscious determinants of his or her way of looking at things. When you know someone intimately, don't you find yourself taking into account their psychology when listening to any story they tell? Third, *intellectual* capacity shapes perception. Some narrators are more capable of discernment when recounting an event than are others. This is as true among storytellers at the office water cooler as among literary narrators. Fourth, a person's *attitude* helps to determine his or her perceptions. When identifying a narrator's point of view, it is especially important to observe attitudes toward the characters and events being reported, as well as toward the listener.

Perhaps of greatest importance to determining point of view is asking whether the narrator was a *participant* in or *observer* of the events being told. Was he or she involved in the action recounted? If so, how involved? Does the storyteller have a vested interest in the outcome of events? Or, by contrast, was the storyteller a neutral observer? In that case, how careful, detailed, and accurate is the observation? Might the storyteller be neither a participant nor an observer but merely a second-hand reporter, retelling what he or she has heard from another?

The more effective a narrator's strategies are, the more we are apt to be unconscious of them. Caught up in the sweep of a story, you think of its telling as inevitable. You can't imagine the tale unfolding in any other way. For our purposes, however, it is vital to figure out why narrators tell their stories in particular ways and not in others. Behind every narrative strategy deployed—from selection of details to quotation of dialogue—lies an intended effect that the narrator wants the story to have on listeners. As a performer, you must understand what motivates the storyteller. What's at risk in the telling? Where does the narrator's passion lie? Similarly, in the role of audience, you should try to comprehend why a narrator tells the story in a certain way. What assumptions has the storyteller made about you? your values? your interests? your intelligence? your psychology?

One way of sharpening sensitivity to these issues is to study the same story told by two different narrators pursuing very different effects. Here is an old story in the hands of two quite different storytellers.

"David and Goliath"

*(As told in I Samuel, Chapter 17, verses 1–52
in the New English Bible.)*

The Philistines collected their forces for war and massed at Socoh in Judah; they camped between Socoh and Azekah at Ephes-dammim. Saul and the Israelites also massed, and camped in the Vale of Elah. They drew up their lines facing the Philistines, the Philistines occupying a position on one hill and the Israelites on another, with a valley between them. A champion came out from the Philistine camp, a man named Goliath, from Gath; he was over nine feet in height. He had a bronze helmet on his head, and he wore plate-armour of bronze, weighing five thousand shekels. On his legs were bronze greaves, and one of his weapons was a dagger of bronze. The shaft of his spear was like a weaver's beam, and its head, which was of iron, weighed six hundred shekels; and his shield-bearer marched ahead of him. The champion stood and shouted to the ranks of Israel, "Why do you come out to do battle, you slaves of Saul? I am the Philistine champion; choose your man to meet me. If he can kill me in fair fight, we will become your slaves; but if I prove too strong for him and kill him, you shall be our slaves and serve us. Here and now I defy the ranks of Israel. Give me a man," said the Philistine, "and we will fight it out." When Saul and the Israelites heard what the Philistine said, they were shaken and dismayed.

David was the son of an Ephrathite called Jesse, who had eight sons. By Saul's time he had become a feeble old man, and his three eldest sons had followed Saul to the war. The eldest was called Eliab, and the next Abinadab, and the third Shammah; David was the youngest. The three eldest followed Saul, while David used to go to Saul's camp and back to Bethlehem to mind his father's flocks.

Morning and evening for forty days the Philistine came forward and took up his position. Then one day Jesse said to his son David, "Take your brothers an ephah of this parched grain and these ten loaves of bread, and run with them to the camp. These ten cream-cheeses are for you to take to the commanding officer. See if your brothers are well and bring back some token from them." Saul and the brothers and all the Israelites were in the Vale of Elah, fighting the Philistines. Early next morning David left someone in charge of the sheep, set out on his errand and went as Jesse had told him. He reached the lines just as the army was going out to take up position and was raising the war-cry. The Israelites and the Philistines drew up their ranks opposite each other. David left his things in charge of the quartermaster, ran to the line and went up to his brothers to greet them. While he was talking to them the Philistine champion, Goliath, came out from the Philistine ranks and issued his challenge in the same words as before; and David heard him. When the Israelites saw the man they ran from him in fear. "Look at this man who comes out day after day to defy Israel," they said. "The king is to give a rich reward to the man who kills him; he will give him his daughter in marriage too and will exempt his family from service due in Israel." Then David turned to his neighbours and said, "What is to be done for the man who kills this Philistine and wipes out our disgrace? And who is he, an uncircumcised Philistine, to defy the army of the living God?" The people told him how the matter stood and what was to be done for the man who killed him. His elder brother Eliab overheard David talking with the men and grew angry. "What are you doing here?" he asked. "And who have you left to look after those few sheep in the wilderness? I know you, you impudent young rascal; you have only come to see the fighting." David answered, "What have I done now? I only asked a question." And he turned away from him to someone else and repeated his question, but everybody gave him the same answer.

What David had said was overheard and reported to Saul, who sent for him. David said to him, "Do not lose heart, sir. I will go and fight this Philistine." Saul answered, "You cannot go and fight this Philistine; you are only a lad, and he has been a fighting man all his life." David said to Saul, "Sir, I am my father's shepherd; when a lion or bear comes and carries off a sheep from the flock, I go after it and attack it and rescue the victim from its jaws. Then if it turns on me, I seize it by the beard and batter it to death. Lions I have killed and bears, and this uncircumcised Philistine will fare no better than they; he has defied the army of the living God. The LORD who saved me from the lion and the bear will save me from this Philistine." "Go then," said Saul; "and the LORD will be with you." He put his own tunic on David, placed a bronze helmet on his head and gave him a coat of mail to wear; he then fastened his sword on David over his tunic. But David hesitated, because he had not tried them, and said to Saul, "I cannot go with these, because I have not tried them." So he took them off. Then he picked up his stick, chose five smooth stones from the brook and put them in a shepherd's bag which served as his pouch. He walked out to meet the Philistine with his sling in his hand.

The Philistine came on towards David, with his shield-bearer marching ahead; and he looked David up and down and had nothing but contempt for this handsome lad with his ruddy cheeks and bright eyes. He said to David, "Am I a dog that you come out against me with sticks?" And he swore at him in the name of his god. "Come on," he said, "and I will give your flesh to the birds and the beasts." David answered, "You have come against me with sword and spear and dagger, but I have come against you in the name of the LORD of Hosts, the God of the army of Israel which you have defied. The LORD will put you into my power this day; I will kill you and cut your head off and leave your carcass and the carcasses of the Philistines to the birds and the wild beasts; all the world shall know that there is a God in Israel. All those who are gathered here shall see that the Lord saves neither by sword or spear; the battle is the LORD's, and he will put you all into our power."

When the Philistine began moving toward him again, David ran quickly to engage him. He put his hand into his bag, took out a stone, slung it, and struck the Philistine on the forehead. The stone sank into his forehead, and he fell flat on his face on the ground. So David proved the victor with his sling and stone; he struck Goliath down and gave him a mortal wound, though he had no sword. Then he ran to the Philistine and stood over him, and grasping his sword, he drew it out of the scabbard, dispatched him and cut off his head. The Philistines, when they saw that their hero was dead, turned and ran. The men of Israel and Judah at once raised the war-cry and hotly pursued them all the way to Gath and even to the gates of Ekron. The road that runs to Shaarim, Gath, and Ekron was strewn with their dead.

For most of us, this story is so familiar that we are apt to miss just how carefully the narrator has deployed strategies of selection, sequence, quotation, and point of view. But look now at how a different storyteller, making different assumptions about the knowledge and psychology of his listeners and pursuing different objectives, employs different strategies.

"The David of Michelangelo"

by Dennis Vannatta

(Copyright © 1991 by Dennis Vannatta. Excerpted from the story collection This Time, This Place *by Dennis Vannatta; available from White Pine Press, Fredonia, New York. Anthologized in* The Pushcart Prize, XV: Best of the Small Presses, 1990–1991.)

[1] DAVID

"I know your pride, and the naughtiness of your heart," says Eliab, his brother.

But David is not listening.

"I killed a lion and a bear that stole one of your sheep," he says to Saul, whose eyes have already begun to glaze over with wonder and madness. "I chased them down. I hit that bear so hard he dropped the sheep right out of his mouth. The lion came for me, and I grabbed him by the beard. I said, 'Whoa, old fellow!' Then I killed him with one blow."

The circle of warriors tightening around Saul and David push Eliab farther back, until soon his mutterings can no longer be heard.

David does not think himself vain. He believes that he has simply told a truth the King will surely be glad to hear.

He does not yet understand the madness in the King's heart.

But David does know that his moment is at hand. After a lion and a bear, a fat Philistine will make a short morning's work.

(He does not have to go naked into the valley of Elah. He could have worn the brass armor, weighing two thousand shekels, provided by Saul—could at least have worn his shepherd's smock, his sandals, and his goatskin cap against the sun. But no. He goes naked into the valley, and just before killing the giant, he turns back toward Saul and Jonathan and

Eliab—his white young manhood shining in the bright morning light like polished stone—and almost smiles. He looks as if he might be posing.)

[2] GOLIATH

He, too, was a shepherd. On his wild rocky hillside in Gath, he would cradle the little lambs gently against his huge chest and nuzzle his face into their necks and breathe the rich, warm, heady odor of young wool. He would study each newborn lamb, rubbing his chin, until he had thought of a suitable name: Wildflower, Mothersmilk, Raincloud. His tender ankles could only painfully support his bulk, so he could not have pursued a strayed lamb far beyond the slope rising above the hut where he lived with his mother. The sheep seemed to know this and would stay near and always come when he called them by name. When it came time for a sheep to be slaughtered, Goliath would weep. But even this the sheep seemed to understand, and they would turn their necks lovingly toward the knife.

When the King's men came to gather recruits for the war against the Israelites, Goliath's neighbors sent them to him as a joke.

"Go to the hut where the widow lives, at the foot of the rocky slope, and there you will find a giant who will slay all your foes," they said, pushing their beards up to hide their smiles.

"Mama!" he cried.

They pounded his fingers with the butts of their spears to make him release the roof pole, and it took six of them to load him into a dung cart. No horse could carry him, and they knew he could not walk all the way back to camp.

He sat weeping and reciting, without hope, the names of his sheep as they hauled him off down the road. His mother wept long after he had passed from sight.

She knew she would never see him, or the dung cart, again.

At the camp of the Philistines, the training captain would slap Goliath's fat buttocks with the side of his sword and squeeze his huge quivering tits, crooning, "Ooo, baby, ooo, baby, ooo," while Goliath bawled and the men chortled.

In his coat of mail weighing five thousand shekels, Goliath could not even stand up without help, much less walk from the camp at the top of the hill down into the valley, where he was to shout his challenge to the Israelites. So they built a frame atop a small wheeled platform, all of gopher wood, and tied Goliath upright to the frame, which they concealed as best they could under his long scarlet cloak. Two long ropes were tied to the frame and then passed through the hands of two files of soldiers, whom Goliath seemed to be pulling down the hill after him. It was they, of course, who were letting him roll down slowly to the bottom of the valley, where Goliath stood, a strange, monstrous villain before the Israelites, who cowered before his challenge for forty days.

"The fattest scarecrow in the world," wheezed the general of the Philistines, holding his sides and laughing to see Goliath pinned to the frame.

Goliath's voice was high and girlish, and he could not have made himself heard to the Israelites trembling in their camp at his approach, were it not for the dwarf hidden under his cloak, who, at the proper moment, rammed into Goliath's anus the sawed-off end of a shepherd's crook. Goliath would bellow then, yes indeed.

"Send me your champion, that we might fight together!" he would bawl.

"They will never send a champion," the Philistine general said. "They will cower in their tents a few more nights, then give over all to me."

When Goliath saw the naked boy stride down the hill toward him, he thought of his mother, and of his lambs, and he smiled.

"Shepherd!" he shouted, with no encouragement from the dwarf squatting under his buttocks. And as the boy began to spin the sling faster and faster over his head, Goliath shouted once more, "Savior!"

[3] MICHELANGELO

Michelangelo has caught him in all the arrogance and cruelty of youth.

His left knee is canted delicately forward and in, almost girlishly—this for Jonathan? His left arm curls upward, holding the sling draped over his shoulder loosely, insolently. His right hand hangs heavily at his side, huge, blood-gorged. There the white marble is almost dark with blood. Though the legs, arms, and torso slant languidly this way and that, the head is perfectly erect, his gaze flat and direct, leveled at Saul, who, just across the valley, writhes in an agony of prescience. Saul knows: the old king under the pitiless gaze of the new.

It is not until a moment later, when he turns from Saul, that David first thinks of the giant. David does not think much of him even then. Hasn't he killed a bear with one blow and bearded the lion?

It is strange, though.

A handful of Philistine soldiers run up behind the giant and seem to give him a shove, then run off up the hill with the rest of their fellows, laughing. The giant seems to glide slowly toward David without moving his arms and legs. He smiles and shouts two words. A Philistine insult, no doubt.

But David does not think much about this, either, and it is not until after he has cut Goliath down from the wooden frame that it occurs to him to hack off Goliath's head and feed his carcass to the fowls of the air, the beasts of the earth.

Goliath surely did not know that his part in the divine plan was to grow fat, so that one day he could have his head bowled down the valley of Elah for the glory of a minor god, bloody and vengeful, bent on hegemony.

And David—a good man, by all accounts, from then on—did not realize that he was doomed to be frozen in stone at a moment of stupid, ruth-
less vanity, forever, in the Accademia, in Florence.

Listening to Narrative Strategies

Perhaps the most obvious difference in the strategies of these two stories is the
different listeners each narrator has in mind. The Biblical narrator expects his
audience to know the geography of his story's world. For the listeners this teller
has in mind, Socoh, Judah, Azekah, Ephes-dammim, Elah, Gath, Shaarim, and
Ekron are specific and familiar locations, but these names mean almost nothing
to a listener who's unfamiliar with them. Because the narrator offers no definitions, he also expects his listeners to know how heavy a shekel is, how much
an ephah is, what a weaver's beam looks like, who Saul and Ephrathites and the
Philistines are. But he does not expect them to know who David or his brothers are, because he interrupts the action to introduce them.

At the level of attitude, the Biblical narrator expects his audience to disapprove of vanity; hence, he goes to great lengths to portray Goliath as a boaster.
More important, he expects them to root for the Israelite underdog. Notice how
he stops the action of the story to give us a detailed description of Goliath:

> . . . he was over nine feet in height. He had a bronze helmet on his head,
> and he wore plate-armour of bronze, weighing five thousand shekels. On
> his legs were bronze greaves, and one of his weapons was a dagger of
> bronze. The shaft of his spear was like a weaver's beam, and its head,
> which was of iron, weighed six hundred shekels; and his shield-bearer
> marched ahead of him.

He also takes great pains to contrast this costume with David's:

> [Saul] put his own tunic on David, placed a bronze helmet on his head and
> gave him a coat of mail to wear; he then fastened his sword on David over
> his tunic. But David hesitated, because he had not tried them, and said to
> Saul, "I cannot go with these, because I have not tried them." So he took
> them off. Then he picked up his stick, chose five smooth stones from the
> brook and put them in a shepherd's bag which served as his pouch. He
> walked out to meet the Philistine with his sling in his hand.

In terms of size, armor, and weaponry, Goliath had it all over David.

This narrator not only expects his listeners to share the opinion that the
Philistines are the bad guys, but he also assumes his audience has a strong stomach for vengeance:

Then he ran to the Philistine and stood over him and grasping his sword, he drew it out of the scabbard, dispatched him and cut off his head. The Philistines, when they saw that their hero was dead, turned and ran. The men of Israel and Judah at once raised the war-cry and hotly pursued them all the way to Gath and even to the gates of Ekron. The road that runs to Shaarim, Gath, and Ekron was strewn with their dead.

Turning now to the story by Dennis Vannatta, "The David of Michelangelo," its narrator also casts his listener in a specific role, making certain assumptions clear by the way he tells the story. First, he assumes familiarity with the Biblical version. He tells little about David, assumes we know about Goliath's armor and only need to be reminded of it, and skips over the actual fight entirely. Second, and more important, he assumes we are thoroughly familiar with Michelangelo's statue of David.

This narrator makes certain assumptions about audience attitudes, too. Like his Biblical counterpart, he assumes we disapprove of vanity and root for the underdog in an unfair contest. He does not assume the taste for vengeance of the first narrator, nor does he assume his listener automatically identifies with the Israelites against the Philistines. Perhaps most important, he assumes his listeners are more skeptical about whether the "god" referred to in both stories is the one true God.

These storytellers make a good many more assumptions about their different listeners. The more you probe their different versions, the more assumptions you find. Notice that what the narrators omit is every bit as important as what they include when trying to determine a storyteller's intended listener.

QUESTIONS FOR DISCUSSION

1. Is there a serious danger that in pretending to adopt the values of the implied listener to a story, you will become convinced of the validity of those values?

2. How does this issue relate to the ongoing controversy over rap lyrics? What other examples from popular culture ask you to assume views you don't really believe in?

3. Are there limits to the values you are willing to assume?

4. Develop guidelines for how much reference work performers have a right to expect of their listeners in your class.

Performing Narrative Strategies

A storyteller can shape a listener's perception by various means. Four of the more important strategies used by a narrator of any story are selection, sequence, quotation, and pace. *Selection* is a teller's judgment of what to include and what to leave out of the story. Even when a narrator begins a tale, "Now I'm going to tell you *everything* . . . ," he or she can't possibly do it. Even when witnesses swear "to tell the truth, the *whole* truth, and nothing but the truth," they have to be selective. Storytellers are not machines, like video recorders. They are human performers who make selections, and these selections demonstrate point of view and judgment. Storytellers are like film editors, choosing which details to include and which to leave out to tell their tale most effectively.

Literary narrators make selections in the same way that we do in everyday interactions. They choose what's most exciting, what's most likely to interest a listener, and what's most apt to represent their own understanding of the action and characters. The life of any story depends on the vitality of details; hence, a narrator's selection is critical to the story's success. To demonstrate the importance of a single detail, you only need to recall someone's telling you the story of an experience and then, later, someone else telling you the same story. The second narrator includes a detail that the first narrator omitted, and you exclaim, "Well, she didn't mention *that! Now* I understand." Any narrator's selection of detail indicates his or her point of view, marking what's important and what's unimportant.

A second narrative strategy is *sequence*. Storytelling is a one-step-at-a-time process. Even if the events being described occurred simultaneously, they cannot be reported at the same time. A narrator must sequence one happening before another in the story's performance. When you look closely, the sequence of events in a story is always telling of the narrator's point of view.

This one-at-a-time focusing process makes storytelling akin to moviemaking. Just as the camera points a viewer's attention to look first at one thing and then at another, a narrator directs the reader's concentration in a meaningful sequence of images and words. The art of storytelling is *temporal*. It occurs over time. The sequence of a story's moments is determined by a narrator. By analyzing that sequence, you may discover subtle clues to the storyteller's values and judgments.

A third narrative strategy is *quotation*. A storyteller straddles the threshold between the characters' world and the reader's. Whenever a narrator quotes a character's speech verbatim (that is, within quotation marks), she wants the audience to hear exactly what that character said. Furthermore, the narrator wants us to hear *how* the character sounds, giving such performative directions as "he bawled" or "she snapped." As a performer, you need to figure out *why* the storyteller stops speaking in her own voice to let us hear characters talking. In every case of dialogue the narrator could have reported only the gist of what the character said. The clearer you are in your own mind about *why* the narrator chooses to quote characters directly, the sharper your performance of the story will be.

The most obvious type of quoted dialogue is *direct discourse,* or verbatim speech within quotation marks. A more subtle form of quotation is called *indirect discourse* and includes any attempt by the narrator to capsulate, approximate, or give the gist of a character's speech. Indirect discourse may take the form of paraphrase (putting a character's dialogue into the narrator's own words) or projection (summarizing dialogue in the character's voice and perspective). Quotation of character speech, whether by direct or indirect discourse, is the revolving door through which a narrator enters and exits the story's world and the reader's world.

A fourth narrative strategy is *pace*. Remember that stories are performance events unfolding over time. A storyteller can speed up or slow down the pace of the story and, thereby, hold or direct a listener's attention. A storytelling performance always moves forward; it cannot hold still. The action inside the story may proceed forward or backward through time and may even appear to come to a complete halt, but a narrator's reporting of that action is constantly in motion.

Think of pace in storytelling as three gears in an automobile. Each permits a different range of speeds, although they overlap in transition. First gear is *description*. Here things proceed very slowly. The narrator pauses to incorporate detail, to offer commentary, or to reflect on the action. Second gear is *scene*. Here the pace of storytelling approximates the speed of the action itself. For instance, in a passage of quoted dialogue between characters, it takes about the same amount of time to narrate the conversation as it did for the characters to speak it originally. Third gear is *summary*. This is the fastest speed of storytelling in which time is compressed or events collapsed to move things ahead quickly. The events spanning six months of a character's life might be summarized in a single paragraph or sentence. Scene, summary, and description—three different paces of storytelling—may be thought of as normal, accelerated, and decelerated time.

It can be important to your understanding of a story to observe how the narrator manipulates pace. When does he or she permit the action to proceed in scene? At what points does the narrator decide to slow things down and describe actions, thoughts, or feelings in detail? What parts of the story is the narrator willing to pass over lightly, in summary? In everyday parlance, narrative pace is marked by such phrases as "to make a long story short" or, in filmic terms, "let's cut to the chase."

Imagine a tale of romance in which a beautiful prince and princess appear on their palace balcony to the pleasure of an adoring crowd of townspeople in the courtyard below. If this is the first time that a character has laid eyes on royalty, the narrator of our romance may decide to slow down the telling to observe every detail of the princess's gown, the prince's features, or the palace's trappings. At the sight of the royal couple, the narrator may choose to take two minutes (or one full page of a novel) to describe a character's perception that only required a fraction of a second in real time. The reason for the narrator to decelerate the pace of storytelling through description is to emphasize the magnitude of the moment.

If we were to create a parody of the romantic tale and look at things through the jaded eyes of a royal couple, bored to death by their daily appearances before the townspeople, the narrator might choose to accelerate time by summarizing how today's appearance is like every other day's—boring.

Imagining a third version of the tale, perhaps a young peasant couple is in the crowd of onlookers. Unlike others around them, they are more enamored of each other than with the thrill of seeing royalty. While everyone else oohs and ahs about the appearance of the prince and princess, this couple is enthralled by their own whispered conversation, oblivious to all around them. The narrator of this story may choose to report their dialogue in scene, exactly as it occurred.

Now imagine all three perspectives—the adoring crowd, the bored prince and princess, and the young lovers—interwoven as three strands of the same story, with the narrator shifting perspectives from one group of characters to another. Depending on point of view, the narrator might choose to represent parts of the action in scene, in summary, or in description. By charting the changing pace of narration, you can monitor the heartbeat of a storyteller's fluctuating passions.

Selection, sequence, quotation, and pace are four storytelling strategies available to narrators for shaping their tales. The selection of detail manufactures plausibility while, at the same time, influencing perception. The sequence of episodes controls a flow of information and, thereby, directs the reader's attention. Quotation, both direct and indirect, permits a narrator to step in and out of the world of characters. Through scene, summary, and description, a narrator can alter the pace of storytelling to focus the listener's concentration on what's most important at a given moment in the ongoing performance.

QUESTIONS FOR DISCUSSION

Now see if you can apply these narrative strategies to further analysis of literary works already introduced by answering the following questions:

1. Return to "Where Are the Waters of Childhood?" on pages 85–86. As a class, discuss the *selection of detail* in this Mark Strand poem. What does it say about the speaker's state of mind, feelings, and memory? How does this selection of detail reveal the speaker's attitude toward his implied listener? What effects is he after in shifting through the senses of sight, smell, hearing, and movement in the first half of the poem? The whole poem is a series of directions. What can you do as a performer to help the audience follow these directions?

2. Return to "The Elder Sister" on page 156. Note all the shifts in time in Sharon Olds's descriptions in this poem. They should sensitize you to the narrative significance of *sequence*. As a class, discuss the importance of sequence to the sense and effect of the poem. Note that the narrator's sequence is not the same as chronology. Why does the speaker begin by looking at her elder sister *now*?

Follow her motivations back in time to her sister's birth, and then return in time to her sister's face in the present. Continue to follow the relations between life-chronology and narrative sequence throughout the poem.

3. Return to the transcript of Marsha Norman's 'Night, Mother on pages 16–21. In this excerpt, the mother narrates several brief stories about her friend Agnes. At one point, the daughter asks why Agnes seems to avoid her (lines 115–116). In the mother's first line of response (line 118), she *quotes* Agnes indirectly and makes no attempt to perform Agnes's voice. At line 122, her first sentence is again indirect quotation without performance of Agnes, but in the rest of the line she quotes Agnes directly. The transcript indicates roughly how the mother performs Agnes. Why does the mother mimic Agnes? One might conclude that in indirect discourse narrators use their own voice, but in direct quotation they imitate the character's speech. How do lines 59 through 61 modify this conclusion?

4. Return to May Swenson's "Bleeding" on pages 91–92. In this narration, the storyteller chooses to hand over almost the entire story to two characters, the Cut and the Knife. Why is it more effective that we hear these characters speak in direct quotation, rather than being told what they said? How should their voices be performed to achieve the narrator's effect?

5. Discuss *pace* as a narrative strategy by answering the following questions:

   a. In the opening of *The Wonderful Wizard of Oz* (page 40), why do you think the narrator chooses to begin with *description*? Using what you know is going to happen in the remainder of the story, explain the narrator's choice of items to describe. How does this understanding shape the effect you would want your performance to have?

   b. In "The David of Michelangelo," (pages 176–179) Dennis Vannatta begins in *scene* with dialogue.

   > "I know your pride, and the naughtiness of your heart," says Eliab, his brother.
   > But David is not listening.
   > "I killed a lion and a bear that stole one of your sheep," he says to Saul, whose eyes have already begun to glaze over with wonder and madness. "I chased them down. I hit that bear so hard he dropped the sheep right out of his mouth. The lion came for me, and I grabbed him by the beard. I said, 'Whoa, old fellow!' Then I killed him with one blow."

   What does the narrator assume his audience knows to give us so little explanation? How should you perform David's voice to achieve the effect the narrator of the story is after?

   c. Return to "At the IGA" (page 43). What motivates the narrator to accelerate her pace into *summary* so that, in the last stanza, probably ten years are collapsed into just five lines? Would more description or dialogue have served the narrative effect better?

Performing Point of View

Point of view describes a narrator's complex relationship to the story being told: What are his or her attitudes toward the action? toward characters? toward the reader? Point of view may be revealed through all the narrative strategies described so far. The key to performance in this genre is trying to understand a narrator's point of view moving through each moment of the story. Remember, your task as a performer is to give voice and body to this *storyteller.*

In many stories, a narrator tries to clear out of the reader's way. The Biblical version of "David and Goliath" provides an example. Everything he says draws your attention into the story's world and away from your own. In other tales, a narrator is more willing to put action on hold in order to offer personal comments, to editorialize, or to pass judgment. In the second version of the David story, for instance, its narrator interrupts his story abruptly when he says,

> ([David] *does not have to go naked into the valley of Elah. He could have worn the brass armor, weighing two thousand shekels, provided by Saul— could at least have worn his shepherd's smock, his sandals, and his goatskin cap against the sun. But no . . .)*

In such moments, the storyteller takes on a distinct personality, and a performer should focus on the interchange between narrator and listener. Some narrators occupy center stage of an audience's attention (sometimes called an *obtrusive narrator*); others seem nearly transparent, providing little more than a frame through which to see the story (an *unobtrusive narrator*). How little we can infer about the unobtrusive narrator in May Swenson's "Bleeding," for example, whereas the more obtrusive narrator of *Huckleberry Finn* is vivid in every detail.

It's dangerous to generalize about narrative point of view because each storyteller approaches his or her tale in ways that are unique to its world, effect, and sense. A narrator's point of view is never static; it's always changing through the dynamic flow of the story. We might illustrate this best by reference back to two earlier stories.

"The Whipping" by Robert Hayden begins with a third-person narrator observing a scene from a distance:

> The old woman across the way
>   is whipping the boy again
> and shouting to the neighborhood
>   her goodness and his wrongs.

Through the third stanza, the narrator retains a certain distance, *apparently* reporting events without a vested interest:

> She strikes and strikes the shrilly circling
> > boy till the stick breaks
> in her hand. His tears are rainy weather
> > to woundlike memories:

It's at the end of that stanza, when the boy's tears water "woundlike memories," that the narration takes a turn. The "woundlike memories" are not those of either character in the story, but of the narrator-reporter. What follows the colon at the end of that stanza is a startling shift in point of view. Read the next two stanzas. Both are in the *first* person, using the "I" pronoun.

> My head gripped in bony vise
> > of knees, the writhing struggle
> to wrench free, the blows, the fear
> > worse than blows that hateful

> Words could bring, the face that I
> > no longer knew or loved . . .
> Well, it is over now, it is over,
> > and the boy sobs in his room,

In the last two lines of this stanza, the narrator shifts back to third-person, observing the boy again from the outside. One can almost feel him emerging from the boy in the repeated lines, "it is over now, it is over." The final stanza remains in the third-person:

> And the woman leans muttering against
> > a tree, exhausted, purged—
> avenged in part for lifelong hidings
> > she has had to bear.

Although several explanations are possible for the shift that occurs in the two first-person stanzas, one thing we can say for sure. The narrator has merged with the boy. In those two stanzas, the narrator's point of view toward the story being told changes dramatically. How you show that in performance makes all the difference to an audience's ability to enter the physical, mental, and emotional worlds of the poem. And how you perform the narrator's release from his immersion in the boy in the final stanza determines this poem's overall effect on an audience. Does the adult narrator, in watching the whipping of the boy, come to any understanding of the old woman?

Or, choosing another example, recall Phyllis Koestenbaum's "Admission of Failure" on page 64. The narrator of that story is, apparently, sitting at a table in Andy's Barbecue Restaurant with her husband and son. She tells her tale in the first-person, present tense, as though the action were occurring in the here and now. She is watching a young, armless man and decides that she wants to change places with him. She fantasizes all the consequences of this impossible exchange: she would sit at his table, drive his car, live in his house, and work at his job. She would even dress in his clothes. But she leaves the restaurant with her husband and son, reflecting on their life together. The prose poem ends with a sudden, unexpected change of viewpoint: "I have worked on this paragraph for more than two years."

This shift in point of view changes everything. It adds a frame of reference entirely invisible until that moment. In fact, until the end, an audience gets the impression that the woman's experience in the restaurant and her projections regarding the "young armless man" are casual and spontaneous. Only in the last line does one learn that the whole narrative episode has been carefully composed. She's been working on it for more than two years. As a performer, you face a difficult decision whether to play the narrator as a writer composing this story or as a character living it. It all depends on your point of view—or hers—or both.

EXERCISE & DISCUSSION

Read the following passage from Barbara Kingsolver's novel *Animal Dreams*. In it, the first-person narrator, Codi, describes her bus trip home to the small town of Grace, Arizona, to attend to the needs of her dying father. Her return home, the first in many years, filled Codi with uneasiness.

"ANIMAL DREAMS"

by Barbara Kingsolver

(Excerpted from Animal Dreams *by Barbara Kingsolver. New York: HarperCollins, 1990. Used by permission.)*

I had lied on the bus. I'd told the woman sitting next to me that I was a Canadian tourist and had never been to Grace. Sometimes I used to do that, tell tales on buses and airplanes—it passes the time. And people love you for it. They'll believe anything if you throw in enough detail. Once I spent a transatlantic flight telling a somber, attentive man about a medical procedure I'd helped develop in Paris, in which human cadavers could be injected with hormones to preserve their organs for transplant. I would be accepting a prestigious medical prize, the name of which I devised on the spot. The man seemed so impressed. He looked like my father.

I didn't do it anymore, I was more or less reformed. What I'd said that morning was the truest kind of lie, I guess, containing fear at its heart: I *was* a stranger to Grace. I'd stayed away fourteen years and in my gut I believe I was hoping that had changed: I would step off the bus and land smack in the middle of a sense of belonging. Ticker tape, apologies, the luxury of forgiveness, home at last. Grace would turn out to be the yardstick I'd been using to measure all other places, like the mysterious wornout photo that storybook orphans carry from place to place, never realizing till the end that it's really their home.

None of this happened. Grace looked like a language I didn't speak. And Emelina wasn't coming. I hefted up my suitcases and started to walk.

This excerpt from a much longer story is itself about story-telling. The narrator, Codi, wants to explain to the reader her feelings of strangeness, aloneness, and pain as she arrives back home in Grace. In trying to tell the truth the best way she can, she ends up telling lies. Not only had Codi lied while on the bus—telling the woman sitting next to her that she was a Canadian tourist new to Grace—but she admits to the reader having told even bigger whoppers in the past.

As a class, discuss the following questions about this excerpt from the Kingsolver novel:

1. From such a short exposure to the unknown narrator, Codi, what first impressions does she make on you? Is she intelligent? How do you know? Do you like her? Why? Is she trustworthy? In what sense?

2. What specific meaning do you attach to the following selection of details:

    - " . . . the name of which I devised on the spot"
    - "He looked like my father."
    - "Ticker tape, apologies, the luxury of forgiveness . . . "
    - " . . . storybook orphans . . . "

3. Codi tells us what she fantasizes a homecoming to Grace might be like *before* she describes her actual arrival. What difference would it make to you if she had reversed the sequence and described the fantasy version *after* the actual event?

4. When performing the first paragraph, which words or sentences represent indirect discourse, Codi quoting her own earlier speech? How

can you mark their difference in performance? What's the distinction between Codi as narrator and Codi as character in her own story?

5. Trace the subtle shifts in pacing throughout this narrative passage. Can you decide precisely where and when the storyteller shifts gears from description to scene to summary?

6. Summarize this narrator's point of view, given the information available to you from this passage.

7. Codi is a self-conscious narrator. That is, she has given a good deal of thought to how stories work, and how they can function in human relationships and personal development. Describe the narrative theory suggested by Codi's talk with the reader.

Analyzing a Story

"The Witch"

by Shirley Jackson

(Reprinted by permission of Farrar, Straus & Giroux, Inc. "The Witch" from The Lottery by Shirley Jackson. Copyright © 1948, 1949 by Shirley Jackson; copyright renewed © 1976, 1977 by Laurence Hyman, Barry Hyman, Mrs. Sarah Webster, and Mrs. Joanne Schnurer.)

The coach was so nearly empty that the little boy had a seat all to himself, and his mother sat across the aisle on the seat next to the little boy's sister, a baby with a piece of toast in one hand and a rattle in the other. She was strapped securely to the seat so she could sit up and look around, and whenever she began to slip slowly sideways the strap caught her and held her halfway until her mother turned around and straightened her again. The little boy was looking out the window and eating a cookie, and the mother was reading quietly, answering the little boy's questions without looking up.

"We're on a river," the little boy said. "This is a river and we're on it."

"Fine," his mother said.

"We're on a bridge over a river," the little boy said to himself.

The few other people in the coach were sitting at the other end of the car; if any of them had occasion to come down the aisle the little boy would look around and say, "Hi," and the stranger would usually say, "Hi," back and sometimes ask the little boy if he were enjoying the train ride, or even tell him he was a fine big fellow. These comments annoyed the little boy and he would turn irritably back to the window.

"There's a cow," he would say, or, sighing, "How far do we have to go?"

"Not much longer now," his mother said, each time.

Once the baby, who was very quiet and busy with her rattle and her toast, which the mother would renew constantly, fell over too far sideways and banged her head. She began to cry, and for a minute there was noise and movement around the mother's seat. The little boy slid down from his own seat and ran across the aisle to pet his sister's feet and beg her not to cry, and finally the baby laughed and went back to her toast, and the little boy received a lollipop from his mother and went back to the window.

"I saw a witch," he said to his mother after a minute. "There was a big old ugly old bad old witch outside."

"Fine," his mother said.

"A big old ugly witch and I told her to go away and she went away," the little boy went on, in a quiet narrative to himself, "she came and said, 'I'm going to eat you up,' and I said 'no, you're not,' and I chased her away, the bad old mean witch."

He stopped talking and looked up as the outside door of the coach opened and a man came in. He was an elderly man, with a pleasant face under white hair; his blue suit was only faintly touched by the disarray that comes from a long train trip. He was carrying a cigar, and when the little boy said, "Hi," the man gestured at him with the cigar and said, "Hello yourself, son." He stopped just beside the little boy's seat, and leaned against the back, looking down at the little boy, who craned his neck to look upward.

"What you looking for out that window?" the man asked.

"Witches," the little boy said promptly. "Bad old mean witches."

"I see," the man said. "Find many?"

"My father smokes cigars," the little boy said.

"All men smoke cigars," the man said. "Someday you'll smoke a cigar, too."

"I'm a man already," the little boy said.

"How old are you?" the man asked.

The little boy, at the eternal question, looked at the man suspiciously for a minute and then said, "Twenty-six. Eight hunnerd and forty eighty."

His mother lifted her head from the book. "Four," she said, smiling fondly at the little boy.

"Is that so?" the man said politely to the little boy. "Twenty-six." He nodded his head at the mother across the aisle. "Is that your mother?"

The little boy leaned forward to look and then said, "Yes, that's her."

"What's your name?" the man asked.

The little boy looked suspicious again. "Mr. Jesus," he said.

"*Johnny*," the little boy's mother said. She caught the little boy's eye and frowned deeply.

"That's my sister over there," the little boy said to the man. "She's twelve-and-a-half."

"Do you love your sister?" the man asked. The little boy stared, and the man came around the side of the seat and sat down next to the little boy. "Listen," the man said, "shall I tell you about my little sister?"

The mother, who had looked up anxiously when the man sat down next to her little boy, went peacefully back to her book.

"Tell me about your sister," the little boy said. "Was she a witch?"

"Maybe," the man said.

The little boy laughed excitedly, and the man leaned back and puffed at his cigar. "Once upon a time," he began, "I had a little sister, just like yours." The little boy looked up at the man, nodding at every word. "My little sister," the man went on, "was so pretty and so nice that I loved her more than anything else in the world. So shall I tell you what I did?"

The little boy nodded more vehemently, and the mother lifted her eyes from her book and smiled, listening.

"I bought her a rocking-horse and a doll and a million lollipops," the man said, "and then I took her and I put my hands around her neck and I pinched her and I pinched her until she was dead."

The little boy gasped and the mother turned around, her smile fading. She opened her mouth, and then closed it again as the man went on, "And then I took and I cut her head off and I took her head—"

"Did you cut her all in pieces?" the little boy asked breathlessly.

"I cut off her head and her hands and her feet and her hair and her nose," the man said, "and I hit her with a stick and I killed her."

"Wait a minute," the mother said, but the baby fell over sideways just at that minute and by the time the mother had set her up again the man was going on.

"And I took her head and I pulled out all her hair and—"

"Your little *sister*?" the little boy prompted eagerly.

"My little sister," the man said firmly. "And I put her head in a cage with a bear and the bear ate it all up."

"Ate her *head* all up?" the little boy asked.

The mother put her book down and came across the aisle. She stood next to the man and said, "Just what do you think you're doing?" The man looked up courteously and she said "Get out of here."

"Did I frighten you?" the man said. He looked down at the little boy and nudged him with an elbow and he and the little boy laughed.

"This man cut up his little sister," the little boy said to his mother.

"I can very easily call the conductor," the mother said to the man.

"The conductor will *eat* my mommy," the little boy said. "We'll chop her head off."

"And little sister's head, too," the man said. He stood up, and the mother stood back to let him get out of the seat. "Don't ever come back in this car," she said.

"My mommy will eat *you*," the little boy said to the man.

The man laughed, and the little boy laughed, and then the man said, "Excuse me," to the mother and went past her out of the car. When the door had closed behind him the little boy said, "How much longer do we have to stay on this old train?"

"Not much longer," the mother said. She stood looking at the little boy, wanting to say something, and finally she said, "You sit still and be a good boy. You may have another lollipop."

The little boy climbed down eagerly and followed his mother back to her seat. She took a lollipop from a bag in her pocketbook and gave it to him. "What do you say?" she asked.

"Thank you," the little boy said. "Did that man really cut his little sister up in pieces?"

"He was just teasing," the mother said, and added urgently, "Just *teasing*."

"Prob'ly," the little boy said. With his lollipop he went back to his own seat, and settled himself to look out the window again. "Prob'ly he was a witch."

Shirley Jackson's "The Witch" offers a fine case study in narrative performance. Its apparent simplicity is deceptive. Actually, the text includes a tale within a tale. At the beginning, we are introduced to the story of a mother and her two children taking a long train ride. Inside that action occurs a second story, the horrific tale told to the little boy by the older gentleman. The two yarns become intertwined in unpredictable ways.

Follow the sequence of actions as the narrator selects details, shares character perspectives, and reveals a clear point of view. The story opens with a portrait of normalcy. What could be less threatening than the scene described in the first paragraph? It's important for the reader to see the characters' seating arrangement: the boy next to the window, a vacant seat next to him; across the aisle, the mother and then the baby sister next to the opposite window. It's also important to realize that the three have fallen into a comfortable routine on their long train trip. Everything is normal, safe, and predictable.

When dialogue is introduced in the form of direct discourse ("We're on a river," the little boy said. "This is a river and we're on it."), our sense of the mundane risks boredom. "Fine," his mother said.

Even though the narrator does not report the mother's tone of voice, we may surmise that it's casual and inattentive. Notice that the boy's next line after her response is addressed to himself. We know, too, from the summary paragraph that follows (which includes indirect discourse) that the boy gets annoyed by clichéd conversation with adults.

The narrator reports only one real action at the beginning of the story (the baby falling too far sideways), and it isn't very dramatic. On first reading, one may even wonder why the storyteller bothers to include this little scene. The most we get from it in terms of characterization is some evidence that Johnny is a nice little boy. (Not every four-year-old boy would run across the aisle "to pet his sister's feet and beg her not to cry.") Later, of course, it proves important that our first impression of Johnny is that of a normal, generous child.

When the boy announces to his mother, "I saw a witch," he gets the same answer as he did to "We're on a river."

"Fine."

As he did the first time, the boy turns away from his inattentive mother and continues talking to himself. In fact, the next short paragraph includes its own complete story:

> *"A big old ugly witch and I told her to go away and she went away," the*
> *little boy went on, in a quiet narrative to himself, "she came and said, 'I'm*
> *going to eat you up,' and I said, 'no, you're not,' and I chased her away,*
> *the bad old mean witch."*

His "quiet narrative to himself" includes characters, action, direct discourse, and a point of view.

Notice that we are nearly one third of the way through the story before anything much *happens*. When the outside door of the coach opens and a man comes in ("an elderly man, with a pleasant face under white hair"), the boy (and we) have some diversion from the boredom of a long train trip. Notice, too, that there's nothing out of the ordinary about this man. Presumably, his arrival in the coach is not unlike similar appearances summarized earlier.

The man stops to talk, in response to the little boy initiating conversation. "What are you looking for out that window?" the man asks.

"Witches," the little boy says promptly. "Bad old mean witches."

What follows next is a mutual testing back-and-forth between the man and the boy. They are sizing each other up. First, the boy observes that the man bears resemblance to his own father (the cigar). Then, in answer to the eternal question, "How old are you?" the boy tests the man: "Twenty-six. Eight hunnerd and forty eighty."

Apparently, the mother has been listening to their conversation because she offers a gentle corrective: "Four," smiling fondly at the little boy. Note that there is nothing threatening to the mother's mind in the conversation so far.

The man passes the boy's test by accepting his answer ("Is that so?" the man said politely to the little boy. "Twenty six.") rather than the mother's.

When he asks another clichéd question, "What's your name?" the boy is again suspicious. Hence, he offers another test by answering, "Mr. Jesus."

Now the mother's corrective, "*Johnny,*" is sterner, wanting to underscore the inappropriateness of his answer.

Apparently, the man ignores her. When the little boy introduces his little sister ("She's twelve-and-a-half"), he and the man confirm that they are on the same wavelength. They've established a relationship unique and separate from the mother. We are fully halfway into the story before the man comes around the side of the seat and sits down next to the little boy. If anything unusual could be said to have happened up to this point, it may be the demonstrations of Johnny's imagination.

From here on, however, normalcy and routine disappear. "Listen," the man said, "shall I tell you about my little sister?"

"Was she a witch?" the little boy asks.

"Maybe," the man says.

The little boy laughs excitedly, and the man leans back to begin: "Once upon a time."

In this brief exchange, a narrative collaboration is established between storyteller and audience. The boy and man are mutually responsible for the tale that is to come. Notice from the first mention of a witch through the piling on of more and bloodier details, it is almost always the boy (the listener) who prompts the telling. At the same time that he is horrified and delighted by the story he hears, Johnny keeps asking for more. Notice, too, that the man clearly marks the genre of his fairy tale from the beginning: "Once upon a time."

For Johnny's mother, however, it is a whole different story. While her son is enjoying the man's gory tale, giggling and gasping, she finds it frightening and threatening. Although they are audiences for the exact same performance, listening to the same words and catching the same tone of voice, the stories that mother and son hear are very different. His is G-rated, just right for a child—funny, engaging, and suspenseful. Hers is R-rated, absolutely inappropriate for a child—violent, macabre, and morbid. When she intervenes to stop the story, the man is surprised. He asks the boy, "Did I frighten you?" And the man and the boy laugh together.

After the man leaves the train coach, the little boy wants to know the definitive interpretation of the story he has just heard. So he asks his mother, "Did that man really cut his little sister up in pieces?"

"He was just teasing," she answers, trying to reframe the narrative genre. She adds urgently, "Just *teasing*."

"Prob'ly," the little boy says, seeming to accept his mother's assertion. Once settled back at his window, however, he offers his own interpretation: "Prob'ly *he* was a witch." The boy found precisely what he had been looking for out the window.

QUESTIONS FOR DISCUSSION

Reread "The Witch" and then discuss the following questions:

1. If you were shooting this story as a movie, what camera positions and angles would you recommend to film the first four paragraphs? Continue through the story and make special note of which characters are in your field of vision line by line.

2. When the man asks the boy, "What are you looking for out that window?" he receives the answer "witches." What difference does the word "for" make in his question? What would the answer likely have been if he had asked, "What are you looking *at* out that window?"

3. The man's story begins, "Once upon a time." What associations do you make with this generic phrase? What kind of story is likely to follow? What expectations does this kind of story have of its audience? Can you account for the different narrative experiences of mother and son by their understandings of "once upon a time"?

4. What do you make of the boy's and the man's extension of their story into the interactions with the mother (for example, "The conductor will eat my mommy." "And little sister's head, too." "My mommy will eat you.")?

5. In each of the following passages from the beginning of "The Witch," identify who is speaking and who is listening. Assume that whoever is speaking is looking directly at his or her listener. Demonstrate or describe how you would perform these passages:

   a. The coach was so nearly empty that the little boy had a seat all to himself, and his mother sat across the aisle on the seat next to the little boy's sister, a baby with a piece of toast in one hand and a rattle in the other.

   b. "We're on a river," the little boy said. "This is a river and we're on it."
   "Fine," his mother said.
   "We're on a bridge over a river," the little boy said to himself.

   c. The few other people in the coach were sitting at the other end of the car; if any of them had occasion to come down the aisle the little boy would look around and say, "Hi," and the stranger would usually say, "Hi," back and sometimes ask the little boy if he were enjoying the train ride, or even tell him he was a fine big fellow.

SUMMARY

Narrative *is* performance. A storyteller selects details, sequences events, introduces characters, and orchestrates pace for the purpose of engaging an audience. The performance of a story occurs over time, moment by moment. Meaning accrues incrementally.

What's distinctive about narrative as a genre is the presence of a storyteller. His or her point of view, knowledge, and reliability shape the tale. As important as the narrator is to any story, he or she can't perform alone. Narrative is a collaborative, ensemble performance between storyteller and listener. "An Old Story," told at the beginning of this chapter, gets cut short because a narrator and a listener can't negotiate their narrative pact. "The Witch," told at the end of this chapter, finds very different audiences in a little boy and his mother. As they collaborate differently in the performance of the elderly man's tale, the perception and meaning of the story itself changes. When we assert that narrative *is* performance, we include both storyteller and audience as active participants in the event. This is so in the everyday stories we tell among friends. And it's true in literary stories narrated off the pages of a magazine or a novel.

CHAPTER SEVEN

PERFORMANCE AS A WAY OF KNOWING

Seems to me it makes sense to push the stuff, keep pushing at it, see how far it might go. You can always pull back to a more cautious, reasonable, sensible position. But when you're doing this explorative work, go ahead and push.
Gail Jefferson, *"On the Poetics of Ordinary Talk"*

In everyday language, people tend to use the word "performance" to describe a self-conscious act of personal display. This might be a well-rehearsed exhibition in the service of art, such as the performance of a musician, actor, or dancer. Or the activity might be sports and the arena basketball, tennis, or gymnastics. Magicians perform. Preachers perform. Sales managers perform. In each of these cases—which could be indexed on a continuum from high art to everyday skills—performance is deliberate and purposeful. But the concept is not limited only to professional training or specialized skills. We also use the word to praise someone's strategic behavior, as when, after a successful dinner party, one spouse says to the other, "Your performance was terrific."

Throughout this book, we have tried to add a second and different understanding of performance to that of purposeful display before an audience. Performance can also be a revealing experience *for the performer.* It can teach as well as demonstrate, generate knowledge as well as appreciation. And the performer stands to learn as much or more from the process as any audience could. For instance, when toddlers practice wobbling in their parents' shoes, they are actually learning to walk by means of a performance act. When youngsters watch TV replays of an NBA player's jump shot and then try to imitate those professional moves on the playground, they're teaching themselves through performance. When college sophomores write their essays in the style of Tom Wolfe or Joan Didion, they are learning the subtleties of grammar, diction, and style through imitation. Such mimicry is the root impulse of performance, accruing insight and knowledge both for an audience and for the performers themselves.

In this final chapter, we expand the discussion of performance beyond those assumptions already made and complicate our understandings of the topic. In future courses, then, you should have opportunities to push out the limits of performance knowledge even further.

Performance as Assent

Throughout this book, we have articulated a view of performance as imitation, or what Aristotle termed *mimesis.* We have maintained that the language of literature—whether spoken in a poem, a story, or a play—is similar in kind, if not always in degree, to the language of everyday life. We have noted especially the intimate connection between a constructed speech in literature and the naturally occurring talk of conversation. Furthermore, we have recommended rehearsal techniques that encourage a correspondence between life as we meet it in literature and life as we know it through experience. We have encouraged performer and text to come together through imitation. To put it another way, we have taught a performance of *assent*. That is, a performer enters the literary world as a sympathetic traveler, yielding to its cultural norms, adopting its behavioral expectations, and speaking its language patterns.

Assent demands a respect for the needs of performer, audience, and text. These three share a common space. They cooperate rather than compete. The performer assents rather than resists. From the beginning of time, dating at least to the larceny of Prometheus, making literature has been considered a collaborative achievement, performed in community. The storyteller and his or her audience enter the created world of language with willing assent.

We're familiar with this approach to performance in everyday life, as well. When listening to a friend share his joy, express her grief, or narrate the story of some personal experience, we try to enter their telling with empathy. Only by placing ourselves imaginatively into the friend's circumstances can we hope to understand her or his feelings.

Here's a good example of literary assent taken from everyday life. American poet William Carlos Williams was also a physician. In the following comments to child psychiatrist Robert Coles, Williams describes his method of treating a child patient. His approach amounts to a narrative diagnosis based on the doctor's giving assent to the patient's performance.

> *A kid is telling me what happened, and where it hurts, and what he does to make the pain better, or what he's tried to do. Some of those kids, they're playwrights, they're storytellers! They'll set the scene for you. They'll introduce other people, not just themselves; I mean, they'll mimic people, or try to use their kind of words. They'll say, 'And then he said . . . and then she said . . . and then I said . . .' They'll work all that into their own list of complaints.*
>
> *Do you see what I'm trying to say? I can't hear a kid talk like that and not be sprung—sprung right out of my own damn self-preoccupations. I'll pick up a good story or novel and the same thing happens: I'm in someone else's world, thank God. I'm listening to their words. My own words become responses to what they say—the novelist or one of my patients. We're on stage! I'm thinking of the moral seriousness [you can see] on the stage, a certain kind of exchange between people, where the words really are charged.* *

Here William Carlos Williams charts a mundane medical history as symptomatic of literary interactions generally. He describes a relationship of assent between doctor and patient and extends the performance analogy to reading.

*Robert Coles, *The Call of Stories* (Boston: Houghton Mifflin, 1989), pp. 104–105.

We would suggest taking the comparison even further by asserting that the silent reader—alone in one's bed or jostled by the subway traffic of rush hour—can experience the same creative collaboration, improvising with the writer on the stage of private imagination. Author Susan Cooper goes so far as to suggest that the personal unconscious may be visualized, literalized, in theatrical trappings:

> The theater. Consider the image. A magical place, quiet and dark most of the time—sometimes for months on end, if its owner is unlucky—but a place which once in a while is brilliant with light and life and excitement. It lies there sleeping, closed up, its doors all locked—until suddenly one day the doors are open and you can go in, and find wonder and delight. That isn't a bad image of the unconscious mind.*

Or, reframing theatrical imagery into cinematic, Michael Herr, in an interview with Michael Kaplan for *Entertainment Weekly* (May 18, 1990), claims that "readers really have the final cut. They always have. They shoot a kind of film in their head when they read a book."

What we're calling "assent" is actually an ensemble performance between writer and reader. The text—whether printed on the page or spoken on the street—becomes their enabling script. In this model, language and structure provide voices and clues without plotting to strangulate character or to hold ransom thought. Collaborative performance, based on mutual assent, precludes any hostile takeover of the reader by an author, insisting, instead, on a negotiated settlement or merger of shared interests.

From the beginning of this book, we have emphasized a performance that literalizes assent and participation. We have maintained that a performer's yielding to character, language, and world can reveal much about another's feelings, attitudes, and viewpoint. An assenting performance requires skill and discipline, just as truly good listening does in everyday life.

Performance as Resistance

Performance also yields knowledge through resistance. Although we have adopted an imitative model for this book, we have not meant to deny the contrary pull of resistance that is present, consciously or unconsciously, in every performance act. At the simplest level, one could say that all performance choices—what you stress, how fast you speak, where you gesture, how you stand—stand out against other possibilities that you *might* have chosen. By emphasizing certain dimensions of a text, you devalue others.

---

*"Fantasy in the Real World," by Susan Cooper, *The Horn Book Magazine* (May/June 1990), p. 305, reprinted by permission of The Horn Book, Inc.

We have recommended playfulness as the operating principle of rehearsal. A performer tries on language and character in the same way that a child improvises super heroes in the backyard. Through purposeful playfulness, you come to accept some performance options and to reject others. The intellectual give and take that accompanies improvisation represents an elastic tension between assent and resistance.

At times, you may want to make performance choices that knowingly and deliberately resist the intention of a literary text. This strategy can yield knowledge for performer and audience alike, as much as the imitative approach we've been advocating. You've already played with one common form of resistant performance, namely *parody* (see Cotton Mather essay on page 93). Often used for comic effect, parody isolates and exaggerates one dimension of a text and, so, resists or distorts the balance of the whole. The long-running popularity of TV's "Saturday Night Live" can be attributed in large part to the show's effective parodies. Actors such as Dana Carvey have built entire careers around the skill of resistant performance.

All performances of resistance, from parody to ideological confrontation, share a common trait: the deliberate insertion of a performer's personal viewpoint into a text's language, thereby altering the world, effect, sense, or genre of the original. In most instances, resistant performances aim to change the intended *effect* by superimposing some different intention on the text's speaker or author. In the 1950s, Lerner and Loewe adapted George Bernard Shaw's play "Pygmalion" into a musical called "My Fair Lady." The cover design for the original cast album showed the heroine of the story as a string puppet being manipulated from above by her teacher, Henry Higgins, who was himself a puppet being manipulated by the adaptors Lerner and Lowe, who were themselves string puppets being manipulated by Shaw. This is a rough metaphor for what we are describing: the characters in a story are manipulated by their narrator, who is under the control of an author, who is subject to the assent *or resistance* of you, the performer.

It may seem irrational to say that the contrary impulses of resistance and assent should be so closely linked in the creative process of a performer. However, the playfulness of rehearsal and the integrity of performance require wide latitude. Sixty years ago, Wayland Maxfield Parrish explained the necessity of freeing up the performer in these words:

> *Reading, thoughtful reading, is more than a mere recognition of words and their meanings. It should rouse into life, in that storehouse of impressions and recollections we call the mind, sleeping images and impulses which may carry our attention far beyond the printed page. The imprints of the type on the page are only symbols of some of the things that passed through the author's mind. For us they can only be stimulators of things we already possess, signals that stir into action the dormant experiences of our past, and cause them to march forward into consciousness, to unite into fresh*

combinations, new forms, hitherto unimagined patterns. If these impressions are thronging at our lips for utterance, our voices will respond with the desired color and vibrancy. *

If you read or watch interviews with performers talking about their creative process, you are sure to hear strategies for playing with texts, both through assent and resistance. Such strategies are nearly limitless and best left to your own discovery or devising. We suggest only a few resistant strategies here.

The first form of resistant play is called *tone copying*, and it dates back to a book by A. E. Phillips entitled *Natural Drills in Expression*, published in 1909. His technique is particularly useful for texts where the style and vocabulary are distinctly different from the performer's natural expression. Tone copying involves translating the author's words into your own, as Phillips illustrates with the following passage from *Julius Caesar*, Act IV, scene 3:

> *Shall we now*
> *Contaminate our fingers with base bribes,*
> *And sell the mighty space of our large honors*
> *For so much trash as may be grasped thus?*
> *I had rather be a dog and bay the moon,*
> *Than such a Roman.*

Phillips would have the performer paraphrase Shakespeare's language into one's own, retaining the sense. Hence, the passage might begin something like "I never heard of anything more high-handed. It's outrageous, scandalous . . ." Stanislavsky would go even further by advising performers to recall situations from their own lives when someone had proposed selling out. Both rehearsal games are meant to free the performer's "self" to become available to the demands of the text. Hence, resisting the original language is a rehearsal technique that ultimately yields deeper assent to the text as written.

Resisting Genre: Narratizing Drama

Another popular strategy involves the resistance of a text's genre. Over thirty years ago, Don Geiger advocated the critical method of "dramatic analysis" for the performance of lyric poetry. His approach recommends treating a lyric poem as a mini-drama in which the speaker becomes a character acting in scene for a particular dramatic effect. By resisting the genre of the poem and thinking of it as a drama instead, performers can pose the kind of questions that translate easily into performance objectives. Who is the character speaking? Where is he or she when speaking? What happens in the course of the drama, and how does

*Wayland Maxfield Parrish, *Reading Aloud* (New York: Thomas Nelson & Sons, 1932), p. 92.

this change the speaker's situation? Why does the character think and act as he or she does?

Playing around with a text in rehearsal, resisting temporarily what seems to be its genre, can result in a new comprehension of that genre. Because dramatic analysis opens up so many performance possibilities, the danger lies in committing too early in the rehearsal process to the first interpretation that comes to mind. You've heard the old adage that "practice makes perfect," but it would be nearer the truth to say that practice makes *permanent*. If you use rehearsal time only to polish your first impression of a text, you lose the greatest enjoyment and learning that performance enables, the discovery of new possibilities.

Resistance is not just a rehearsal technique. It may be a strategy for final performance as well. If it can be helpful to treat a lyric poem as a little drama, it can be equally helpful to think of the solo performance of drama as narrative. We have in mind here not so much the performance of a single speech from a play but, rather, when you want to perform a whole scene, giving voice to all the characters in it. Solo performance represents a resistance to the genre of the play, a form of literature that usually assumes a different performer for each character.

The two genres are not always as distinct as you might suppose. In the last chapter, we looked at a short-short story by James Kelman. Here's the same story laid out in the form of drama. If you check back to pages 167–168, you see that we have neither deleted nor added anything to it.

"An Old Story"
(reconfigured as drama)

by James Kelman

Speaker #1: She'd been going about in this depressed state for ages so I should've known something was up. But I didnt. You dont always see what's in front of your nose. I've been sitting about the house that long. You wind up in a daze. You dont see things properly, even with the weans, the weans especially. There again but she's no a wean. No now. She's a young woman. Ach, I dont want to tell this story.

Speaker #2: But you cant say that. Obviously the story has to get told.

#1: Mm, aye, I know what you mean.

#2: Fine then.

#1: Mmm.

#2: Okay, so about your story . . .

#1: Aye.

#2: It concerns a lassie, right? And she's in this depressed state, because of her boyfriend probably—eh?

#1: I dont want to tell it.

#2: But you've got to tell it. You've got to tell it. Unless . . . if it's no really a story at all.

#1: Oh aye christ it's a story, dont worry about that.

Is "An Old Story" a short-short story or a mini-drama? Reread "Bleeding" on pages 91–92. Here we have a speaking narrator, but her only communicative function seems to be to provide dialogue tags.

Now think through what would actually be happening were you to perform a dramatic scene by yourself. For starters, everything is funneled through an individual consciousness, or voice, or speaker—yourself. Like the actor, you spend much of your time *showing* us the characters as you imagine them with your voice and body. But even in the starkest of scenes, there comes a moment when you can't show something to the audience; you have to *tell* them something—who throws what, and who gets it in the face. When a single person tells us a story, demonstrating vocally and physically how the characters talk, and when that person shifts back and forth between demonstrating what they said and how they said it on the one hand, and telling us in his or her own words what can't be shown, on the other, this is storytelling or *narration*.

Having resisted the genre of your scene by moving it closer to narration, it can be a valuable exercise to bring to bear everything that narrative has to offer. Much of narration is given over to compensating for the fact that the listener isn't present at the scene being described. Read through the following narration by a famous storywriter, Flannery O'Connor, paying particular attention to the uses she makes of narration:

From "A Good Man Is Hard to Find"

The grandmother didn't want to go to Florida. She wanted to visit some of her connections in east Tennessee and she was seizing at every chance to change Bailey's mind. Bailey was the son she lived with, her only boy. He was sitting on the edge of his chair at the table, bent over the orange sports section of the *Journal*. "Now look here, Bailey," she said, "see here, read this," and she stood with one hand on her thin hip and the other rattling the newspaper at his bald head. "Here this fellow that calls himself The Misfit is aloose from the Federal Pen and headed toward Florida and you read here what it says he did to these people. Just you read it. I wouldn't take my children in any direction with a criminal like that aloose in it. I couldn't answer to my conscience if I did."

Bailey didn't look up from his reading so she wheeled around then and faced the children's mother, a young woman in slacks, whose face was as broad and innocent as a cabbage and was tied around with a green head-kerchief that had two points on the top like a rabbit's ears. She was sitting on the sofa, feeding the baby his apricots out of a jar. "The children have been to Florida before," **the old lady said.** "You all ought to take them somewhere else for a change so they would see different parts of the world and be broad. They never been to east Tennessee."

The children's mother didn't seem to hear her but the eight-year-old boy, John Wesley, a stocky child with glasses, said, "If you don't want to go to Florida, why dontcha stay at home?"

Much of this narration is given over to descriptions of the characters in the scene, the dialogue itself, and narrative tags identifying the speakers. If this were a scene from a play with only the dialogue given, as a solo performer you would probably have to tell your audience most of this information.

But narration makes it possible to present a scene in ways not available to the playwright. Reread that opening narration. In addition to telling us what we can't see because we aren't present in the scene, O'Connor's narrator takes us into the old lady's thoughts, explaining not only who she is but what motivates her actions in the scene that is to follow.

In addition to exploring a character's motivation verbally, narratizing a play permits you to focus on one or all of the character's thoughts. Notice, for example, that in presenting this particular scene, the narrator lets us eavesdrop on the grandmother's thoughts, but no one else's.

Finally, notice that this narrator does not introduce all the characters at the start of the scene, but gives us the information we need to follow the action at the precise moment when we need it.

These few paragraphs do not cover all the possibilities of narration, of course, but they do give us enough to get started on narratizing dramatic scenes. The following lines come from Henrik Ibsen's play *Hedda Gabler.*

Tesman: [to Hedda] Only think—ill as she was, Aunt Rina embroidered these for me. Oh you can't think how many associations cling to them.

Hedda: [at the table] Scarcely for me.

Miss Tesman: Of course not for Hedda, George.

Tesman: Well, but now that she belongs to the family, I thought—

Hedda: [interrupting] We shall never get on with this servant, Tesman.

Miss Tesman: Not get on with Berta?

Tesman: Why, dear, what puts that in your head? Eh?

Hedda: [pointing] Look there! She has left her old bonnet lying about on a chair.

This famous exchange comes early in the first act, and innocent as it seems on the surface, it is a telling moment in the action of the play. Undoubtedly, you would want to do a longer scene than these few lines, but keeping our selection short makes it easier to explore what is to be learned from narratizing drama. If you are unfamiliar with the play, it helps to know that Tesman, an aspiring college teacher, and Hedda have just returned from their honeymoon. Hedda has married beneath herself socially, not for love but for security. Secretly, she despises Tesman and his doting aunts, referred to here as Miss Tesman (Aunt Julie) and Rina. Because Hedda has been listening in the next room to Tesman and his aunt, she knows that the hat in question is Miss Tesman's and not the servant's.

To develop a solo performance of these lines, the performer would have to adopt a narrative stance. That is, no matter how cleverly one might suggest Hedda, Tesman, and Miss Tesman in the scene, the audience would not be watching their actual conversation, as an audience would be in a theatre, but apprehending it through a solo performer. It is possible that there are scenes in drama that an audience could follow in solo performance without the performer providing any information other than the words of the characters. But this scene certainly isn't one of them. At the very least, the performer would have to explain what had transpired before this particular exchange and who these people are.

In the section from O'Connor's "A Good Man Is Hard to Find," we noted that the narrator did not treat all characters equally but built the scene around one particular person, the grandmother. In narratizing drama, you can try for the same effect by featuring one character over the others. In the scene from *Hedda Gabler*, if you decided to focus on Hedda, your narratized script might look something like this:

> Hedda was beginning to think this dowdy, old woman would never leave.
> As if fussy George were not enough to drive one to distraction, she must
> stand there, trapped in her own parlor, while they go on prattling over a
> pair of silly—no, grotesque—bedroom slippers. She turned away from
> them and wandered distractedly to the table. "Air," she thought, "I need

air," and began beating a desperate little tattoo on the back of the chair where Aunt Julie had left her hat.

But George would not leave her alone. "Only think," he crowed, thrusting those threadbare carpet slippers— maroon!—at her with their ridiculous cross-stitching in hideous green. "Aunt Rina lay and embroidered them sick as she was." He hugged them tenderly in his fat hands. "You couldn't believe how many memories are bound up in them."

She had never felt more isolated, more alone. "Scarcely for me," she countered.

Perhaps a note in Hedda's voice struck a minor chord of sympathy in Aunt Julie. George had been pampered enough. "Of course not for Hedda, George," she said. And taking the slippers from him, she hastily rewrapped them in brown paper.

"Well," George sighed reluctantly, "but now that she belongs to the family, I thought—"

"Belongs to the family! Belongs to the family!" The words bit into Hedda's mind. As she tapped the chair in desperation her eyes fell on Aunt Julie's hat. Two green doves cuddled together in an outlandish nest of maroon feathers and netting. Suddenly a cruel thought occurred to her, so cruel she began to laugh. "We shall never get on with this servant, Tesman!"

Aunt Julie looked at her blankly. "Not get on with Berta?"

"Why, dear, what put that idea into your head? Eh?"

"Look there," Hedda chuckled, gingerly picking up Aunt Julie's hat as if it were a dirty rag. "She has left her old bonnet lying about on a chair."

Since the solo performer controls the focus of the scene, you can not only decide which character to feature, but whether to feature any one particular character of all of them. One way to make such a decision is to work out a narratization for each of the characters in your scene. For example, with this play, present the scene from Tesman's point of view. What thoughts might go through his head if he were afraid of Hedda or impatient with her or more interested in his aunt, Miss Tesman? Even though Miss Tesman has the fewest lines in the scene, that doesn't rule her out as providing an interesting point of view.

One distinct advantage of resisting the genre of a play by narratizing it is that the exercise focuses your attention on what is motivating each character to do what he or she does and says. How these different narratives "feel" in rehearsal helps you decide on the point of view you use in the final performance. Don't be afraid to start with too much narration. One problem you must explore in rehearsal is how to convert as much narrative telling into performative showing as possible.

Your ability to do so depends in large part on how vividly you can imagine the characters and how precisely you can mark the differences between them. Before you narratize a scene from a play, practice the technique on an everyday conversation. In the first chapter, we asked you to pair up and imitate as precisely as you could the participants in "It's Gun Be Hard to Do." This time, you should practice by yourself imitating both speakers, adding enough narration in your own voice that the class can follow the exchange.

Here's a conversation characterized by its apparently mundane interaction between a mother and her daughter. The subject is "dangley earrings," which the daughter named Mary (age 11) wants to wear, but which the mother, named Joan, discourages.*

1	Mary:	Mu:m why doesn't Dad let me wa-wear long earrings whil-m <u>at</u> school
		(...............)
	Joan:	<u>Da</u>ngley ones (.) he doesn't like because you
5		look (.....................) isn't gir:l like (..........) okay
	Mary:	((laughing)) isn't <u>girl</u> like
	Joan:	It <u>doe</u>sn't look like a young <u>lady</u> (.......)
		when you wear the dangley ones that flip flippy
		flop (..........) it (.) just (..........) doesn't. (.) maybe
10		in a couple a ye:ars maybe th<u>e</u>:n
	Mary:	Mom (.) hhhh.
		(.............)
	Joan:	M<u>a</u>ry (.) my understanding that (.) the
		agreement was <u>on</u>ce a week.
15		(.....)
	Mary:	When- when did (.) <u>oh</u> he didn't say that when I
		got my <u>ears</u> pierced I had no id<u>ea</u> that
		was
	Joan:	When you- Mary (.) when you got your <u>ears</u>
20		pierced my understanding was p<u>o</u>sts <u>on</u>ly.

*Conversational transcript by Deleasa Randall, used with permission.

```
    Mary:      Nuh uh uh nobody ever said that to m:e
    Joan:                        and then that
                          (..........)
    Joan:      We:ll (.) that was my understanding (...) was
25             posts only and the:n: (.....) afta your time (.)
               with the initial (.....) pierce posts (.....) you
               went directly (.......) to (...) dingle dangle
               turc-
    Mary:             └Nobody ever said the post thing to me
30                        (.....)
    Joan:      Okay well (...) this (.) I'm tryin to explain
    Mary:      Why does it matter to Dad anyway to ⌈me
    Joan:                                          └It does matter
               (.) it does matter it (.) reflects (.) you're(.)
35             p:art of a family Mary (...) and it's reflection
               upon us as parents (.) upon the family unit.
               (..........) and (.....) we don't (.) want you to look
               (.) like a street walker (.) with your (..........)
               your (.) high heeled sneakers and your (.)
40  Mary:      I don't have high heeled ⌈sneakers
    Joan:                                └I'm (.)
               just giving example first you start off with
               the dang (.) flippy floppy earrings (.) and then
               you go into (.) high heeled sneakers
45             and then you put a wig h- -
    Mary:      I wouldn't want high heeled sneakers=
    Joan:      =well then you put a wig hat on your head
    Mary:      I wouldn't want a wig hat
    Joan:      and then you put cher your bright lips on hhhh
50  Mary:      I don't want to wear lipstick=
    Joan:      =then you put you:r: (...) black leather jacket on
```

		(.....)
	Mary:	I don't <u>have</u> a black leather jacket (.) and
	Joan:	and then you add
55		chains to it
	Mary:	you'd <u>never</u> <u>let</u> me get a black leather jacket=
	Joan:	=and then put your tatoos on
	Mary:	<u>e:</u>ither
		(.....)
60	Mary:	You'd <u>never</u> l<u>e</u>t me get a ta<u>too</u> <u>ei</u>ther
		(...)
	Joan:	Well there you go.
		(........................)
	Joan:	See <u>listen</u> l<u>:i:s</u>ten to you you know
65		(............)
	Mary:	Well you're s:<u>a</u>ying stuff that you know as a <u>fact</u>
		you'd never let me <u>d:o:</u>
		(.....)
	Joan:	hhhh
70		(............)
	Joan:	When you're of age (.) you will (.) have that
		choice to do because
	Mary:	o:h how old is: <u>tha:</u>t
	Joan:	<u>Mary</u> I was the s:<u>a</u>:me (.......) ⌈the s:<u>a</u>:me
75	Mary:	⌊No you w:<u>e</u>ren't
		(.....)
	Joan:	<u>Ye</u>s. (.) the s<u>a</u>me <u>a</u>ttitude an everything (.) you
		never let me to do anything ((mock voice))=
	Mary:	=well ⌈you <u>d:o:</u>nt
80	Joan:	⌊but b<u>elieve</u> me (.) bul<u>:ie:v</u>e me when <u>I</u>
		be<u>ca:</u>me of <u>a</u>ge (.) an got out on my own=
	Mary:	=how old was <u>th::a</u>t <u>thi</u>rdy

	Joan:	$(\ldots\ldots\ldots)$ No Mary
85		$(\ldots\ldots\ldots)$
	Joan:	I was eigh<u>teen</u> when I married your father=
	Mary:	=eighteen is <u>o</u>ld
		$(\ldots\ldots\ldots\ldots)$
	Joan:	⌈Well I
90	Mary:	⌊I don't think I can wait that long
	Joan:	You c<u>a</u>n't?
		(.)
	Mary:	<u>N:o:</u>
		$(\ldots\ldots\ldots\ldots\ldots)$
95	Joan:	Well let's do it gra::dually (.) let's work at
		it (.) gr::a:dually
		$(\ldots\ldots)$
	Mary:	⌈S:even <u>ye</u>:ars gradually?
	Joan:	⌊Well we can hhhhh (.) <u>M:a</u>:ry it's (.) your
100		(.) lookin at the <u>lo:ng</u> term $(\ldots\ldots)$ ya <u>t</u>ake=
	Mary:	=well that's what <u>yo:u</u> said
	Joan:	ya take <u>three</u> months
		(.) ya take six months ya take it gr:a:dually
		$(\ldots\ldots\ldots\ldots)$
105	Mary:	I'm n<u>o</u>t a <u>gra</u>:dual <u>per</u>son
		$(\ldots\ldots\ldots)$
	Mary:	I like to get things <u>d:o</u>ne (.) <u>f</u>ast
	Joan:	Fast? (.) <u>O</u>ka::y

In converting this dialogue to a narrated scene, you have all the options available to any literary narrator. At the very least, you have to make clear who's talking. The greater the vocal difference you are able to give Mary and Joan, the fewer dialogue tags you will need. But for the first speeches, be particularly careful to identify the speaker.

Certainly your audience can be better listeners if you begin not with the conversation itself, but with a brief description of the world in which this talk takes place and what outcome each participant is after. As the opening of "A Good Man Is Hard to Find" illustrates, you don't have to tell everything at the start. Rather, like that narrator, you feed information to the audience when they can best use it.

Beyond providing this minimum background information, you can decide from what point of view you want to tell the story. A narrator may have the ability to report on such internal matters as a character's thoughts and motivation. You may decide to let the audience into the mind of either Joan or Mary or both. You may, on the other hand, comment on the dialogue the audience is hearing, either to explain it or to criticize its speaker. A vividly imagined reading of the transcript may even suggest action the characters might be doing.

As you work out your reading of this conversation transcript, rehearsing Joan's and Mary's performances should reveal a good many items to comment on. Notice in line 4, for example, that Joan rejects Mary's description of the earrings as "long," referring to them as "dangley." Does this suggest to you that trouble is brewing between these two right from the start?

In line 6, Mary laughs after the mother has explained, "Dad's objection to wearing long earrings because it isn't gir:l like." You might interrupt at this point to comment on the laugh. Is it intended to be dismissive, or is Mary actually amused?

At first it may be difficult to gauge just how much narration is enough. You certainly want enough to make it easy for the audience to follow the conversation, but not so much that the dialogue gets buried in your commentary. With experience, this decision becomes easier, but your own common sense should be a reliable guide. Because this is a narratizing exercise, it is probably better to have too much than not enough.

Resisting the Text: Intertextualizing

Another technique for resisting a text, called *intertextualizing*, asks the performer to divide what seems to be a single voice into its constituent attitudes or, more radically, to break up a single text by intercutting other texts into it. One form involves intercutting the language of a literary speaker with the performer's own voice, underscoring, arguing with, or explaining the text. This approach is common in the lecture-performance where a performer cuts into a text to explain or demonstrate his or her own understanding.

We have seen students intercut a work of literature with other texts by the same writer or texts by different writers. For example, a scholar who wanted to demonstrate the stylistic influence of Abraham Lincoln on the poetry of Vachel Lindsay intercut passages from "The Gettysburg Address" with Lindsay's "Abraham Lincoln Walks at Midnight":

It is portentous, and a thing of state
Four score and seven years ago

That here at midnight, in our little town
Our fathers brought forth on this continent

A mourning figure [who] walks, and will not rest,
A new nation, conceived in liberty,

Near the old court-house pacing up and down,
And dedicated to the proposition,

Or by his homestead, or in shadowed yards
That all men are created equal.

He lingers where his children used to play,
Now we are engaged in a great civil war,

Or through the market, on the well-worn stones
Testing whether that nation, or any nation

He stalks, until the dawn-stars burn away,
So conceived and so dedicated.*

Intertextualizing can be particularly effective if you use texts the audience is already familiar with. The juxtaposing of individual lines, phrases, and sentences can transform the world, sense, and most definitely the effect of both texts. Imagine two students performing "At the IGA" and "An Old Story" as a single, intertextual script along the following lines:

At the IGA: An Old Story

This is where I would shop if my husband worked felling trees for the mill.
She'd been going about in this depressed state for ages so I should've known something was up.
Hurting himself badly from time to time.
But I didnt.
Where I would bring my three kids. Where I would push one basket and pull another.
You dont always see what's in front of your nose.

*Marjorie Taylor, "The Folk Imagination of Vachel Lindsay." Unpublished Dissertation, Wayne State University, 1976.

Because the boxes of diapers and cereal and gallon milk jugs take so much room.

I've been sitting about the house that long.

I would already have put the clothes in the two largest washers next door at the Norge Laundry Village.

You wind up in a daze.

Done shopping, I'd pile the wet wash in trash bags and take it home to dry on the line.

You dont see things properly, even with the weans, the weans especially.

And I would think, hanging out the baby's shirts and sleepers, and cranking the pully away from me . . .

There again but she's no a wean. No now.

How it would be to change lives with someone.

She's a young woman. Ach, I dont want to tell this story.

Like the woman who came after us in the checkout, thin, with lots of rings on her hands, who looked us over openly.

But you cant say that. Obviously the story has to get told.

Things would have been different.

Mm, aye, I know what you mean.

If I hadn't let Bob climb on top of me for ninety seconds in 1979.

Fine then.

It was raining lightly in the state park.

Mmm.

And so we were alone. The charcoal fire hissed as the first drops fell . . .

Okay, so about your story . . .

In ninety seconds we made this life.

Aye.

A trailer on a windy hill.

It concerns a lassie, right? And she's in this depressed state, because of her boyfriend probably—eh?

Dangerous jobs in the woods.

I dont want to tell it.

Or night work at the packing plant.

But you've got to tell it. You've got to tell it.

Roy, Kimberly, Bobby.

Unless . . . if it's no really a story at all.

Too much in the hamper, never enough in the bank.

Oh aye christ it's a story, dont worry about that.

One of our students interested in performing the contrast between the public and private sides of the poet Sylvia Plath intercut one of her most emotionally intense poems with passages from the cheerful letters she was writing at the time to her family and friends. Yet another variation would intercut one text with others that argue against the ideas in the original. As you can see, this type of resistance empowers the performer's own viewpoint in relation to the text, offering new opportunities for individual creativity, along with greater responsibility for the consequences.

Finally, we must point out that the act of performance itself is a defiant resistance to the uniformity and linearity of print. Performance *insists* that the language of literature is, like the language of life, embodied, vocalized, and localized. Performance defies any notion that language is neutral or mechanical, two connotations associated with print. Rather, performance is a public demonstration on behalf of the individuality and humanity of all utterance, both everyday and literary.

LANGUAGE IN PERFORMANCE

The title of this book may not say it *all*, but we hope that it says a good deal. *Performance in life and literature* is, fundamentally, the same operation. And it's the same language that we perform. Author Alice Thomas Ellis says, "Books are an embroidery on the way you talk."* Further, we would maintain that literature amounts to a reframing of everyday conversation. Central to both are the requisite elements of language and performance, or words and speech.

Contemporary theories of communication drawn from disciplines as diverse as speech, literature, linguistics, psychology, and anthropology focus on *language* as situated in the concrete circumstances of some place-and-time *world*, intended by a particular speaker to create a specific *effect*, making *sense* to an individual listener, and framed by conventional understandings of *genre*. Everything that surrounds language—the voice that utters it, its social context and cultural history—is the domain of performance. One theorist puts the centrality of language to contemporary thought this way:

> . . . *language occupies center stage in theoretical thinking and research. Language is seen as that which makes the world it tells about. Moreover, it makes this world through implicit as well as explicit dialogue; that is, it functions and has functioned always in a social context.***

Performance provides both a means of expressing language *and* a laboratory for studying it. By engaging in the act of performance, as you have done repeatedly in this class, both as performer and audience, we hope you have come to some fuller understanding of how language communicates, as well as how it creates. The threshold between everyday conversation and artistic expression,

---

*Interview with Alice Thomas Ellis in *Women Writers Talk*, edited by Olga Kenyon (New York: Carol & Graf Publishers, 1990), p. 64.
**Roy Schafer, *Retelling a Life: Narration and Dialogue in Psychoanalysis* (New York: Basic Books, 1992), p. 148.

between life and literature, is the most exciting place to live if one wants to witness the word becoming flesh. This sacred transformation cannot occur on its own. It requires you, the performer, to collaborate in a profoundly creative process. Novelist William Gass sums it up this way: "In order to have this experience [of literature], one must learn to perform the text, say, sing, shout the words to oneself, give them, with *our* minds, *their* body."*

We hope in this course you have experienced the transport that is possible when performing the common language of life and literature. If so, you have caught a glimpse of the eternal that is inside any single moment of human utterance, whether spoken in the homemade words of casual conversation or composed in the artistic forms of literature.

*William H. Gass, "Of Speed Readers and Lip-Movers," in *The New York Times Book Review*, April 1, 1984, p. 33. Copyright © 1984 by The New York Times Company. Reprinted by permission.

Two Personal Narratives

One artistic form popular today in the mass media and in theatrical practice is the *personal narrative*. This genre, born in and through performance, purposely blurs any distinction between life and literature, aspiring to tell the truth by heightening real-life experience into a staged conversation with an audience. Performers shape the personal material of their everyday lives into a verbal art that stands on the threshold between life and literature. Here are two personal narratives composed in and for performance by contemporary artist-scholars.

"An Unsolicited Gift"

(by Barney Downs, University of South Florida)

For a while I went to a dream analyst who encouraged me to record my dreams. When I told him of a dream in which I was thinking of boarding a train, he said, "Don't. Do you realize what that may be symbolic of? Trains can represent a desire to die, a desire to leave this life." I thought about that, and then it came in a flash: "That idea *was* at work within me! I was getting older. I was no longer in my prime. I'd probably done all I ever thought I would do. I *was* thinking about leaving. The question was, did I want to die?"

Later, I dreamed I was on a train, in a club-car. There was a party. There were several couples. We were having a wonderful time, laughing, drinking, frolicking around. I knew that I needed to leave, but my partner wouldn't consider the idea. I said, "We must leave. I don't want to be here. This is not right." The deepest part of me was frightened. I looked out the window and saw hordes of weary soldiers, all marching in the direction the train was moving. It was cold, bleak, dark, and snowing, and they were weary from battle. You could see numbed pain on their faces. We were all heading toward a battle which could not be won. Certain defeat was written in their bodies. Again I tried to get my companion off the train, but she was embroiled in pleasure and wouldn't listen to me. Finally, I sat back helplessly, thinking, maybe it will be all right.

That same dream would haunt me for over a year.

I was waiting on the phone for a report from my dermatologist. I had a little spot on my thigh. When he first saw it he said, "That's a bug bite."

Six months later, he said, "That's not a bug bite." It had grown larger, to the size of half a dime, burgundy-colored. I hadn't even realized it was growing. "Let's do a biopsy," he said. "Call me in two weeks and I'll give you the report."

I was waiting on the phone, and getting bored. I started making slash marks on a piece of paper. One, two, three, four—slash. One, two, three, four—slash. Soon I had the whole sheet filled. Is he that busy? How long could it take for him to find my biopsy report? When he came back to the phone, he said, "You have Kaposi Sarcoma."

I felt a ball of fire in my belly. I was frightened by the way my body was responding, and I was frightened by my thoughts. I knew what Kaposi Sarcoma was. I had visited an AIDS support group, and the young man who sat next to me had a Kaposi Sarcoma lesion on the tip of his nose. He was a sweet-faced, gentle man who wore a baseball cap to hide the fact that he had lost his hair in chemotherapy. I had a hard time looking at him, because my eyes were drawn involuntarily to his nose. He looked like Snoopy in a road company of *Peanuts*.

I asked, "What should I do?" He said, "Go to your family physician. You will have to get an HIV blood test to determine whether you have AIDS." I asked myself what else it could be but AIDS?

Fortunately, I was able to see my family physician that same day. Getting out of the car, my knees buckled, and I had to catch myself from falling. I thought this only happened in movies.

"How much time do I have? How long can I teach?" I asked. She said, "We don't know what kind of infection this is. It could be the classical form of Kaposi Sarcoma, or the AIDS-related form. They are two entirely different diseases. The classical form is found in older men with a Mediterranean heritage. Do either of your parents have a Mediterranean background?"

I said, "No."

She asked. "Are you gay?"

I said, "Yes."

She asked, "Do you participate in anal sexual intercourse?"

I said, "No."

"Of course it can affect men without a Mediterranean background, but the incidence is not as great. You are nearing sixty years, you are in the proper age bracket for the classical form. The first thing to do is to test for HIV, and then we'll work from there. It will take two weeks to get the HIV results."

Before the two weeks were up, I got a call that the lab had lost my blood sample. I would have to come in for another test.

After another two weeks my doctor called me in. "I always give the report in my office," she said. "I never give it on the phone, whether it is positive or negative."

She sat across the desk from me. On the walls were pictures of athletic teams with inscriptions: "We love you, doctor." "We owe it all to you, doctor." "It couldn't have happened without you, doctor." She said the results of my test were negative, but that one test wasn't sufficient. The disease can have a window. A window does not register the presence of the disease, it avoids detection. I must continue getting the HIV blood tests on a monthly basis.

Over the next few weeks, I become overwhelmingly tired. I had night sweats. I sometimes had to change my pajamas several times during the night. Walking took great effort. If I used the stairs, I had to use the railing to pull myself up. I felt my body hunching over, my usual stride diminished. Once at a shopping mall I was shocked to see the reflection of a shrunken figure painfully inching his way. I realized I looked exactly like one of the soldiers in my dream sludging toward a battle he knew he couldn't win.

I visited my massage therapist, Don McCann, who was also a mental health counselor. "What are you trying to do," he asked, "punish yourself for being gay?"

"What can I do about this?" I asked. "Nobody can do anything about it until they find out what it is."

He said, "You can't think about having AIDS. You can give it to yourself just by dwelling on it, by believing that you deserve to be punished. You must give up the belief that you are infected with AIDS."

"That's like asking someone to sit in the corner and not think of elephants," I said.

"Why don't you see a vitamin therapist. I know of one over in Lakeland," he said.

Vitamin therapy was a husband and wife team effort. The wife came from a Latin country, and spoke with an accent. She was portly and motherly to me and her five-year-old son who wandered around the room. She had a very different sort of scientific approach. She placed a combination vitamin/mineral on my lap. Then she asked me to hold the thumb and little finger of my left hand together, so that they touched. If she could pull this contact apart while I tried to hold it firmly together, it meant that the vitamin/mineral on my lap needed to be part of my diet right now. If she couldn't, it meant that the pill wasn't necessary. Every month I went back, and the little bundle of pills that I took home cost close to $200.00.

"Yes, you have AIDS," she said. "No, you don't have cancer," she announced, after she had placed first the AIDS packet and then the cancer packet on my lap. "My sister," she said, "has pneumonia. She is seeing a physician now, and she won't ask for my advice. I know I could help her, but she won't ask for my advice. What am I going to do?" Before I could respond she continued. "But, darling, this is so good for you," she said, pushing my packaged month's supply of pills toward me in exchange for my check. "You will like it, believe me. Already I can see a difference in your eyes. The color of your eyes has improved."

In the meantime, my physician had lined up an oncologist for me to see. A cancer specialist. He looked at the little spot. "Well, there is nothing we can do until we learn whether this is AIDS-related or not. Once we know, we will either excise it or give you some kind of radiation treatment. But you know, I had a Lutheran minister in here last year with the same condition as yours, your age, a married man." He laughed. "A Lutheran minister! So you see, it is not always AIDS-related."

As I was getting dressed, which consisted merely of putting on my trousers, the doctor left the room. In the hall, deliberately looking through the open doorway, was his wife. Deliberately looking at me. Before I saw the doctor, I had spoken with her briefly about the method of payment. Then she turned me over to the receptionist who recorded the diagnosis which had brought me here. Now, the wife was looking at me pointedly. Her gaze seemed to say, "So this is what *you people* look like." Something about her curiosity was evil.

This is what it's like to have AIDS, I thought to myself. Does it delight her? Does it give her satisfaction? Does it make her feel superior to look upon a person in fear?

After a few months of HIV testing, my family physician informed me that she was closing her office. She was selling her practice so she could return home to be with a sister who was struggling with cancer.

"She was abandoned by my alcoholic parents," she said. "She was abandoned by her husband, and I can't leave her now."

Fortunately, I had a friend who was a physician. Dr. Diane accepted me into her practice. Her first advice: "Go to an AIDS specialist. Go to Dr. Dolly." I had heard about Dr. Dolly. When her patients were in pain, terrified, and alone in the hospital, she would get into bed with them. "Yes," I thought, "that is the kind of doctor I want."

Dr. Dolly's waiting room was relatively small. The lighting was subdued, the colors soft. Light pearl gray covered the walls, along which were benches upholstered in cushioned leather, like the seating at a built-in restaurant table. To one side of the reception desk was a vertical fish tank, large enough to contain a human body. It was the strongest source of light in the room, with its bits of color dashing from one area of interest to another.

Waiting to be called was a man—middle-aged, balding, paunchy, nondescript. His most remarkable feature was terror. Perched on the edge of his seat, his eyes were wide, making them available to every bit of information they could gather. You knew this was his first time. You knew he didn't know what to expect. You knew he was the victim of the changes all round him.

Earlier when I was at the washroom lavatory, a tall figure with great amounts of cascading hair and a wildly patterned blouse passed behind me. I thought, "A woman is in here. Does she know she is in the men's john?" Not until we returned to the waiting room, did I realize that person was a man, costumed and coiffed in the manner of a rock star. His face was handsome and strong, containing bravura. He seemed bored, eager to get it all over with. Clearly he had been here before. Clearly he had something better to do than this.

The very first thing Dr. Dolly said to me was, "These tests are all wrong. They are too unreliable. You must take *this* HIV test," she said, referring to a multi-dimensional process she recommended. "It will take two months for us to get the results." She explained that the test consisted of taking cultures to determine whether the HIV antibody was in my DNA. This would give us absolute proof whether the antibody was lurking about anywhere.

As I was leaving the office, there was a man seated on the slab bench against the wall. It was clear he did not have the energy to sit upright. His head rested against the wall. He looked as if he had been poured into place, as if he didn't have a skeletal structure. His face was ashen. I felt I needed to do something, but I did not know what. He glanced up and caught my eye. I gave him a "thumbs up." He closed his eyes briefly, opened them again, and smiled.

In the meantime, my new family physician, Dr. Diane, referred me to another cancer specialist holding an association in a large unit devoted to that disease. "He treats Kaposi Sarcoma all the time," she said.

The doctor was tall, pleasant looking, and *very* assured. He carried himself with the ease of a prince in a Viennese operetta. With him was a shorter, younger man, obviously in training. The specialist looked at the lesion and laughed. "Oh, this is nothing. You should see some of the cases I get. Their bodies are covered with it."

He examined my throat, felt the neck glands, and looked at my records. "Your body is putting up one hell of a fight."

"You mean I have something to fight?" I said. "You mean you believe I have the AIDS infection?"

"It is not as if the medical establishment is not looking for cures," he said brightly. "Something will be found. Any day now."

I laughed, "Sure!" The young man next to him lowered his head and did not look at me.

A friend of mine, a nurse, knew of my condition. One day she came to me and said, "Would you like Jose to pray over you?"

And I asked, "Who is Jose?"

And she said, "A spiritualist, who is teaching a course on how to utilize spiritual forces in recovery and healing."

I said, "I'm not interested in the course, but do you think he would pray over me?"

She checked into it, and said, "Come next Wednesday."

Jose lived on the outskirts of the city, in a modest little bungalow, with a small, ancient, faded auto in the open carport. Once inside, the living and dining area was fairly large and unobstructed by any traditional furniture with the exception of a sofa. Folding chairs, open and closed, were scattered about. The house seemed to have been converted into a sort of temple. Central to the design was the placement of an elaborate sound system. Within the focus wall which held the sound system were a series of shelves holding vigil lights, pictures and statues of deities from many different cultures. It was a little pantheon of beliefs. Jose was dressed all in white: slacks, with a short-sleeved Filipino shirt hanging over his trousers. As I sat, he placed his hands on my shoulders and began chanting. This went on for several minutes.

Afterwards he always asked, "How do you feel?"

And I always said, "Better." I didn't know whether it was the result of energy he was giving me or just the comfort of having someone touch me. I thought, "What the hell, it can't hurt."

Over the next few weeks he would never take any money. One day he said, "Would you like to go to Mexico? Would you like to go to Chichen Itza? It is a wonderful place for spiritual rejuvenation. We are going to do a firewalk."

Our group numbered about fifteen. Most of the participants were studying for the "priesthood" with Jose. All of them had regular jobs and saw this as a way of heightening their spiritual sensitivity.

Chichen Itza is the site of Mayan ruins. At first glimpse, a member of our group shouted, "I've been here before, I was here in another life, I was thrown off the top of that parapet as a sacrifice to the Gods. It will take me a little time to feel comfortable with the place. You understand, don't you?" We all nodded in agreement. "But I am home," he sighed jubilantly.

I was having trouble walking up the monuments. I have difficulty with heights. I practically crawled on my hands and knees. My fear was that I would fall off the top of one of those things.

The day came for the firewalk. The first thing we did was to chant. Then we were told to enter a meditative state during which Jose would counsel us for our trip. I fell asleep. This worried me and I breathlessly confessed what happened to Jose. "Don't worry, it will work whether you were conscious or not," he said.

The bed of coals was approximately two feet wide, and eight feet long. Papers and bits of wood were placed on top of the coals and ignited. Once the flames burned out, the coals were glowing. We took turns walking across the coals. I wasn't among the first, but those who were, were ecstatic: "It was wonderful." "I made it." "I didn't feel a thing." "I am doing it again."

When it came time for me, I literally flew. It wasn't altogether comfortable. When it was over, those of us who felt less successful rushed into the bathroom of the little nearby cottage, soaking our feet in the tub. We laughed in excitement and embarrassment. Inspecting my feet I did find a few tiny blisters. A few others had larger blisters; many had no blisters at all.

That night, I was proud and happy. I felt, "Yes, I have control over my body. I really didn't burn myself. Well, not to any significant degree. It *is* mind over matter. And that was what I was hoping to do with this disease. Mind over matter. You've got balls, Barney." I slept at ease, and happily, for the first time since my diagnosis.

I do not know how I came across the theories of Bernie Siegel. He is the oncologist who developed the concept of the Exceptional Cancer Patient. He has written a number of books on a self-help process in which the patient admits to being responsible for his own illness. Once you do that, you can accept the responsibility for your own health and recovery. The backbone of Siegel's concept is meditating four times a day. During this meditation you envision yourself in white light. You see yourself healed. You develop images of conquering the little demons of disease crawling about inside your body with your own small white warrior-knights carrying your banner of victory. I was beginning to know peace.

Louise Hay developed a powerful affirmation for people with AIDS: "I am part of the universal design. I am important and loved by life itself. I am powerful and capable, and I love and appreciate all of myself."

I would say this aloud, time and time again, with feeling and conviction. As soon as I got into my car, I would let loose.

Once when my sister was visiting me, I asked her to join me. She said, "I can't."

"Okay, just take one little phrase at a time. You don't have to memorize the whole thing."

She said, "It's not a matter of memory; I can't say it."

"What do you mean you can't say it?"

"I can't say it. I can't form the words, they won't come out of my mouth."

Today my sister has a serious illness that is crippling her entire body. I've sent her the Louise Hay affirmation tapes. I don't ask if she plays them. She never mentions them. I believe she still can't say the words.

Later in the year, it was necessary for me to go back to the dermatologist who initially diagnosed the Kaposi Sarcoma. I had to pick up the slide on the basis of which the diagnosis had been made. I didn't want to see the man. I called the nurse and made arrangements for the slide to be at the desk for me to pick up.

When I arrived, she asked me to be seated and said, "The doctor would like to see you." I felt like leaving without the slide. He had become the epitome of all that I hated and feared in this experience.

The doctor asked me to sit down when I entered his office. He started speaking technically about my case. I listened for a few minutes, then interrupted him. "I'm angry with you." He didn't say anything. "I am angry with the way you gave me my diagnosis. I am angry with the way it was so depersonalized. I am angry with the way I was led to believe that I was about to die."

Again he didn't say anything. He held out the hand which was resting on his lap and softly said, "Help me."

I put my hand in his, and we sat there.

I went to Don McCann for a regular therapy appointment. I didn't know if he was going to counsel or massage. It didn't matter. I ached beyond redemption, physically and emotionally. He said, "You need to do rage work."

I said, "I haven't got the energy."

"Get the club and bang the punching bag, stick out your lower jaw, and growl. You know the procedure."

I did it, hating the whole idea.

"And what images do you get?"

I said, "I don't get any images."

He said, "Oh well, you've got undifferentiated rage. Once you lop off some of that, you'll get down to some of the specific things you are angry with."

I *was* angry. God, I was angry. I banged away at that thing. I let go. I growled, I barked, I roared. I was saturated with rage. It was dripping out of my mouth.

Then he said, "Say what is coming to mind, say what you feel."

I said, "I am angry! I hate God! I hate sex! I hate my parents! I hate God for having created all this! I hate it that no one ever taught me anything! I hate it all!"

I went on for I don't know how long. When I was finished my throat was raw, and I had no voice.

He asked, "How do you feel?"

I said, "Wonderful!"

I walked out of there with a light step, energized, and provoked to think about my sexuality, to remember incidents I had not thought of since they occurred.

My first sexual response was heterosexual. I was making tracings of realistically drawn women from comic books. I drew them without their clothes, and I masturbated looking at them. I was in grade school.

My mother found them. "Did you do this?"

"Yes."

"Don't do that again."

I didn't. I drew pictures of men without clothes. I masturbated looking at them. It didn't occur to me that I was making a sexual choice.

I remembered my first homosexual experience. I was in my early twenties. He was bisexual. We had known each other for several years. When it was over he asked,

"What do you think of that?"

"It's not all that important or special, is it?"

He laughed.

"Why do people do it?"

He was silent, which surprised me. He was ten years older than myself, a professional anthropologist, and I knew he knew everything. Then he spoke. "I don't know. I guess it's for the intimacy. I think it's because you feel closer to someone."

After that, I never went back to confession. I don't know why. Did I feel it was something I couldn't confess? Was it too overwhelmingly wrong? Was it too incongruent with my conscious self-image?

I remembered Uncle Al, in a car. My family was driving somewhere. Uncle Al sat in the back, and he was making some comment. It was about me, although he didn't *say* who. He was saying how despicable gay people were. There was silence in the car. Nobody said anything. My body was frozen with fear.

Later, when my mother asked, "Are you gay?" I said, "No." "Well, I hope not," she said.

I thought about how I had always repressed my sexuality. I thought of how it became a thing I did apart from my real life. Something that I did away from the sun of ordinary social experience. It was something I was dreadfully ashamed of. Because of it I despised and hated myself.

And why did I have sex? I wanted to be held. I wanted to touch and be touched. I wanted intimacy.

There were times too, in the midst of sex, when I thought, "Nobody wants me to do this, and I am doing it *for that reason*. It is *fun* for that reason. F___ 'em all."

I had locked myself in a closet. A closet of fear. A closet of hatred. A closet of isolation. I saw myself as something less than human. I committed the ultimate crime: the crime of hating myself. Of hating my vehicle for existence. Of hating my body. Of hating the gift of my being.

With Don McCann we formed a therapy group consisting of two men and six women. We did rage work, mostly. On one occasion, however, I was given a task. "Stand up in front of everyone," Don said, "describe yourself, and end every sentence with, 'And I am lovable.'"

I stood up in the small group and looked at the others. I had no idea where I would go with this. "I may have AIDS—and I'm lovable. I am gay and God knows what else sexually—and I am lovable. I haven't got much hair—and I'm lovable. My teeth are yellowing—and I'm lovable. I'm aging—and I'm lovable. Oh my God, I've got a 17-year-old car—and I'm lovable. And I'll never be a full professor—and I'm lovable. And I'll never make a lot of money—and I'm lovable. And I make about the lowest salary in the whole department, even after being there over twenty years—and I'm lovable. And I live in a little match-stick house, while many of my colleagues live in what seem to be splendid looking palaces—and I'm lovable. And I haven't had a sustained, intimate, sexual relationship for a very, very long time—and I'm lovable. And I don't know where I am going—and I am lovable. Sometimes I hate God—and I am lovable. And I don't think I have done a hell of a lot with my life—and I am lovable. And I would so dearly love to have loved myself—and I'm lovable. And I am not at all the splendid kind of person some people see me as—and I'm lovable. And at times I'm not a very good teacher—and I'm lovable. Although sometimes I teach with a great deal of joy and abandon—and I am lovable. And I am not physically prepossessing—and I am lovable. And I haven't got a splendid theatrical voice—and I am lovable. And I am a terrible actor—and I am lovable. And I don't know what it is all about, after all this time—and I am lovable. And I am trying like hell—and I am lovable."

Afterward, the group was invited to respond. They were warmly supportive, noting elements in my sharing that surprised me: honesty, courage, beauty. But it was the insistent refrain that hung in my heart. There was nothing that could not make me lovable.

It was October, exactly one year from the time of my initial diagnosis, and I was seeing Dr. Dolly for the report on the second super-duper HIV test. She had moved; she needed more examining rooms. Business had improved. I looked at her closely to see what kind of message she was about to give me, to see whether it was favorable or unfavorable. I couldn't tell. She was thoughtful and closed. She took out my chart, and started leafing through it. Reading it. Then I was amazed to realize she was reading the report for the first time. She looked up, passive, still without a message.

"You are negative. You don't have it. After this second test, the likelihood of your developing the disease is so mathematically remote that it doesn't warrant a third test." Then she smiled broadly and said, "You don't belong here. Go on," she joked. "Get out of here." And as I closed the door behind me, she called out, "And keep healthy."

Somehow, even before that revelation, I was at peace. While I was scanning her face, my heart wasn't thumping. I was at ease. I had an entirely different sense of myself than I had a year ago. My sense of self, life, God, the world around me—all was altered. I had grown, and I knew I had.

And I knew that I could never, ever have gotten to where I was without this gift—of fear: the fear of not knowing whether I would be, the fear of this particular disease, the fear that connected me with the reality of the sexual path that I had chosen and with the life that I had created for myself. That fear forced me to see. There was no denial here. Something was shattered. It wasn't as if an innocence was shattered. The facade of deceit, hate, and fear was shattered.

As I sat in my car in the parking lot of Dr. Dolly's office, and these thoughts rushed through my head, a great calm fell on me. I knew, finally, that I had stepped off that train.

It wasn't until years later, as I pieced this experience together and struggled to entitle it that the phrase "an unsolicited gift" came to me. How appropriate, I thought, for that is the definition of grace.

sista docta

(conceived and performed by Joni L. Jones, choreographed by Llory Wilson, drummed by Alli Aweusi)

(Alli enters drumming from the back of the house through the audience while I set the stage. He finishes drum solo and takes a seat upstage left, where he remains throughout the performance. He resumes drumming softly while I improvise a greeting—ask how many sista doctas there are in the house and dedicate the performance to a particular sista docta. The opening poem is "Status Symbol" by Mari Evans, with my additions indicated in bold.)

"arrival"

i
Have arrived
MA—NU
PHD—NYU
Tenure Track—UT
i
am the
New Negro
cowries and silk
kente and linen
Christmas and kwanzaa
i
am the result of
MTV, BET, PC, AME
President Lincoln
World War I
and Paris
the
Red Ball Express
white drinking fountains
white guilt
Affirmative Action
Target of Opportunity Money

sitdowns and
sit-ins
Federal Troops
Marches on Washington
Brown vs. The Board of Education
Central High
bussing
and
prayer meetings
today
They hired me

i t
is a status
job . . .
grants, conferences, receptions
meetings
office computer and voice mail
meetings
summer break, semester break, spring break
meetings
medical plan, dental plan, retirement plan
meetings
along
with my papers
They
gave me my
Status Symbol

the
key
to the
White . . . Locked . . .
John

(I walk upstage, remove comfortable jacket and drop it near Alli. As jacket drops, Alli begins to drum and walking movement commences. Movement ends with elbow punctuating the final drum beat. Transition occurs as Alli starts new rhythm, while I do Yoruba movement upstage to Alli. At his signal, that movement stops and I begin a slow motion movement transition into "family." Movement continues while I speak in the different voices of my sisters and my daughter.)

"Why are we here Joni?"

"The sound on the tape—"

"So you're doing a performance and you want us to talk about your work and you're going to use that in the performance? Is that it?"

"What I like about what Joni does is that she is probably the only person that I know right now intimately who finds joy in her work."

"I find joy in my work. I just don't enjoy the people."

"Then it seems to me you don't find joy."

"I like that moma and I get to go to plays, and sometimes I go to her classes and sometimes I get to help her direct. What I don't like is that moma travels alot and I have to stay with babysitters and one time she was at a conference and she couldn't make my costume for halloween."

"If we get into the don't like, I don't like the uh, the uh—"

"Bureaucracy."

"—bureaucracy, the white establishment mentality which I hate—"

"Well, I'm going to say something into this tape that everybody here already knows and that is that white folks are toxic and oppressive. They can't help it. It's in their genetic coding."

"But Joni works with white folks."

"I wouldn't be going to none of their parties and putting on pantyhose. I wouldn't be doing none of it."

"But Joni can hang with white folks."

"You can hang with white folks?"

"what I like abt my work is . . ."

(I walk in a circle as I improvise to myself about what I enjoy in my work. This improvisation concludes with the word "transformative" as I stand directly facing the audience. Alli begins a rhythm while I do the circular arm movement and head shake from earlier dance. This marks the transition into "the faculty party." While moving, I give instructions on how the audience will participate in this section. Prior to the performance, audience members were randomly handed cards with their lines on them. At this moment in the performance, I explain that they are to stand and to perform the roles of white faculty, using the lines on the cards. The cards have been numbered one through eight, and they are to speak in order while I move from person to person with a stomping movement. The following lines are delivered by the randomly selected audience members.)

"the faculty party"

"I really liked your presentation last night a great deal!"

"After last night, I just wanted to say I continue to be impressed with your performances. I am glad to have you as a colleague."

"As I've said to you before, your teaching is solid and your service seems right on target."

"Now, you went to well respected schools, you've taught at recognized institutions—why do you think you're different from us?"

"I just wanted to tell you, I think you should be careful of how white women might be using you."

"That's great! You say you'll be doing a book chapter on Lorraine Hansberry. That's really great—now, who is Lorraine Hansberry?"

"You know we're moving. Well, it will be good to be in a city where the only people who stay home during the day aren't on welfare."

"Yeah, I think the move will be good for us. We just found a great house. It looks just like a plantation!"

(I sporadically continue the stomps as I head upstage to the rolling chair, naming some of the things I said earlier about liking my work. This ends with the word "transformative" as I sit in the chair. The following section is done in the chair. I roll during each quotation and freeze the movement when I say the speaker's name. This is the same movement used during "family talk" except that I am now seated.)

"girl talk"

". . . if I know my name, I know that in the academy, like in America, the sister is caught between the rock of racism and the hard place of sexism."

Johnetta B. Cole

"It made me feel alienated, as a black *woman* in *white* universities, teaching *every white boy* to be Biff and Happy! Is *that* pedagogically sound, in this time?"

Anna Deavere Smith

"being an afro-american writer is something to be self-conscious about"

Ntozake Shange

"Black women intellectuals . . . must recognize the call to speak openly about . . . our work as a form of activism."

bell hooks

"I've realized people in academic circles aren't really talking to me. They're trying to figure out if I'm smart or not."

Anna Deavere Smith

"While courageous individuals have organized and fought to make the walls of academia less impenetrable, these very victories have spawned new problems . . ."

Angela Davis

". . . the absence of race and culture in much of our communication theory and research, in fact, has impoverished that same theory and research."

Navita James

". . . how often do we truly love our work?"

Audre Lorde

". . . every black writer knows the very people you may most want to hear your words may never read them . . . "

bell hooks

"How do we convert a racist house into a non-racist home? The answer could save our lives."

Toni Morrison

(Alli starts tape recording of answering machine messages. Between each voice is the beep from the machine. I run from stage left to stage right, and begin movement that continues through this section.)

"the machine"

"Dr. Jones—I know you're busy, but I would like for you to be on the board of First Stage productions. Girl you know we could use someone on our board like you."

BEEP

"Dr. Jones—I'm calling for Texas Folklife Resources and we were wondering if you would mc for us again—you were so good with that dance series—so we thought you might mc this celebration we are having for this local blues singer. Give me a call if you can do it."

BEEP

"Dr. Jones—I wanted to remind you that Black Arts Alliance is having a board meeting tomorrow at 6:00. You said you teach until 6 so we know you'll be late."

BEEP

"Dr. Jones—I'm sorry to bother you at home, but—well—I just don't know how to play Sula—I mean—what's black about her? Do you know what I mean? I'll try you at your office."

BEEP

"Hey Joni—I'm doing that Langston Hughes program again and I was hoping that you would read in it again this year. I know you are busy, but I would love to have you. We would begin rehearsals right away."

BEEP

"Dr. Jones—My rehearsals have changed and I need to give you the revisions. Drop by anytime you get a minute. Oh—and do you have time for advising tomorrow? I have to turn in that form with your signature by Friday. Well, I'll see you tomorrow."

BEEP

"Joni—I have a favor to ask. Will you write the introduction to my book on African-American holidays? And can you proofread my book on the Black Panthers? They're both almost done—I just can't seem to find the time to write. I know you can relate. Check you later."

BEEP

"Joni—just a reminder. There's a budget council meeting at 2:00. Usual place. See you there."

BEEP

"Joni? Is this Joni Jones? Or Dr. Jones? Look, I'm the woman who ran the meeting tonight, and well, I'm sorry. I really didn't mean to offend you. I mean, it's just that . . . well, you know. Some of us, when we start getting those degrees and things . . . you know, we start acting all uppity! You know how black folks are . . . and I know you're not like that but some of us start getting those doctorates and well, look, I should be saying this in person, I mean—"

BEEP

(During the last message, I continue the movement traveling upstage. I do a slow-motion-movement transition into the next section. "the stats" is accompanied by the same movement used during "the faculty party." The movement travels diagonally downstage.)

"the stats"

In 1987, the percentage of doctorates awarded to African-American men and women was (pause) 2.0% (stomp stomp stomp)

In 1992, the percentage of tenured faculty who were African-American women was (pause) 2.5% (stomp stomp stomp)

In 1985, the percentage of full professors who were African-American women was (pause) 0.6% (stomp stomp stomp)

In 1993, out of 2342 UT faculty, how many were African-American? (pause) 55 (stomp stomp stomp)

Of that 55 how many were African-American women? (pause) 15 (stomp stomp stomp)

Who was the first African-American woman to be hired by the Department of Speech Communication at the University of Texas? (pause) ME! (stomp stomp stomp)

(Alli begins same transition rhythm while I do Yoruba dance traveling upstage. I pick up a "conservative" jacket while dancing, and end the dance at Alli's signal. The drumming also stops. I put on the jacket and it is obviously too small. I deliver the next section while trying to dance the opening movement from the "arrival" sequence.)

                    i
          Have Arrived
                    i
              am the
          New Negro

                    i
          am the result of President Lincoln
          World War I
          and Paris
          the
          Red Ball Express
          white drinking fountains
          sitdowns and
          sit-ins
          Federal Troops
          Marches on Washington
          and
          prayer meetings
          today
          They hired me

          i t
          is a status
          job . . .
          along
          with my papers
          They
          gave me my
          Status Symbol

          the
          key
          to the
          White . . . Locked . . .
          John

          (I slowly take off the jacket and drop it.)

                    "what i like abt my work"

          (I again improvise a conversation with myself about the joys of my
          work. I again walk slowly in a circle during this improvisation

which ends with the word "transformative" while facing the audience.)

"to ed."

(The following is my poem which I deliver standing very still while facing the audience.)

she said she was my sister
but
sisterhood
is being redefined
without my consent

she pressed my hair
and she wasn't even my moma
no comfort of familial straightening
no warm momahands on Saturday night
before Sunday school gotta look good

she pressed out the kinks of me-ness
of slash marks and nouns into verbs
and umph umph umph

she thused and therefored my hair to a
stiff straight flatness
a spit polish shine
Dixie Peach
the overpressed awkwardness
apparent in every word

did she know how hard it was to find this nappy freedom
to close away that straightening comb in the kitchen drawer

after all
there was the thousands of years of silence
after all
there was my daily institutionalization
after all
there was the phd where i was dissed to death

i hope my edges go back real soon
go back from sweat and living

she said she was my sister
but
sisterhood
is being redefined
without my consent

(I pick up the tight jacket and walk slowly upstage to Alli. I pick
up the comfortable jacket and fold them both over my arm. Alli
begins rhythm. The closing is modeled after the closing of Ntozake
Shange's *for colored girls who have considered suicide/when the rainbow
is enuf.*)

"return"

And this is for sista doctas
Who are making our own arrivals

(I bow, Alli increases the volume, and I dance out of the space
through the audience.)

DRAMATIC PERFORMANCE OF EVERYDAY CONVERSATION*

Robert Hopper

Everyday life is a source for dramatic and poetic performance. This appendix supplements the examples of everyday interaction provided in the book. These conversations actually occurred, and were tape-recorded. The scripts that appear here have been copied verbatim from recordings. You may perform these scenes; and you may subject these texts to any of the kinds of analysis shown in the book or discussed in class.

These scripts work best when you read them aloud. If you attend to the extra symbols, and practice with a partner, you quickly learn to perform the scenes much as the original actors did. Read aloud repeatedly those scenes that draw your interest. Your instructor may ask you to commit scenes to memory and perform them in class.

How to Read the Script Notation

These scripts look like play scripts. Speaker identification is shown at the left margin. In addition to words, these scripts use markings devised for describing conversational timing, emphasis, and expression. Some words are misspelled to show how they are pronounced (e.g., "probly"). Syllables of laughter are spelled out (e.g., "hah hah hah"). Audible exhaling is shown by hhhhh, and audible in-breath is shown by ·hhhh.

Use this guide to script symbols until you become familiar with them.

Performance and Analysis of the Scripts

Performance and analysis feed one another. Whenever you get stuck in textual analysis, read aloud the passage in question. As you rehearse actual speech rhythms, new ideas occur to you. Write these down in a rehearsal journal, and use the notes to discuss your performance.

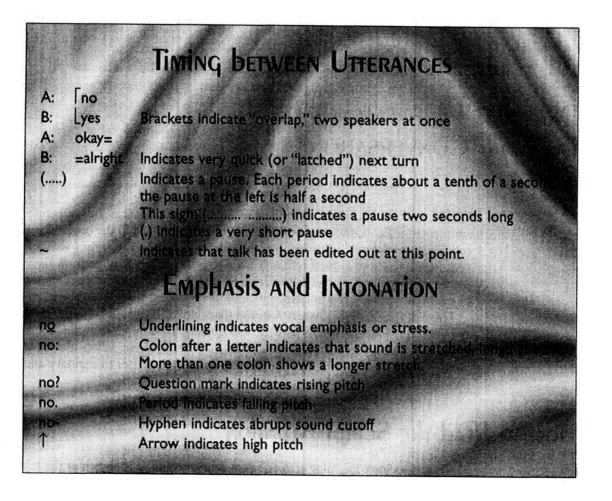

Timing between Utterances

A: ⌈no
B: ⌊yes   Brackets indicate "overlap," two speakers at once
A: okay=
B: =alright   Indicates very quick (or "latched") next turn
(.....)   Indicates a pause. Each period indicates about a tenth of a second;
       the pause at the left is half a second
       This sign (......... ....) indicates a pause two seconds long
       (.) indicates a very short pause
~   Indicates that talk has been edited out at this point.

Emphasis and Intonation

no   Underlining indicates vocal emphasis or stress.
no: Colon after a letter indicates that sound is stretched, lengthened.
       More than one colon shows a longer stretch.
no?   Question mark indicates rising pitch
no.   Period indicates falling pitch.
no-   Hyphen indicates abrupt sound cutoff
↑   Arrow indicates high pitch

Here are some questions that may guide your thinking and your performance choices. To respond to these questions, find a brief passage in the script that provides evidence for your answer. Quote the passage in your writing to explicate how the characters do things with words. (Avoid descriptions like "all the time;" instead, show and describe one instance.)

- What is the nature of the interpersonal relationship between these people? Locate one moment in the text that especially shows this relationship state.

- Does the relationship change during this scene? At what point can you observe this change in the talk? Does it change for just one person, or more than one? How can you tell?

- Is there a "turning point" in the scene? Write the line number in the script when the change occurs, and explicate what gets changed. How do the actors accomplish the change? Do the characters change at the same time or at different moments?

- Do the characters show surprise, anger, or other emotion? What in the script shows such emotion, and how? Does the other actor in the scene seem to notice the emotion? How can you tell?

- What effects do the speakers have on their listener(s)? Does this change during the scene? When, and how?

- Does one person know something the other doesn't? How can you tell?

- Where are the speakers? Where is your evidence for this? Do they use a phone? Do they move during the scene? Are there cues in the text for actions that the parties do besides their speech?

- Do the actors "move around" in time during the scene, shifting from present to past or future? How does one such shift affect the performance?

- Does your character show a certain type of personality? Copy a particular utterance that shows this characteristic most forcefully.

- Do the speakers emphasize key words and "throw away" echo ideas? (See Chapter 4.)

- Are there instances of narration in your scene? If so, what narrative strategies does the speaker use? (See Chapter 6.)

Rehearsal Notes

It is best to rehearse over as many days as possible: An hour of rehearsal each day for ten days is much better than five hours each over two days. Rehearse on your own, as well as with performance partner(s). One way to rehearse on your own is to make a recording as soon as you and your partners can read the script accurately. Then attempt to speak *in unison with the tape* as it plays "your" speaking turn.

While continuing to use the script, alternate between talking in unison with the tape and reading aloud without the tape. This not only helps you achieve accuracy, but speeds memorization. When you can perform accurately using script and tape, then you should attempt to talk along with tape *without* looking at the script.

Push accuracy as far as you can. Keep returning to the script to check details. Tape-record your rehearsals and listen to them while looking at the script. The following areas especially represent challenges to accurate performance of the scripts.

Speech overlap and laughter. Most performers find it challenging at first to speak in overlap with another speaker. The first problem is timing the overlap. It helps to try to start a bit *earlier* than the script shows; otherwise you often find yourself gulping for breath at your cue and coming in a bit late. Practice each overlap repeatedly at about half speed—a technique musicians use to learn difficult passages. (Some tape recorders can even play at slow speed to aid such rehearsal.)

Slowing down and repeated rehearsal are also necessary for passages with laughter. The script does not just give general instructions to laugh, but shows the precise number of laughter syllables, and some detail on how to pronounce them (e.g., "hah hah hah"). Careful practice in laughing and breathing (e.g. ·hhh) helps you discover the rhythm of breathing that your character is using. This rhythm is often quite consistent throughout the scene. "Inspiration" literally means "breathing."

Pauses. The script shows you a precise length of each pause. You may start by noticing that for long pauses there are sets of ten dots, each of which represents a second. The sign (.......... ....) indicates a two-second pause. When you begin rehearsing, count seconds aloud in whatever way you have used to play hide and seek, or to shoot time exposures with a camera. Most people use something like "one thousand one, one thousand two" to count a two-second pause. At the start of rehearsal, actually count the pauses aloud. Later, count silently.

You can use the same counting technique for medium-length pauses. Remember that "one thousand one" has four syllables. Hence for a pause of half a second, indicated by (.....), you might count "one thous" between vocalizations. After about a dozen repetitions, you can perform a medium-length pause without counting.

For short pauses, such as (..), perform a short break in your speaking rhythm. As you rehearse, keep going back to the transcription, and to your recording to see your pauses remain accurate.

Finally, notice that some pauses on your script appear within a line of dialogue spoken by one actor, while others have their own line. Here's an example of each:

1==> D: But- (........) I feel like I should go visit Ja:n

because I feel like that's what God wants me to do

(..........)

2==> M: We:ll do you mean you're not gonna go if I don't go:?

The first pause in this instance clearly falls within a speaker's turn. It appears after the word "but," after which it is clear D will continue speaking. The second pause is roughly the same length, but it occurs at the end of a sentence. During or after this pause either person could talk. This pause appears on its own line in the script because it's not really within anybody's speaking turn. Both actors must collaborate on such a pause.

A pause that appears on its own line is a *transition-relevant pause*, and it is not really either speaker's turn. A speaker change would be okay at this moment. Many transition-relevant pauses are significant to the way a scene is played. These pauses may occur at a crisis, a disagreement, a turn of events, and so on. In the example above, the pause comes after D (who has just realized M may not go with her to visit a terminally ill friend) asks M to declare whether she will visit the friend. After the pause, M turns the challenge around. At transition-relevant pauses, it is critical that you and your performance partner collaborate accurately. As you learn to perform these pauses ask yourself why they are occurring, and what effect they seem to have. These questions will help you discover things about your character's motives. The best way to check your accuracy in pauses is to rehearse in unison with the tape recording you made at the start of the rehearsal process.

At first each of these details—pauses, emphases, and so on—may seem needlessly picky. But as soon as you begin to mimic the actual performance details of your character's speech, you find that you begin (almost by accident) to discover some keys to the kind of character you are performing. You will begin to experience emotions as the character.

You may also begin to find things the character says creeping into your everyday speech. Students have reported to us that these exercises not only make them better performers, but more important, they become more accurate listeners.

If you rehearse regularly, it does not matter if you are an experienced actor. In some ways, students without previous stage experience have an advantage because they are less likely to try to sound dramatic, which can get in the way of accurate re-creation.

Experienced actors might still learn from this process, however. We have used these scripts as workshop experiences for the case of traditional plays. A few days of working on these scripts before starting to rehearse a traditional dramatic presentation can be useful in helping actors to make their speech sound like real life.

New uses for these techniques are still evolving; maybe you will invent one. These scripts, in combinations with tape recordings of them, have been used for a number of teaching and thinking experiences. We are now experimenting with this technique to aid the learning of foreign languages. We also use it to teach gender roles and other matters related to cultural diversity. Try performing someone very different from you. Walk a mile in their vocal moccasins.

Short Subjects on Courtship

These separate items may be performed together.
The first segment, the easiest to perform, is useful as a practice exercise.
The last segment may be performed as a monologue.

I Love You

	Sam:	So what time's her pl<u>a</u>ne come in?
	Tia:	Eleven thirty?
		(..........)
	Sam:	Eleven thirty, so what time are you gonna pick me up.
5	Pam:	Um a quarter to eleven.
		(.......... ....)
	Sam:	Okay.
	Sal::	Is that alright?
	Sam:	Yeah.
10		(.....)
		Yeah that's good.
		(..........)
		Alright
	Tia:	I love you.
	Sam:	I love you too.
15		(.......... .....)
	Tia:	See you in a <u>li</u>ttle bit then.
		(....)
	Sam:	Okay.
20	Sal::	A:lr<u>i</u>ghty.
		(..........)
	Tia:	Get a lot do:ne.
	Sam:	Okay.
	Tia:	I'll call you when I get ready.

25	Sam:	Alright.
	Tia:	Everything alright?
	Sam:	Yeah.
	Tia:	Okay, you sure,
	Sam:	Yeah.
30	Tia:	Uhm.
	Sam:	Alright.
	Tia:	I love you.
	Sam:	I l<u>o</u>ve you too.
	Tia:	Bye.
	Sam:	Bye.

PUMPING

	Rick:	Y<u>e</u>::<u>ss</u>? <u>h</u>eh <u>h</u>eh heh
	Pam:	Ri:ck?
	Rick:	˙hhh Ye(h)es?
	Pam:	You quee:r w(h)at're you doin
5		(....)
	Rick:	U:h I dunno what're you doin you queer bait heh heh=
	Pam:	=Nothing?
	Rick:	<u>E</u>h <u>e</u>h <u>ih</u>
	Pam:	What's go'n on.
10	Rick:	˙hhhhh O:h u:::h just sittin arou:nd jammin some tunes
	Pam:	Are ya=
	Rick:	=Mm hm?
		(...)
	Pam:	↑Hm:. (..) how fun
15	Rick:	What're y<u>ou</u> guys doin
		(...)
	Pam:	<u>We</u>ll- <u>u</u>m we've been looking for: apartments all d<u>a</u>:y and no:w

		(..) we're cooking ((rhymes with 'kicking'))
	Rick:	You're- you're punting
20	Pam:	Cooking
		(..)
	Rick:	Kicking
	Pam:	Cooking.
	Rick:	Cooking huh huh
25	Pam:	↑Ye::s.
	Rick:	Oh ho ho ho=
	Pam:	=Pumping, we're pumping. ↑Thuh huh huh ·hhh huh,
		what could that mean
	Rick:	U:h I don't kno:w u:h
30		(...)
	Pam:	Huh?
	Rick:	U- you got me heh heh heh
	Pam:	hhh You're the one that said the word.
		(.....)
35	Pam:	Right?
		(...)
	Rick:	Well 'at's what th- I thought that's whatyou said though
		(..)
	Pam:	Oh really
40	Rick:	Mm mm?
	Pam:	What does that word mean
		(....)
	Rick:	Pumping?
	Pam:	Pumping
45		(..........)
	Rick:	Puppy? or pumping.
	Pam:	Pumping.
		(..)

	Pam:	Isn't that what you said?
50

Pam: Isn't that what you said?

(..)

Rick: Pumping?

(..)

Pam: Yeah

Rick: S<u>e</u>xually heh heh heh

55 Pam: Is that what you mea(h)nt

Rick: ·<u>h</u>hh no(h) not at a(h)ll.

Pam: O(h)h,

Rick: ·<u>h</u>hhh Is that what <u>you</u> meant?

Pam: N<u>o</u>. not at <u>a</u>ll. ⌈huh <u>h</u>eh <u>h</u>eh <u>h</u>eh.

60 Rick: ⌊heh heh

Pam: ·h<u>hhhh</u>⌈hh

Rick: ⌊·hhhh⌈hh.

Pam: ⌊So <u>how</u> was your da:y

Rick: O:h it was <u>ni</u>fty

REST OF OUR LIVES

Sue: And then you walk in the doo:r. You walked in the doo::r

and I was so happy de see ya, you know?=

Ed: =I was happy de see you ↑too.

Sue: And th<u>e</u>n: you just all the sudden turned into Doctor Jekell and

5 Mister Hyde or whatever and just ch<u>a</u>nged your whole attitude

(..........)

Ed: Wud you think- (..........) okay I got p<u>i</u>ssed

when you poured the beer in my la:p

(.......... ....)

10 Ed: That made me mad.

Sue: And I didn't m<u>e</u>an to d<u>o</u> tha:t either,

I didn't even mean to ↑do that. That was a ↑acciden:t.

                              (........... ....)
      Ed: That wa(h)sn't- completely accident
15   Sue: Well ↑I was sittin there just going like this and you g- (.....)
               you move my a:rm like that you're- no: I know
               you're going ((BANG BANG BANG BANG)) ⌈like ↑tha:t.-
      Ed: ⌊huh hah
      Sue: And I was just- trying to be sweet and I uhh-
20   put- moved your arm aw:ay and you spi- spilt your beer:,
               and then you took your beer and went just like that.
                              (.......)
      Ed: hh huh huh huh huh ·hhh heh
      Sue: hhuh huh ⌈huh huh
25   Ed: ⌊huh huh
      Sue: An it jus- uh- (....) you know, jus ↑stupid stuff like that,
               I don't know
                              (.......... ....)
      Ed: We're jus stupid people.
30   (.......... ....)
      Ed: I jus- after everythin: (..........) one side of me tells me (..........)
               to never have anything to do with you again, (.......... ....)
               and I've felt that way, and the other side of me tells me (..........)
               you like her more than anybody else in the world,
35   (....)
               and you know damn well that y'all can be happy together
               if you work at it
                              (.....)
               and it'll come easy in time.
40   (.......... ....)
      Sue: Well ⌈this-
      Ed: ⌊So which side do I talk to hh listen to
                              (.......... ....)

45   Sue: Y'know mostly I've thought that too, but and- then again I've
      thought about- good Lord if we can't even ughhh (..........) get
      al:ong. (....) withou- one day without havin a argument, there's
      no way were gunna be able to get along for the rest of our li:ves

LAPSE REVISITED

      Gor: I'd gone out a couple times with this girl in Alpha Rho
          like a couple a weeks ago: and u:h like- taken her to parties
          and stuff and then- ·hhhh toda:y I told her I didn't
          want to g(h)o ou(h)t with her anym(h)ore huh
5   (.......)
      Nell: Oh we⌈:ll hhh
      Gor: ⌊Oh actually:s (.) I'm glad she got- the message because
          we had nothing in common and we would like
          talk on the phone and we'd go- (..........)
10   Nell: Hheh hih hih hih ·hh
      Gor: So. (........)
      Nell: Ehh hh
                 (.....)
      Gor: Ehh hh
15   Nell: So you gave her to the big punt huh
      Gor: ·hhhh ⌈Thee old one two ⌈kick hh
      Nell: ⌊hhh   ⌊Huh huh huh huh huh
          ·hhh Dr:op kick ⌈hah- huh ⌈huh
      Gor: ⌊Na(h)a- ⌊huh huh huh
20   ·hhhhh No:. I mean she's a nice girl an everything but
          then she sent me dumb gl- (.....) see I'd like for a while then I like-
          just like didn't call her: for like all last week (....) and like- er-
          what- er- um- (..........) and the:n so she sends me this valentine
          I got on Saturday it was like (..........) is something wro:::ng and

25		then- you kno:w if you wanna- not go out anymore
		lemme kno:w 'zlike Oh good thiss my ticket to freedom I'm-
	Nell:	Ehh hh hh hh ·hhhhh
	Gor:	((SNIFF))
	Nell:	Gordon Gordon Gordon:
30	Gor:	I dunno
		(...)
	Nell:	Did ↑you get a valentine in the paper?

I Saw Him

	Pat:	And I got in I guess about ten thirty (..........)
		And I went to ↑bed.
		(....)
5		Cause I mean you know I had to get up and everything
		and my parents came home I guess about ele-
		my mom and my sis came home about eleven
		·hhhhh and she changed she did all this stuff
		and you know how your parents walk around the hou:se
10		you know at night
	Dee:	Yeah
	Pat:	Well Mom was walking around the house-
		and she sees this truck parked out in front of our house.
		(..........)
15		and it was Brad's truck he parked out in front a my house.
		that Friday night.
		(..........)
		But I don't know what he did.
		(........)
20	Dee:	Like- (....) he wasn't there? he just-
	Pat:	I don't ⌈know if he was in his truck or not.
	Dee:	⌊parked?

		(.....)
	Pat:	See ↑I was asleep.
25		(..........)
	Dee:	Thats is bizarre did you ever ask him?
	Pat:	No: (.) huh uh I never had the ner:ve.
		(......)
	Pat:	because you ↑know how <u>p</u>arents are. (....) you know- (...)
30		with things
	Dee:	⌈Yeah.
	Pat:	⌊Like your mom goes oh Dee you know huh (...) a ↑car drove by
		and the car could be dark blue and she- I mea:n could be
		light blue and she'll say that's bl<u>a</u>:ck, you know=
35	Dee:	=Y<u>ea</u>h (.) Yeah
	Pat:	So I don't- I just- you know (..........)
		I never had the really the ner:ve
		(..........)
	Pat:	I mean, an I s<u>a</u>w him the other da:y.
40		and I just- I just- I was like in shock you know?
	Dee:	Mm hm
	Pat:	And I couldn't get my h<u>a</u>nd ↑up to w<u>a</u>ve to him
		·hhh and I just kept starin at him and he kept starin at me:?
		(.......)
45	Pat:	And it was like- cause I was in my <u>mo</u>ther's car
		and he'd <u>ne</u>ver seen me in that car.
		(..........)
	Pat:	And I was like sta:rin at him (...) he's like staring at me
		through his rear view mirror cause I was beh<u>i</u>nd him
50		(..)
	Dee:	Uh huh
	Pat:	And it was so ↑funny:- And then I was just- oh my god

I couldn't wave and I <u>shot</u> myself afterwards I was
so ma:d

55   (....)

Dee: O(h)o- jee(h)z

You Ain't Got No Buddies

Dan: Hello-
Al: Hey
Dan: H<u>e</u>:y.
Al: H<u>e</u>:y.=
5   Dan: =What's happnen=
Al: =Hey buddy?
Dan: Is this my buddy=
Al: =E:h you ain't got no buddies=
Dan: =What's happenen.
10   Al: Hey.
                              (..)
Dan: H<u>e</u>:y.=
Al: =Did u::h-
Dan: You ready for thanksgiving
15   Al: Ye::s
Dan: <u>Awr::ght</u>.=
Al: =Want some cheeseburgers and some- some onion rings, please
Dan: heh h<u>u</u>h huh huh ·hhh well ah was funny I was gonna call you: uh
           myself.
20   Al: Oh were you?
Dan: Ye:s. And na- here I <u>a</u>m, callin you- no you're calling m<u>e</u> I
           guess
Al: Naw I just wa:nta see- uh Kelly supposed to be over there for
           one oh four, did they make it y<u>e</u>sterday

25		(....)
	Dan:	U::h you know I don't know? ~
	Dan:	About the ceiling, huh
	Al:	Yeah=
	Dan:	=Okay.=
30	Al:	=About that thing and=
	Dan:	=And that w<u>a</u>ter leak and all that=
	Al:	=Yeah
	Dan:	Oh okay=
	Al:	=And all that stuff. So I just wanta let you kn<u>o</u>w that-
35	Al:	⌈you know-
	Dan:	⌊it's bein taken care of=
	Al:	=that they a:re (..) supp<u>o</u>sedly: gonna be come- what, you alls
		goin down tuh Laredo?
	Dan:	Yes ind<u>ee</u>d as a matter a fact ⌈yuh, leavin this afternoon.
40	Al:	⌊Ah good
	Al:	↑Oo:. On a jet plane? or-
	Dan:	U:h No, no we're drivinn O<u>h</u> gee(h)z, of cou(h)rse h<u>u</u>hh
		·hhh No we can't aff<u>o</u>rd that uh- that uh- that- that uh
		b<u>u</u>zz plane that they send down there.
45		No we're gonna- yeah we're gonna take off
		we got one a the g<u>i</u>rls here watchin the pl<u>a</u>ce for us
		(..)
	Al:	Oh yeah?
	Dan:	D'You know Donna, don'tcha
50	Al:	Donna (.) Donna with the big- wangers
		(....)
	Dan:	Yeah-⌈yeah, up in two o four?
	Al:	⌊↑A:::h.
	Dan:	The ⌈bi- you know
55	Al:	⌊Two-

Al:	Two oh four.=
Dan:	=Big girl.
Al:	Bi:g.=
Dan:	=We're talkin big everything's big on her=
60	Al:	=O:h Lord=
Dan:	=huh heh heh huh ↑huh huh huh huh huh=
Al:	=How sweet, how sweet
Dan:	In<u>dee</u>:d, indee:d, a:h yes: your- your type for sure
Al:	Yes
65	Dan:	·hh So what are you doin, for turkey day
Al:	O:h goin de go down to mom in law's.
Dan:	<u>O</u>h y'are.
Al:	Ye:ah=
Dan:	=Well 'at's uh- I guess sh- you have to d<u>o</u> that
70		every now and ⌈then huh?
Al:	⌊Ye:ah yeah we do it every goddamn time
	That's all right s'enj<u>o</u>yable.
Dan:	<u>h</u>hh hah huh huh huh huh (..) ·hhh well why not
Al:	E:h why not hail, Go eat goo:d and all that shit
75	Dan:	<u>O</u>h yeah yeah well at's my-
	my j<u>o</u>b every year is to make pecan pi:es.

THE UGLY HALF

Kay:	Colorado Data. This is Kay?
Red:	Hi, Kay, where's the ugly half.
Kay:	↑Hah hah hah hah, O:kay, Red, hold on just a moment
Red:	Thank you ~
5		((muzak))
Gil:	Hi ya Red
Red:	Hiya Gil
	(...)

	Gil:	Di'you get a call from <u>her</u> yet
10	Red:	I got through to her: little wh<u>i</u>le ago.
	Gil:	Okay
	Red:	u:m (......) <u>u</u>hh basically I think all she's lookin for is cable length and d<u>e</u>tail, which I didn't realize she was gonna w<u>a</u>nt,
	Gil:	Well now the- to- fill you in on the picture (....) ↑I've done
15		business with Sally in the p<u>a</u>st when we were doing three west cosmos, cable work and stuff
	Red:	Okay
		(......)
	Gil:	A:nd the reason I tried to hh <u>wa</u>rn you, <u>her</u> t<u>a</u>ke on this whole
20		scenerio is that uh course she should a been involved from the <u>very</u> very beginning
	Red:	Mmm.
	Gil:	And that myself as a vendor had n<u>o</u> business doing <u>any</u> work at Rocky Mountain Bell, or installing <u>any</u> cables or even a
25		prototype project without prior approval of their group,
	Red:	heh heh heh heh heh heh
	Gil:	You follow me?
	Red:	O::kay, horseshit
	Gil:	Well- that's- t<u>h</u>eir thing=
30	Red:	=Yeah okay
	Gil:	=Alright we're the contracts people we're the one that issue the bucks, and ya- you know what would happen Gil if I decided not to <u>pay</u> you now. (...) and you tell me that you have a piece of equipment over there already? (....) I said well
35		obviously Sally we may have to go <u>else</u>where maybe Mister Winter would have to cough it up outta <u>his</u> budget (.....) She goes well thats not the way we're talkin about she goes there's certain ways that this stuff should be d<u>one</u> and <u>no</u>body followed the rules on this one.

40		(....)
	Gil:	⌈I said Sally I can appreciate that
	Red:	⌊Mm mm, true enough
	Gil:	We're tryin to fix it no:w, (...) you know- (.....) cut us some slack,
		you know what I mean
45	Red:	Mm hm?
	Gil:	So- she's bent more over priorit- uh ha over the (...) the
		⌈process, tha:n the actual reality of what's goin on.
	Red:	⌊Yea:h
		(.......)
50	Red:	Okay ~
	Gil:	↑Ha swear
		(.....)
	Red:	O::kay so I stepped on her toes. hhh
	Gil:	We all did I mean I should have- known, soon as they mentioned
55		her name I should have- told you the way she was, but=
	Red:	=O:h well, I've never- (....) done any of that kind of stuff before
		you know as I said I had talked to Juana I talked to Cathy I
		talked to ·hh Sol and Joe they all knew what I was workin on=
	Gil:	=Sure=
60	Red:	=They said, you know ·hhh clear the floor:, make sure you got
		space so that we can do this stuff ·hhh Dave said you know while
		you're doin it get the printers off duh floor
	Gil:	↑Sure
	Red:	I said okay. (..) yeah, no problem
65	Gil:	Yeah
	Red:	So
	Gil:	We just didn't follow proper p (....) procedure=
	Red:	Yea::h I know protocawl hhh
	Gil:	So: I gotta- now look at thee other projects since she's lumpin
70		them together and get my lengths (....) for- for thee u:h (..) A N S

(....)

Red: Okay, do you need <u>me</u> to get you anything else I know I got you
the <u>one</u> the other day but is that sufficient or is there somethin
else I can help you with from here that'll (..) ·hhh get ya (.) you

75 know numbers and sizes and stuff ~

Gil: Maybe I'll just come over tomorrow and do it (....) get the
measurements and get her off our back.

Red: Okay, (..) yeah if you've got time otherwise I'll go <u>pace</u> em off

Gil: ⌈Ya:h, I can do it tommorrow

80 Red: ⌊And then like tell you how long but ·hhh okay if you've got a
chance stop in in the morning I should be here all morning

Gil: Okay=

Red: =So you know we can- <u>anything</u> you <u>don't</u> have <u>lengths</u> or
information on, that I can give you, you know well go ahead and

85 get her the info she needs to shut her up

(...)

Gil: Yeah

(.....)

Gil: She's just du:h, (.) at's just the way she is.

90 Red: Okay

Gil: So she was <u>fumin</u> yesterday shoulda

Red: Oh, ⌈well, I got a hold of her about lunch today =

Gil: ⌊huh ↑huh huh hoh

Red: =and ·hhh ↑a::h. She was a little abrupt but not bad, so=

95 Gil: =Aw that's good (..) okay

Red: ·hhhhhhh Okay ⌈I will see y'in the morning

Gil: ⌊Alright

Gil: Sounds good

Red: Alrighty

100 Gil: Buhbye

Red: Thanks,

ON SMOKING

	West:	Health Information Service may I help you?
	Lee:	Got your number yesterday off the t-television?
	West:	Uh uh
	Lee:	And u:m (.....) I was wonderin- um a- what type of help do y'all
5		assi<u>st</u>
		(...)
	West:	A:h well we offer uh a variety of publications, and we can put
		you in touch with different agencies? ·hhh tell me exactly what
		you're- what you're- looking for and maybe I can help you a
10		little bit mo:re ·hh in terms of what we can do:.
		(....)
		Or do you have a b- specific question about something?
	Lee:	·hhh Well this is the smoking line right? ~
	West:	·hhh U:m You want some information on smoking?
15	Lee:	⌈Uh huhh
	West:	⌊Or or on smoking cessation?
		(.......)
	Lee:	Uh huhh
	West:	Oka:y- u:m- are you a smoker no:w?
20	West:	Ye:s.
	Lee:	Oka:y u:m (...) uwhere do you li:ve. Do you live <u>in</u> Memphis?
		or do you live in: Tennessee?
	Lee:	Uh hu:h Jackson
	West:	Okay. (.) Jackson.
25	West:	·hhhhhhh Oka:y and um (......) Tell me a little more about yourself
		have you tried to stop smoking befo:re?
		(..)
	Lee:	Yes I ha:ve but- ·hhhh I: noticed that like when I eat?
	West:	Mm hm:?=

30	Lee:	=U̲:m. ·hh I- (...) I: w̲ant a cigarette but if I- if I'm eating
		chocolate or some-in ⌈some type of ca:ndy?
	West:	⌊Um hm
	West:	Mm hm
	Lee:	I- it takes the taste away oh- you know for a whi:le
35	West:	Mm hm:=
	Lee:	=And I won't need to smoke or if I'm wo:rkin I'm steady workin
	West:	Uh hu:h=
	Lee:	=I won't need a smoke like tha:t
	West:	Mkay h̲ow o̲ld are you:.
40	Lee:	I'm ninetee:n?
	West:	You're ninetee:n?
	Lee:	Uh huh=
	West:	=And h̲ow long have you been smo̲king.
	Lee:	I just started about t̲wo ye̲ars ago,
45	West:	Okay and how many packs a c̲igarettes a day do you smo̲:ke.
	Lee:	I don't (.) I just smoke about a h̲alf a pa:ck.
	West:	·hhh Okay well- you know its- it's really- u:m great that you
		called and ·hhhhh u:m its and it's easy when you're- (.......)
		smo̲king as little as you're smoking to stop, and it's a real good
50		idea to go ahead and stop now since you're so young. Instead of
		w̲aiting until you get older and of probably smoking mo:re. So
		·hhhh um I'll be glad to send you some information and some
		information about ·hhhh u:m you know the benefits of stopping
		smoki:ng and um (.......) some t̲ips on how to quit
55	Lee:	Uh huh ~
	West:	·hhhh Lemme explain to you that- ·hhhh um (..) tha- the- (..) t̲ars
		and the nicotine in cigarettes ·hhhhh a̲re addictive its just like
		taking a drug. (....) uh that you get addicted to.
	West:	·hhhh and so it takes you a while to get it out of your system
60		and n̲ot be addicted to it.

Lee:	Um hum
West:	A:nd um (...) you know- that's- -that's why you have the craving for cigare:ttes.
Lee:	Uh huh=
65 West:	=And uh ·hhhh a lot of times- smokers do- s- stop and then u:m (....) try to- u:h- substitute with candy or- other things and that- can tend to cause a weight gain.
West:	So- (..........) you know you-you probabably ·hhhh need to be aware of that when you've substituting something else=
70 Lee:	=But me: I'm only- What- like about a hunern ten or fifteen pounds maybe I need to g(h)ain ⌈a little weight
West:	⌊Maybe you do:.
West:	Maybe you're work just fine for you(h)u
Lee:	Yeah
75 West:	Anyway- I'll be glad to send you some information and I hope that it'll help, Let me get your name and address.
Lee:	hO:kay
West:	Okay
	(.....)
80 West:	What's your name?
Lee:	Jasmine Lee,
West:	Okay,
Lee:	124 South Street,
West:	Okay
85 Lee:	Jackson, Tennessee ~
West:	Oka:y, a::nd ·hhh Let me see: (...) u::m (..........) I need to ask you a couple of questions just for our office- files, ·hhhhh um you said that you were ninetee:n?
Lee:	Ye:s
90 West:	Okay ·hhh And um I need to ask you a couple questions about your education and ethnic background have you um graduated

	from high school?=

	from high school?=
Lee:	=No but I would like to go back if I had a chance
West:	Oka:y ·hhh and- your ethnic background are you white (.) black
	(.) asian, (.) hispanic?
Lee:	Mi<u>x</u>ed hh
West:	Okay wull-
Lee:	Mostly black
West:	Okay, let's put that. ~
	Okay- hhhh great I will send you some information and I hope it
	helps
	(.....)
West:	And- good luck I hope you- make it huh huh
Lee:	Yes ma'am.
West:	·hhhh Okay th<u>a</u>nks=
Lee:	hhh<u>u</u>h. Thank⌈you
West:	⌊Byeb<u>ye</u>
Lee:	Bye

Line numbers: 95, 100, 105 appear in left margin.

You'd Vote for the Devil If He Was Republican

D:	Wedo, we sound <u>i</u>gnorant, we have nothing to talk about
	that's (..........) ⌈int-
M:	⌊relevant?
M:	·hh Sa⌈ :y.
D:	⌊intellectual.
M:	What are you goin be doing March twenty fi:rst.
	(..........)
D:	Well ↑I don:t ↑kno:w Mother lemme check my calendar.
D:	↑I don't know what I'm gonna ⌈be doing
M:	⌊I need: two more
	people to do: <u>p</u>honing for Phil Gramm.

Line numbers: 5, 10 appear in left margin.

(...)

	D:	I: am not voting for Phil Gramm.
		I'm not working for the ma:n, I don't- like him.
15	M:	Why not.
	D:	Because ↑I just ↑don't no:w you find somebody else,
		I'm not voting- I am (..) twenty-three years old
		and I can vote- for who I want to now.

(.....)

20	D:	You can't make me you can't make me you can't make me=
	M:	=There's a little orange marmalade in there-
		Okay, I just thought maybe you might li:ke to.
		He's very intelligent and he's been in Congress for a long
25		⌈ti:me
	D:	⌊↑Mother:- you like him because he's a Democrat and
		he turned Republican you'd vote for- (.......)
	M:	Well listen (.) if- if he win:s the:- u::h (...)
		nomination for the: ·hhhhhhhh to run for Senator on the
30		Republican ticket then will you vote for him?

(...)

	D:	I don't know?

(.....)

	M:	Well see it's between he and Mossbacher.
35		⌈And if he-
	D:	⌊I like Mossbacher.
	M:	Well I know but if Mossbacher doesn't get the nomination=
	D:	=I ↑kno:w, what you're saying I don't know
		if I'll vote for him or ↑not.
40		(..)
	D:	I don't particu'rly like the man.

(.....)

	M:	Well what do you know about him.

	D:	↑We:ll? (...) I've just seen him and I don't know if I like him
45		or not.
		(.......... .....)
	M:	We:ll=
	D:	=I ↑may vote- s- a straight Democratic ticket hh
		(..........)
50	M:	Well, (...) whatever turns you o:n.
	D:	huh huh ·hhhhhhh You are such a d- .hhhhhhhhhh
		⌈You'd vote for-
	M:	⌊I-
		(.......... .....)
55	M:	What.
	D:	You'd vote for (....) hhh the devil if he was Republican
	M:	No I wouldn't I- I did get a real nice letter from uh
		Mossbacher he was the speaker at the Republican
		Ladies Club last week ⌈I didn
60	D:	⌊Why don't you like Mossbacher
		(...)
	M:	Misty I do like him he's a nice young man, but he's
		a baby.
	D:	he is ↑not a ↑ba:by ⌈mother:?
65	M:	⌊He is a baby thi- he's just runnin
		this time to get his name out, he-he doesn't have- (....)
		have any idea that ⌈he's gonna win this
	D:	⌊We:ll I agree:: I- I agree:
		but you gotta start somewhe:re.
70	M:	Well that's fi:ne, (..) ⌈but-
	D:	⌊That's what they were sayin about
		Mark White a- few years ago now look where he is.=
	M:	=Hey did you see his pla::ne?
		(....)

75	D:	Who
	M:	Mark Whi:te.
	D:	Oh Mark White makes me s:ick.=
	M:	=Did you see his three and a half million dollar jet?
	D:	⌈N:o::.
80	M:	⌊that's <u>out</u>fitted like a cadilla:c?
	D:	Oh yeah
	D:	Yeah
	D:	U:h hh he makes me ill.
		(..........)
85	M:	We:ll, maybe we better not talk about politics
		(..........)
	M:	While we're ⌈being recorded
	D:	⌊Well I-
		(.......... .....)
90	M:	We:ll. hh anyway I need somebody
	D:	W- We:ll, I need to go:.

CAT IN THE HOUSE

	Mel:	Hello?
		(......)
	Sam:	Hey chief did you say that cat over at three hundred Alice was in the house?
5		(....)
	Mel:	Yeah (..) ·hhh when <u>we</u> were there it was
	Sam:	Was that yesterday?
	Mel:	Yeah
		(....)
10	Sam:	O::ay the n<u>ei</u>ghbor lady says she's been puttin food out for it but tuh, she never has s<u>ee</u>n it (...) and u::h when I told her you said

it was <u>in</u> the house she said ↑oh dear I don't think that cat's

suppose to b<u>e</u> in the house cause ·hhhh she's puttin food out by

the g'ra:ge and they propped the g'rage door open so the cat

could get in and ou:t

           (....)

Mel: Woah.=

Sam: =And uh somebody must=

Mel: =Maybe that's why that cat wan'd to get out so bad.

Sam: Maybe that's ri:ght.

           (....)

Sam: heh heh ·hhh okay, he is ahhem ⌈it was in the house, huh?

Mel: ⌊It was-

Mel: It was in the the house when I was there, yeah

Sam: O:kay I:'ll better tell her that ↑that cat in't supposed to be in

there.

           (.....)

Mel: Ca- uh=

Sam: =She said so. She said they told her the cat was supposed to be

in the garage and she's just puttin food on the patio, ·hh she said

the food's been ↑gone every time she goes back over there but

there's other cats and dogs wanderin around problably eatin it

           (......)

or possums.

Mel: (....)

Sam: ⌈heh heh ·hhh

Mel: ⌊Nkay, well it sounds like she probly <u>not</u> supposed to be in there

then

Sam: Yeah it does ·hhh well, Harvey said if we got any more questions

talked t'him just now and he said maybe he oughtta call the

people in Chicago and be sure.

Mel: Mm hm

	Sam:	But I'll talk to:, John Benn and his wife next door again
		·hh tell her what you said
45	Mel:	Okay
	Sam:	Thanks again
	Mel:	Good enough, see ya later=
	Sam:	=You betcha (.) b'bye̲p

LIKE A PRETZEL

	Sam:	Don't worry about him
		(........)
		He's u:h (..) you know if he wants to be that wa:y well (......)
		then he's gonna
5		(..)
		There's nothin you can do about it
		(....)
		I me:an (..........) let's f̲ace it you're not the k̲ind of girl that he
		wants you to be
10		(..........)
		A::nd there's nothing you can do about that.
		·hhhhhhh unless you just be:nd like a pre̲tzel
		(.....)
		H̲huh huh ⌈huh huh hah hah hah ·h̲hh
15	Sue:	⌊↑huh ↑huh ·hhhh- but pre̲tzels brea:k
	Sam:	Yeah (.) huh ⌈huh
	Sue:	⌊huhu̲h ·hhh
	Sam:	Yeah- (....) we̲ll u:h (....) what are you do̲in all week
		(..........)
20	Sue:	We:ll, i'nt the week almost over?
		(..........)
	Sam:	Wha̲t are you doin this weekend.
		(....)

	Sue:	Nuthin I d'know Mimi was gonna come in town:,
25		and I was gunna read Shakespeare and that's about it.
	Sam:	·hhh Yeah, I got to u:h (..........) read some stuff a my own too
		(....)
	Sue:	I- (........) now I kn<u>o</u>w, okay: well- (....) so you think I should just
		blow him <u>o</u>ff then
30	Sam:	Un hn? (..) If you don't like him,
		If you want to k<u>ee</u>p him k<u>ee</u>p him (.......) you know but
		⌈u:::h ·hhh don't don't start treatin m<u>e</u>=
	Sue:	⌊But- what if he zih-
	Sam:	=like you want to go out with me: you know if if if he's your guy
35		and you like him a whole bunch ·hhhh you kno:w,
		don't be <u>t</u>easin me: and manipulatin ↑me
	Sue:	·hhhh Well what if he's a friend of mine.
		(...)
	Sam:	⌈That's ↑fine
40	Sue:	⌊And I don't want to lose his friendship and he:-
	Sam:	That's fi:ne, but you know you can't let him just- you know, run
		your l<u>i</u>fe
	Sue:	So what'll I do I just say Bobby no more n gimme back my key,
		yuh can't come over any more unless I ⌈invite you
45	Sam:	⌊Yeah he has a <u>key</u>
		to your house?
		(..)
	Sue:	He: ⌈<u>too</u>k one
	Sam:	⌊<u>hh</u>ih
50		(...)
	Sam:	We::ll- yi:h=
	Sue:	=And I took it b<u>a</u>:ck, and- and we had a f<u>i</u>ght, and then he took it
		again- ·hhh and I just think I'm ⌈just gonna haf ta
	Sam:	⌊Well the guy is w<u>a</u>lkin all over

55   you, if you don't like him you know, then ↑dump him
                     (....)
    Sam: U::m <u>but</u> you know- I mea- he's a nice guy, you don't want to be
            mean to him ·hhhh <u>but</u> <u>just</u> u::h (..........) show him the way it ↑is.
                     (.......... .....)
60 Sam: You know?
                     (..........)
            I don't know wh<u>a</u>t to tell ya (...) you know (..) I can't make
            decisions for ya
                     (.......... .....)
65   I think you're nice girl I like you and I'd like to start taking you
            out (...) and u:h (..........) but if <u>he's</u> around (....) then we're jus
            going be- friends, you know, we'll just be buddies and u:h (.....)
            ⌈then we'll give y-
    Sue: ⌊Al:right, well how about ·hhh if he's just around as a friend or
70   just sometimes ·hhh and I can go out with everybody and
            anybody
                     (........)
    Sue: That's fine
    Sam: Okay ~
75   (..........)
    Sue: Well you wanna go eat sushi tommorrow?
                     (.......... ....)
    Sam: U:::::m. I don't know, man you got all these <u>guys</u> surroundin you
            (.....) I just don't know. (.) I really don't ·hhh Let's go out and u::h
80   (.....) go t'Sixth Street or sum'n
                     (..........)
    Sue: Why- I wanna go eat sushi.
                     (..........)
    Sam: You <u>do</u>, huh
85   (....)

	Sue:	<u>D</u>on't worry I'll pay for my own.
		(..........)
	Sam:	You are such a bitch, you are <u>such</u> a bitch.
	Sue:	Wait a minute, wait a minute, this has gotten a little too far,
90		↑why am I a bitch?
		(.....)
	Sam:	You'e manipulative.
	Sue:	~ Because I don't wanna go to Sixth Street, or because I'll pay
		for my own.
95	Sam:	Well th<u>a</u>t's not it, you know (.) I don't know (..) I don't know.
	Sue:	Because you say you don't wanta t<u>a</u>ke me out and spend money
		en investment on me ·hhh well you know why can't=
	Sam:	=Well girls <u>are</u> an investment you know=
	Sue:	=Why can't we be <u>fri:</u>ends, ·hhh why- why do I have to be your
100		investment why can't I just be one of the guys and we're goin to
		eat sushi together
		(....)
	Sam:	Okay: let's go eat sushi tomorrow
		(....)
105	Sue:	Okay.
	Sam:	Okay?
		(....)
	Sue:	You know and I think Mimi might come to town and she loves
		sushi ↑too the ↑three of us can go.

TALKING COKE MACHINE

DJ:	Three nine zero. K B A K, the local lines are available
	now's your turn. (....) You wanta get <u>i</u>n, you been trying to get in
	and you hadn't been able to now's your chance let's take a
	long distance call, Hi you're on K B A K where you calling from.

5	Bel:	↑Lipton
	DJ:	↑Lipton. Good to h<u>ea</u>r from you.
	Bel:	Oh yeah.　　　　～
	Bel:	·hhhh U:::m you were mention' while ago about- Johnny Carson
		talkin about Coke machines? ⌈What does he say ⌈about th<u>e</u>m.
10	DJ:	⌊Huh　　　　⌊O h h huh
		Na(h)w it was a ·hhh that's what they were calling thee
		De Lorean automobile right after John De Lorean=
	Bel:	=↑O:::h.=
	DJ:	=was (.) arrested for: cocai:ne- trafficking=
15	Bel:	I thought maybe he had an experience that I had with one
		recently ·hhh As you know I can b<u>a</u>rely see
		my h<u>a</u>nd in front of my f<u>a</u>ce ·hhhh a:nd I get out <u>rare</u>ly.
	DJ:	Um=
	Bel:	=Well ·hhhh my daughter parked in front of u:h u:h grocery store
20		and I got out to get me a Coke while she was in there
	DJ:	Yeah?
	Bel:	And I put my two quarters in, ·hhh got my <u>can</u> Coke and just as I
		started to open it ·hh ↑that damn thing started talkin to me
	DJ:	Huh the Coke machine did?=
25	W:	=↑Yeah
		(....)
	Bel:	Thank you for gettin a Coke and bl<u>a</u>nkety blank ·hhhh and I
		turned around real quick to see if- you know there is somebody
		ar<u>ou</u>nd me ↑I didn't realize that it was <u>it</u>
30	DJ:	Yeah ·hhhh yeah they got some talkin Coke machines now
		I didn't realize they had on:e- in this area but they-
		·hhhh there was a story came out about a year and a <u>half</u> ago
		·hhhh about talking Coke machines.
	Bel:	Well this is in front of Super Bee in Lipton

35	DJ:	↑Huh huh huh huh huh huh⌈huh huh
	Bel:	⌊hu:h
	Bel:	This one (.) just scared the fool out of me=
	DJ:	=I'll bet it did
	Bel:	Cause there I was I thought I'z out there by myself, and sure
40		enough I was, but ·hhh at- ·hhhh lady in that talkin machine was
		sure telling me uh- a:ll about it
	DJ:	I'll I'll be dar- I've had a few- I've had a few conversations with
		Coke machines in my time.=
	Bel:	=huh ·hhh I have too but not like that
45	DJ:	Nawhh
	Bel:	Hah. When they take my money and not gimme anthing in
		return?=
	DJ:	=Yeah or right if the Coke machine says thank you for buying a
		Coke ·hhhh you kick it and say but I wanted a Doctor Pepper
50	Bel:	Hah ↑hah ·hhhh but a:nyway when I- my daughter got in back in
		the car I's tellin her about it and she laughed at ↑me ·hhhh
		she said poor Mama you go so seldom you don't even know the
		Coke machines⌈talk to you anymore
	DJ:	⌊hah hah
55	DJ:	My ↑car talks to me
	Bel:	Oh I've heard those too.
	DJ:	Yeah my car talks to me, real sweet voice=
	Bel:	=Uhah hah ·hhhh u:m- bu di- have ↑you ever: read this book um
		·hhhh Dooms Day Nineteen Ninety Ni:ne.
60	DJ:	No I haven't
		·hhh I've heard about it but I haven't gotten to read it yet.=
	Bel:	=I wished you'd read that, that's a most hair raisin thing
		when you read it- ·hhhh and stop an think a-=
	DJ:	=Oh Lordy I can't afford to read a hair raisin book I don't have

65		any hair left to rai:se.
	Bel:	Maybe it'll ↑grow you some.
	DJ:	u↑Hah hah hah hah=
	Bel:	=Hah hah ·hhh bu:t u:::h (.) It was u:h (....) went to pre:ss in
		nineteen eighty and it told things that was goin to happen in
70		eighty three?
	DJ:	Yeah
		(...)
	Bel:	And by gum it ↑did.
		(........)
75	DJ:	Hmmm.
	Bel:	And I want you tell- and about the earthquakes anyway it's the
		coming up ·hh of it won't be the end of ti:me in nineteen ninety
		nine ·hh but we'll ha:ve ou:r (..) bienium is that what it's called
		~
80	DJ:	I'll check around and see if I can find it
		(....)
	W:	Anyway I- I get that from my- on my blind readin machine
		you know
	DJ:	Alright
85	W:	And that was so: interesting I want you'd know I's- awake all
		night listening to it (...) I couldn't st- it's o:n cassette
	DJ:	Yeah=
	Bel:	=Way I get- ·hhhh and it is just super
	DJ:	All right.
90	DJ:	·hhhh Well that sounds good take care of
		yourself I gotta move ⌈along.
	Bel:	⌊huh All ↑righty
	DJ:	Bye bye now
95	Bel:	Bye bye
	DJ:	It i:s thirteen away from two o'clock three nine zero
	K B A K:	still your line is available. What cha waitin for?

LAPSE FOR WORDS

	Den:	Hello?
	Gor:	Denise?
	Den:	Yeah.
	Gor:	Thiz Gordon
5	Den:	Hi
	Gor:	Hi how are you.
	Den:	.hhh I'm okay how you doin h
	Gor:	Alright (.) I have the cold now?

                                  (...)

10   Den: Hu:h?=

            Gor: =I've a- I got a cold while I was at A and M.

            Den: .hhh Oh goo:d ⌈hih hih ·hh ·hh ·hh

            Gor: ⌊Yeah really, um

            Den: ⌈·h h h h

15   Gor: ⌊D'you enjoy your parents coming up here

                                    (.)

            Den: Ther've- They've left already

            Gor: Oh really

            Den: Yea:h

20   (....)

            Den: ⌈But-

            Gor: ⌊D'y'ave a goo- (....) you had a good time?

            Den: Yeah I di:d, I had a lot of fun.

                                    (....)

25   Gor: T's good

            Den: It was grea:t

                                    (....)

            Gor: We:ll. I got your card. h

                                    (..)

30	Den:	Yeah. hhhh
	Gor:	A::nd ((SNIFF)) I guess you prob'ly read me right.
		It pro'ly is some'n wrong
		(.....)
	Den:	Hang on jis second okay I'm a switch phone
35	Gor:	Okay
		((long pause))
	Den:	Okay.
	Gor:	.hhhh ⌈U:::m
	Den:	⌊Ann I got it
40		(....)
	Den:	Okay.
	Gor:	I- actually w'd rather talk to you in person but I don't think
		I'm gonna be able make a meeting cause I- now have a
		headache and- ⌈fever and everything
45	Den:	⌊Yeah hh
	Gor:	·hhhhhhhh Bu:t u:m (.....) I think maybe u- u I w- um
		would like tuh- stop really goin ou:t- at least for right no:w
	Den:	Yeah
	Gor:	·hhh U::m I jus- hhhhhh (.....) u::h ·hhh I feel really ba:d cause I-
50		u:m (..........) ((SNIFF)) I wish- I think I just we don't have
		as much in common as: I think we both tho:ught
		(...)
	Den:	Yeah
	Gor:	Bu:t- u:m cause I know sometimes we're both
55		at just a lapse for words and=
	Den:	=huh huh
	Gor:	I'm a speech major I ⌈duh(h)
	Den:	⌊Mm: hm:
	Gor:	U:m (......) bu:t- and I wish I had more time-
60		and tu:h even to get to know you better

	Den:	Yeah
	Gor:	U:m but I mean I'm- so busy and you're so busy and
		I feel ba:d that I can't do anything and so I'll
	Den:	⌈Yeh
65	Gor:	⌊feel bad when I can't call you and ·hhhh and whatever and uh
	Den:	I know
	Gor:	Or go out and do anything with you even like tha:t.
	Den:	Yeah I know what chyou me:an.
		(..........)
70	Gor:	But uh (..........) I still wanna be in good friend with ya hhh
	Den:	Yeah
		(.........)
	Gor:	⌈But
	Den:	⌊I just- (.......) I think part of it- I think part of the problem the
75		hhhh huh- the loss f- for words and all that, is (..........) u:h
		I mean like last time we went out I was so tired hhuh
		·hhh you know (.....) and (...) u- I'm jus- (.......... ...) s:o (....)
		I work so hard all week, you know
	Gor:	Oh yeah
80	Den:	Then I just collapse on weekends huh huh ·hhh so:
		I mean (..........) you know I- I really (..........)
		I think the busyness is a lot of it
	Gor:	·hhh Yeah=
	Den:	=Because- I just ge:t (.......... ...) I dunno huh huh
85	Gor:	Yeah (.) it's hard tu:h ((SNIFF)) do anything much I-less
		besides schoolwork an:d- and something else on top of that
	Den:	Yeah (..) it is
	Gor:	And you're doin so much and (.) I'm doin so much and ((SNIFF))
		I'm pro'bly- (..........) overdo. (.) too much ~
90		(.......... .....)
	Den:	We:ll huh

	(..........)
Gor:	((SNIFF)) We:ll um
Den:	hhhh ·hhh
95	Gor:	Don't ⌈wanta ruin your da:y or anything
Den:	⌊So
	(......)
Den:	No: hhh I mean- (.......) I just-
Gor:	And I apologize for- you know not talkin to
100		you earlier ⌈even
Den:	⌊That's okay
	(..........)
Den:	I understand.
	(..........)
105	Den:	I me:an I just need a little ti:me. too
Gor:	Yeah
	(......)
Den:	And (..........) y'know hhh
	(..........)
110	Gor:	Who knows maybe later or some ⌈thing
Den:	⌊Right
	(..........)
Den:	Maybe hhuh ·hhh Maybe after the show's over
	and I have a little ti:me=
115	Gor:	=Huh huh
	(..........)
Den:	Would be:- (....) really nice
Gor:	Yeah
Den:	Yeah
120		(.......... ....)
Den:	So
Gor:	Okay well I'm g'let you go

Den:	Yeah
Gor:	Um, take care, I will s still talk to you, hope you'll still talk to me
125 Den:	Sure a course
Gor:	Nkay
Den:	And (.....) we'll have to go out sometime
Gor:	Okay, good deal=
Den:	=Have fun
130	(..)
Gor:	Alright
Den:	Okay
Gor:	Good, see you later
Den:	I'll talk to you later,
135 Gor:	⌈Bye
Den:	⌊Bye bye

Birthday Party

M:	Tell my honey to get on the telepho:ne=
D:	=He ain't gone come momma (..) Jafari is not gone come cause he playin with those dominoes, he lo:ve dominoes.
M:	Tell him Granny- ~ Tell Jafari that- if he'll get on the
5	telephone, I'll (.) buy him a birthday cake
	(....)
D:	Jafari
	(....)
	Jafari
10	(......)
	Granny say if you get on the telephone she'll buy you
	a birthday cake
	(...)
Boy:	She ain't gon buy me that=

15	D:	↑U::h huh hah hah ·hhh Mo:mma ·hhh he say she a:in't gone
		buy me that n he was shakin his he:ad no.
	M:	huh ↑huh ↑huh
	D:	Like he'd know what you were up to
	M:	Tell him I'ma have his birthday party here at the ↑hou:se.
20	D:	Granny say she gone have your birthday party there at the
		house
		(...........)
	Boy:	Hu:h.
	D:	He say (.) hu:h.
25		(.....)
	D:	But he don't want his birthday par:ty to be- at home,
		he want it to be at Macdonalds or Show Bi:z.
	M:	↑Uh huh
	D:	So I don't know yet momma I might still give it at the house
30		like I normally do or I might just go on to give it at Showbiz.=
	M:	=I think he'll like it better at Showbiz=
	D:	=Yea::h, I think ⌈so too
	M:	⌊I'll kinda help you with that too.
		(....)
35	D:	⌈Alright
	M:	⌊How mu- how much do it cost.
	D:	I'n't know I need to call they said about thirty or forty
		dollars.
		(...)
40	M:	↑That's not ↑much?
	D:	I know I- I told u::h daddy last year that ↑we paid more-
		havin it at ho:me, ·hh than we do havin it at Macdonalds or
		Showbiz and they get (.) food and icecre:am
	M:	An:d then they see Buffalo ⌈Bo:b ain't it
45	D:	⌊hhuhh Billy Bo:b, Momma ⌈huh
	M:	⌊hh huh

		(........)
	D:	Jerry. Momma ca:lled Billy Bob Buffalo Bo:b.
		(....)
50	M:	↑huh ↑huh
	D:	·hhh Yeah, he'll get chance to see Billy Bo:b, and (..) he'll have a nice time but he can only invite so many people you know but- ·hhh you know we won't- have that many people anyway.
55		(....)
	D:	Jus:t like Coree:n and
		(...)
	M:	Well ↑I'll help I'll help on his uh: birthday pa:rty
	D:	Mm alright.
60	M:	Help on my baby's birthday party
	M:	(.........)
	D:	⌈Al:right
	M:	⌊This is gonna skunk goes to see Billy Bo:b
	D:	So he can cry:?
65	M:	You can invite Coree:n?
	D:	And Chris:topher:
		(....)
	D:	⌈An Lush-
	M:	⌊Now who is Christopher.
70	D:	He's uh Vanessa baby
	M:	Okay that's right, (.) Christopher?
	D:	Lushan:dra
	M:	Lushandra
	D:	⌈An:d=
75	M:	⌊Then- Ethel li'l bo:y? (..) li'l girl?
		(...)
	D:	Ah-=
	M:	=Is he walkin

		(..)
80	D:	N: yes (...........) but on- only thing about that is I don't know
		if Ethel n them gonna come an I don't wanna be,
		you know
	M:	Yea:h suh Ethel is not dependable.
	D:	Uh unh. (....) an Kim not either so I don't know about the
85		neighborhood ki:ds ⌈goin to Showbiz
	M:	⌊Now Lisa bring her little baby
	D:	Yeah Lisa probably bring her little ba:by
		(......)
	D:	And who else
90		(....)
	M:	U::h
	D:	I'm tryin to think uh little Vick can bring her little boy
		(....)
	D:	Is he walkin
95	M:	Oh ye:ah. ~
	D:	Momma u:h Janey's up here tryin to do the Bugaloo.
	M:	My goo:dne:ss
	D:	huhh You need to see her (.) she look so ↑funny?
	M:	Wha- what's J- what's Jafari doin
100	D:	He laughin at her

DAD

	Dad:	Hello
	Wil:	Dad?
	Dad:	Yeah
		(..)
5	Wil:	Huh- ↑um (..) you know how bad the roads are now
	Dad:	Yeah just came home.

<pre>
                    (..........)
              just drove in,
                    (......)
10   Wil: Uh⌈huh
      Dad: ⌊Not too bad.
                    (....)
      Wil: Right.
                    (...)
15   Dad: They: aren't chyet,
                    (.......... .....)
      Wil: ⌈w-
      Dad: ⌊They're pretty good.
      Wil: ((off phone)) Mom
20   (.......... ...)
      Dad: So I'd magine granma n granpa (.) still plan on comin
                    (..........)
      Wil: Well- how bout- we com- come back here tonight.
                    (........)
25   Dad: What for.
                    (....)
      Wil: Because Shari n Teri gonna be here (...) and Fay n Al
                    (.......... ....)
      Dad: ↑hhu:h hee huh huh well it would be late- pro'ly by the time you
30   get back there and tomorrow we have your birthday party here.
      Wil: Not mine
      Dad: In the aft- I mean Carol's (..........) with the folks out here n
      Wil: What time's that=
      Dad: =It's spose be my day anyway (.....) u::m (..)
35   Wil: W'l I know but you're gunna have us all next weekend ~
      Dad: Since the roads are bad I figured you might as well stay here
              and you wouldn't have to be ·hhh goin around back n forth,
</pre>

so forth
         (..........)

40   Dad: Sides I'd like to see ya.
              (...)
            Si:des, I cn- ·hhhh I can lift uh (......) all the weight
            you got on there, fiftyfour times.
              (......)

45   Wil: Yeah hh
              (.......... .....)

     Dad: I worked out on it twice.
              (.......... ....)

     Dad: So I gotta go feed your horsie and put him in he's out she's
50   outside

     Wil: Well Mom doesn't think it's a good idea we go anywher:e today.
              (.......... .....)
            cause it's sleeting right now, ice
              (.......)

55   Dad: Yeah I just now drove in here. (..) the roads aren't- they're
            better now than they were this morning
            but that dudn't mean they're goin stay good I mean
            I think they're goin get worse but it's been kinda raining
            so they're ·hhhh clearer now than they were before
60   (.......... ....)

     Dad: Highway fifty's no problem comin in, but- that doesn't mean it
            won't- get worse (.) later tonight (...) if it snows a bunch
              (..........)

     Wil: Well-
65   Dad: They're not good (.......... .....) just haf take it slow
              (...)

     Wil: What about comin back here tonight.
     Dad: ·hhh Well I just don't think that makes any sense, Honey

	Wil:	I̲ do
70		(..........)
	Dad:	Well, (...) I don't, I just think at's kinda ridiculous
		(.....)
	Wil:	⌈hhhh ((pouty puff))
	Dad:	⌊N We got that party tomorrow
75		(.......)
	Wil:	⌈so I'm nuh-
	Dad:	⌊And Sunday's supposed to be my day anyway
	Wil:	Well you're gonna have us a̲l̲l̲ next weekend
		(..........)
80	Dad:	Well ne̲x̲t weekend yeah,
		(......)
	Wil:	(h)Yeah (.......... ....) from Thursday on,
		(..........) ~
	Dad:	O̲kay (..........) well we'll see ya in a little bit (...)
85		when granma n granpa (..) pick ya up
	Wil:	Okay
	Dad:	Okay ⌈Bye bye.
	Wil:	⌊wai- Dad?
	Dad:	Yeah
90	Wil:	What time are they goin pick us up
	Dad:	U:h, quarter four,
	Wil:	Ahright
	Dad:	Kay bye bye
	Wil:	Alright bah

YOU MAD AT ME

Amy:	You mad at me
Guy:	N̲o̲ not at all.

	Guy:	You gave me this <u>look</u> when I just filled in-
		when I filled in Suzy then=
5	Amy:	=Yeah because I didn't (....)
	Guy:	Well you shouldn't a brought it up
		⌈with her sitting in the room
	Amy:	⌊I realized that afterwards but if I gave you the <u>look</u>
		you don't have to go into detail ⌈about it
10	Guy:	⌊I ↑didn't
		(..)
	Amy:	⌈You ↑di:d.
	Guy:	⌊I just said who he ↑was.
	Amy:	You set there and told her who he was,
15		what Suzy knew about him and everything
	Guy:	No I didn't say anything except fo:r what you would get on
		the bare bone hello who are you, ↑Oh really so what do you do
		well I'm working over at the Air Force base as a doctor.
		I don't think that's very much information to give out
20		(.......... ....)
	Amy:	No: it was my fault to mention it ⌈I admit
	Guy:	⌊That's right
	Amy:	Bu:t you didn't have to go and elaborate when I gave you
		⌈such a look
25	Guy:	⌊I <u>didn't</u> elaborate beyond your look
		(........)
	Amy:	⌈You ↑di:d.
	Guy:	⌊All I ↑sa:id was that he worked or was in thee ↑Air Force
		(....)
30	Amy:	You didn't have to say what his name is you didn't have to say
		have you <u>heard</u> about him
		(.......... .....)
	Guy:	Well beca:use you brought it up (....) and she's sitting there (.....)
		I don't know, I think it's rude to talk about people when:- when

```
35        everyone ⌈in the room doesn't know
   Amy:          ⌊I'm sorry you shoud've said that's nice and
          then that's it and just changed the subject
                        (..)
   Guy:   ⌈I see-
40 Amy:   ⌊Because you realized when I gave you that look that I didn't
          mean to say it
                      (..........)
   Guy:   You gave me that look after I aready started my explanation
          ⌈not before.
45 Amy:   ⌊Because I just thought you'd say that's nice and that's ↑it
                      (..........)
   Guy:   ⌈I'm sorry
   Amy:   ⌊And you go and have to tell Pam and the whole- (.....) story
   Guy:   But I didn't ↑tell her the whole story.
50                    (..........)
   Amy:   You ↑did.
                        (.....)
   Guy:   That I would ↑call him and that Suzy was excited.
                        (...)
55 Amy:   He's Jewish? (..) He works at the Air Force base?
   Guy:   Right. And he's a ↑doctor.
                      (..........)
   Guy:   ↑That's not the whole story?
                        (.....)
60 Amy:   So how'd you- (..........)
   Guy:   The whole story is all of the background how Suzy was dying for
          him
                      (..........)
   Guy:   ⌈She wants his body
65 Amy:   ⌊Yeah well you said that
                       (......)
```

	Guy:	Did you: give Suzy the advice I suggested?
		(..........)
	Amy:	No
70	Guy:	Are you going to?
		(..)
	Amy:	No
		(.....)
	Guy:	I don't believe you
75		(.......... ....)
	Amy:	You're irritable
		(...)
	Guy:	What?
	Amy:	You're irritable
80	Guy:	Sorry I'll drink more tea
	Amy:	That makes you more irritable
	Guy:	↑Tea makes me irritable?
	Amy:	Mm hm, It's got caffeine
		(...)
85	Guy:	I'm sorry
		(..........) ((Kiss)) (.......... ....)
	Guy:	So: why else are you mad at me
		(..........)
	Guy:	That the only reason why you're mad at me
90		(..........)
	Amy:	Yeah, it really bo(h)thered me
		(..........)
	Guy:	Ahhrhh, then don't bring these things up with
		⌈me around=
95	Amy:	⌊Okay I'm sorry I didn't mean to ↑blabbermouth
	Guy:	Tc h̲hhhhh (...) ·h̲hhhhhhh O::::::h. well ↑I always hate being the one
		left out, therefore I don't like to leave out people

Amy: All right Suzy and Stan are picking us up at five til six,

(......)

100   Amy: Plus I'm <u>e</u>dgy because I have to call my mother

(..........)

Guy: I see

(......)

Amy: What time's your show at seven r- nine right?

105   (....)

Guy: We don't have to- if ⌈we're late I'd like to

Amy: ⌊We'll be late then

Amy: And I'm also I'm edgy because Pam sits there and goes

·hhh yo:u're cleaning up your bathroom you <u>a</u>re cleaning out the

110   bottom. Well exc<u>u</u>se me, I think someone always cleans out the

bottom of the bathtub

(..........)

And who is <u>she</u> to go inspect the bottom of my bathtub.

(..........)

115   I guess the last time my bathtub must not of <u>met</u>

ixspection (..) or she wouldn't a s<u>a</u>id it to me

And then she tells me you're cleaning it a::ll out

(.......... ....)

Amy: I'm sorry I don't think she should of said it the way she said it

120   (..)

Guy: You're right

(......)

Amy: ⌈You actually agree with me

Guy: ⌊Come sit down with me over here

125   (....)

Guy: Yes dear

(..........)

Amy: I'm really pissed by that, I really a:m. I can't t<u>a</u>ke that

		(....)
130		I don't think that's right.
		(..........)
	Guy:	You're right, it's not
		(..........)
	Amy:	Why are you all of a sudden agreeing with me
135		(...)
	Guy:	You're ↑right
		(......)
		I can't agree with you when you're right
	Amy:	But last night you were telling me I was wrong ~
140	Guy:	You're ↑right- I ↑agree
		(..........)
	Amy:	I mean her dad must have said something about my ↑bathtub.

MENTALLY RAPING A GIRL

	May:	Those guys that work there are so crazy
	Bob:	Mm huh?
		(...)
	Bob:	I think they're pretty funny but that's only way to make it
5		through the job that's- that's how I act back ho:me
		at the grocery store
		(......)
	Bob:	Act- act Like a nut all the time
	May:	Well- ⌈I me:an ↑they were sort of insulting ~
10	Bob:	Uh well, yeah that's true they're- (....) they're (..........) they're-
		they're funny to the point to where they really are- it-
		they (...) haven't ever insulted me but they but they (....)
		for girls I can see where ya'll could probably get insulted

May: They really (.) can lay some stuff on.
15 (..........)
Bob: What they tell you
(..........)
May: Well Patti and I were standing there (......)
we were like halfway down the line (...) you know
20 I mean we weren't anywhere near the counter,
to where we could- place our order or whatever (......)
and he starts shouting ↑hey you in the white sweater
↑hey you in the white sweater and I was talking to Patti
I wasn't paying any attention (......) a:nd he was-
25 ↑hey what are you deaf?
(....)
May: And then everyone turned around and looked at me(h) huh hnh
·hhh and- I noticed then cause everyone was looking at me and-
he goes huh huh I didn't answer he goes wh(h)at are you dumb?
30 Bob: ⌈Huh huh huh huh
May: ⌊↑huh huh deaf and dumb ↑huh huh huh ·hhh ↑I was so mortified.
I just sorta looked at him he goes what do you want
and I looked at Patti and hah hah hah hah ·hhh
he goes huh hnh well doncha have a mind of your own?
35 Bob: eh huh huh
May: I was so- and then he- we got- finally got up there and
he said (..) well do you want everything on it, I said no not
onions, and he said I- well I can't believe you have a da:te.
Bob: ih heh heh heh
40 May: huh (.) huh I was so embarrassed
(..........)
Bob: hh huh huh hunh
May: And then Patti said well (...) don't get just the cheeseburger get
the cheeseburger platter, and so I- ↑I didn't know the difference

45	I said okay (.) the platter he goes, you're gonna eat a <u>who:le</u>
	platter huh hah are you ·hhh And he sta(h)rted making pig noises
	((SNORT SNORT)) ~
Bob:	When e- when ever a good lookin girl comes in you can <u>a</u>lways
	tell (..) he's over there staring (..) and- (....) you know- mo- mo-
50	most <u>guys</u> will stare for a <u>sec</u>ond or something but he just (....)
	z:oo:ms in and he can't (......) he can't af<u>fix</u> his <u>e</u>yes anywhere
	else (......) If I- if I 's a girl I'd just walk right up t<u>o</u> him and sa:y
	he:y bastard leave me alone
May:	We:ll- I m<u>e</u>an it's ↑not like he just sta:res. (...) It was like- (...)
55	uhh I don't kno:w.
	(.....)
Bob:	You kn<u>ew</u> what he wanted to do to you right
May:	Yea:h.=
Bob:	=Through the stare.
60	(....)
May:	It ↑wasn't- it <u>wasn't</u> a stare. It- it's like he looked you <u>up</u> and
	down. up and down. up and down and then he sorta goes like
	thi:s sorta goes like tha:t
	(....)
65	May:	⌈And
Bob:	⌊My:- <u>E</u>nglish teacher in high school called th<u>a</u>t the mentally
	r<u>a</u>ping a girl
	(........)
May:	Its very unnerving ~
70	Bob:	So what else is happenin today
	(.......... ....)
May:	This a weird tree
	(.......... ....)
May:	I mean it looks li:ke (...) from where I a:m right here
75	it looks like the thing is about ready to p<u>ou</u>nce on me

		(.......... ....)
	May:	If this tree had a mind I'd say it was dirty ~
	Bob:	Smell something?
	May:	Yeah
80		(....)
	May:	Like- (..........) d<u>o</u>g doo doo huh haha
		(....)
	May:	Hope it's not you
	Bob:	Mm=
85	May:	=And I hope I'm not laying on it
	Bob:	Mm, Oh well, you trying to tickle me with that stick?=
	May:	=heh heh heh (.......... .....) heh heh tickle you?
		Am I just being a- an annoyance
	Bob:	You're <u>always</u> an annoyance
90		(...)
	Bob:	But it's startin to work (.) hhuh ↑huh huh
		(.......... ....) ((noises))
	Bob:	You're right it d<u>o</u>es smell <u>hi</u>h
	May:	huh hah hah⌈hah hah hah hah ↑hah hah
95	Bob:	⌊heh
	Bob:	hah hah hah hah ha ·hhh ↑I(h) to(h)ld you.=
	Bob:	=I don't know where it's coming from
	May:	eh <u>hi</u>h <u>hi</u>h hih huh huh I think it's you:.
		(...)
100	May:	And it sm<u>e</u>lls just like <u>pu</u>ppy poop huh (..)
		You know when you're tryin du:- housebreak a do:g ~
	May:	Well d<u>o</u>n't wipe it over here. G<u>o</u> wipe it over there somewhere.
	Bob:	I'll go⌈wipe it on you
	May:	⌊↑Wipe it on the trees.
105		(.......)
	Bob:	↑Pyoo:: <u>i</u>h huh⌈huh huh huh <u>h</u>hh
	May:	⌊heh heh heh heh

May:	That's it Bobbo hike your leg
Bob:	Tell me about it baby.
110 May:	SHHH (...) there are people in the museum
Bob:	So
May:	who wouldn't understand
Bob:	There's nothing <u>to</u> understand

(.....)

115 Bob:	↑Who was Elizabeth N<u>ey</u>?

(....)

May:	She was sculptress=
Bob:	Nye?=
May:	=She did um (....) the st<u>a</u>tue of Sam Houston and Austin that- (...)
120	is in the Capital? ~
Bob:	Hm

(.......... .....)

Bob:	And wh<u>a</u>t's Shipe Park named after. [pron.: shīp]

(....)

125 Bob:	Somebody named Shipe?
May:	Or a lady, or a lady named Shipe?
Bob:	Yeah

(....)

Bob:	Or a dog named Shipe
130	(.......)
Bob:	Who- (..........) who does his d<u>u</u>ty so I can step on
May:	↑huh huh huh huh huh

GONNA KEEP SCORE?

Val:	We're not gonna keep sc<u>o</u>re?
Ric:	Nope=
Val:	=Why:

(.....)

5   Pat: Wel- well w<u>ai</u>t a second.

   Val: Just <u>u</u>se the ↑newspaper or something.

                               (.......... .....)

   Pat: G<u>o</u>t it (..) I got it. (.) A genuine Lee Perlmutter (.) original (.) scorecard.

10   Val: H<u>u</u>h, thats somethin

                               (.....)

   Pat: N<u>o</u>. (...) But I'm no- I don't know what the g<u>un</u> laws a:re (..) in a:h (..........) in ⌈Fl<u>o</u>rida.

   Val: ⌊This isn't set up very good but I guess uh (.)

15   push this back a little bit

                             (..........)

   Val: Does that intimidate you

   Pat: What.

   Val: T<u>a</u>pe recorder

20   Pat: No it doesn't

   Val: Okay, Gloria, you d<u>o</u>n't have to put that d<u>o</u>wn.

   Pat: It does't intimidate us in the slightest

          I just won't talk about <u>sex</u> or anything nasty

   Val: ↑You can do that

25   Pat: Mm, (..........) talk about nothing like that in front of a- tape recorder

                           (..........)

   Pat: It's <u>N</u>ixon's first mist<u>a</u>ke.

                            (......)

30   ↑Woo:: ⌈you

   Val: ⌊I just have to tell you you're s<u>u</u>nk.

   Pat: Why=

   Val: =I have a gr<u>ea</u>t ha:nd.

                      (.....)

35	Pat:	Mm hm?
	Val:	=I don't know if I shuffled this very good.
	Pat:	You probably didn't cause I don't have a b(h)ad hand either
		(..........)
	Val:	I mean like ahhh I only nee:d y'know a couple cards?
40	Pat:	O:h that's good. Hopefully you won't get them. ~
	Val:	Hey
	Pat:	What
	Val:	I haven't had something in a long time
		(..........)
45		besides a piece of thatcold pecan pie.
		(.......... ....)
	Pat:	Oh yeah?
	Val:	I want a ↑kiss.
		(.....)
50	Pat:	Oh. hhh that.
	Val:	Whattayou ⌈↑mean.
	Pat:	⌊I's thinkin let's go
	Val:	huh huh
55		Mmmmm. (.....) ((SMACK—noisy kiss))
	Pat:	((to recorder)) Hear that?
	Val:	Shhh, don't say that she has to write it down.
	Pat:	((cartoon voice)) Observed behaviors of the assexual fema:le
	Val:	Assexual, what're you talkin assexual, who's assexual,
60		speak for yourself.
		(.....)
	Pat:	You will be when I leave for Florida
		(...)
	Val:	How do you know
65		(...)
	Pat:	I'm gonna strip you. hhhhh

	Val:	I'm a romp with everybody I can find
		(..........)
	Pat:	Don't need that ((discarding))
70		((pause; Val picks, thinks, discards))
	Val:	But ↑Gary said he didn't think anybody would go <u>with</u> me.
		((Pat shakes ice cubes in drink)) ~
	Pat:	Aw- uh- I hate to tell you this Val, most college guys who are
		basket cases look to get <u>butt</u>
75		(.......... ....)
	Val:	↑But-
	Pat:	↑Bu::t?
	Val:	↑We'd make good ti:me? I- I mean I'd show'm a good time?
		(.......... .....)
80	Pat:	You better watch your mouth.
	Val:	But if he was a fri<u>e</u>nd a mine don't you think he'd- understand?
		(..........)
		and just go:? And have a good time? And that's it?
	Pat:	=Possibility? ~
85	Val:	Gin.
	Pat:	Bitch
	Val:	We're not keepin score.
	Pat:	I don't like this game.
		((Pat goes to kitchen, shuffles pans)) ~
90	Val:	I assume that you're eating Thanksgiving at <u>your</u> house right?
	Pat:	Um. If I'm <u>in</u>. (........) You're ass<u>u</u>ming correct.
		(..........)
		<u>How</u> are <u>we</u> gonna work that out.
	Val:	Same way we did last year.
95		(.....)
	Pat:	What
	Val:	You eat at your house I eat at mine.

	Pat:	Um um no I'm not talking about <u>that</u>
		and I'm not talking about right <u>now</u> ~
100	Val:	You mean later on like who's house are we gonna go to
		for what?
	Pat:	Yeah.
		(..)
	Val:	I don't know=
105	Pat:	=Okay. I figure how's this. (........) The <u>Je</u>wish holidays (.........)
		we spend at your house. and <u>Ame</u>rican ones we spend at mine.
		(....)
	Val:	Well I don't <u>kno</u>w I mean Thanksgiving is important to my family
		too.
110	Pat:	I k<u>no</u>w but we'll spend Roshashana (...) and Passover with <u>them</u>
		(.........) I think it's only fair my parents dese<u>r</u>ve it
		(.........)
	Val:	Well, maybe like- like I can tell my mom to (.........)
	Pat:	Well maybe we can all get together as a (.......)
115		I keep forgetting we're gonna be a <u>big</u> family then.
	Val:	Yeah but your mom always likes to have the Hensleys over: and
	Pat:	F___ the Hensleys I can't stand those pricks.
		(......... .....)
	Pat:	Maybe we'll get lucky.
120		(.....)
	Val:	What.
	Pat:	They'll all <u>die</u>
	Val:	I k<u>new</u> you were gonna say that that is dis<u>gu</u>sting
	Pat:	I know it is but it's (.) the truth.
125	Val:	Um: (...) no I was gonna say maybe my mom would have (.....)
		Thanksgiving dinner on <u>Thurs</u>day, I mean <u>Fri</u>day. (.........) y'know?
		(....) so we could get fat- two days in a row.

	Pat:	That's a possibility
	Val:	I don't know we'll see. We'll see what happens.
130		(..........)
	Val:	I mean I see your point about the Jewish holidays
		cause your family doesn't exactly have Passover Seder.
	Pat:	Um hm (.) and so- that makes it perfect.
		(.......... ....) ((kitchen noises))
135	Val:	Well we could combi::ne. (..........) or else (....)
	Pat:	Y'know (.) I'm just saying (.......) ((POTS BANGING))
		it would mean more to my parents
		(.......... ....) ((kitchen noises))
	Val:	Well?- (.......... ....) maybe- ((bang)) (..........)
140		they'll be a- at different times of the day?
		Like (....) we'll leave your house at two? (........)
		and then (........) go over to my house and um:
		(...) y'know at four someth'n
		(..........)
145	Pat:	Yes:, we can blow up like f___ing balloons.
	Val:	Well we don't have to eat you know massive meals at both
		(.......... ....)
		I don't know, I don't know how people do that.
		(..........) ((BANG))
150	Pat:	Neither do I
	Val:	I'm sure this is a very (..........) big (.....) universal problem.s

PLAIN OLD BUG

	Tad:	I see a- (...) a- a- maybe bunda bee.
	Abe:	It look like a wasp or a mosquito to me.
		(.......... ....)
	Tad:	Whatever it is, it looks likes it's giwuh- ih- ih- ih

its a- its not a fly:. It's a bitn' bug or a shupin bug.

Roy: If it's a stinging bug- it's a bee ⌈or a ant.

Tad: ⌊or or- or =

Abe: =It's a flying stinging bug

Roy: That's a bee:.

10 Tad: It's just a plain old bug.

Abe: How do you know?

Tad: Because ·hhh it- (.......) plain old bug =

Abe: =Cause it- cause I saw a stinger on it

(..........)

15 Roy: Then it's a bee

Abe: It's a wasp

(........)

Roy: Yeah (..) it can't be

Tad: Where's that lock?

20   (..........)

Tad: Hey look   ~

Abe: Hey, lets play jungle in th- in- let's pla:y um (..)
⌈that were being

Roy: ⌊Wile, Wile, West

25   (....)

Abe: No, we're monkey, you dum dum=

Tad: =huu huu hee heh heh heh heh hoo hoo hoo

(.......... ...)

Roy: ↑i:, i: ↑ee (..) ↑ee

30   (...)

Tad: hoo hoo hee yeh

(......)

Roy: hoo hoo hee

Abe: No you gotta be on the inside a the cage because (........)

35	Tad:	hoo hoo ⌈hoo
	Roy:	⌊hroinch
	Tad:	duh dutu ↑du du du ⌈du du dah
	Roy:	⌊See I'm a monkey ~
	Abe:	Look (........) Hey look. (..) Look, we're ⌈monkeys
40	Roy:	⌊whn ↑whn, whn:.
	Tad:	Hey wanna see some?
		(.......)
	Roy:	hn, hnn, hnn.
	Tad:	Don duh duh ↑dan don.
45	Abe:	Hey, did ya see ↑that?
		(..)
		I was only holdin on with one foot.
		(..........)
	Roy:	Show me.
50	Abe:	Okay (..........) without my hands hanging down like ↑that.
		(........)
	Abe:	And without them holding o:n.
		(........)
	Abe:	Watch
55		(........)
	Roy:	doo: doo ↑doo do- duh
		(..........)
	Tad:	Go like this
		(...)
60	Tad:	Like this (.) like this: ~
	Abe:	Hey, let's play zoo.
		(...)
	Roy:	↑I'm a uh- (...) ah- we=
	Abe:	See I'm the zookeeper. You two are the monkey:s.

65		(..)
	Tad:	I'm the monkey w- we're different animals in here
		·hhh and we fight
		(....)
	Tad:	I'm a tiger yer a li:on.
70	Abe:	Uh uh I'm a gorilla
		(....)
	Roy:	Who are you
	Tad:	Hey, (..) hey: ⌈I have a idea yr-
	Roy:	⌊I'm a monkey=
75	Tad:	=Eyh I have idea?=
	Roy:	=uh ↑runga (..) ↑mm::.=
	Tad:	=A muh- (..) see a monkey (..) is a gorilla's (..) son:.
		(........)
	Abe:	⌈That's right gorilla's don't hurt monkeys
80	Roy:	⌊Then wuhn the monkey grows up he begins tuh be a gorilla=
	Abe:	=Gorillas don't hurt monkeys.
		(..........)
	Abe:	Listen, gorillas don't hurt ⌈monkeys
	Roy:	⌊↑No:, gorillas- (....) er- (..........)
85		monkeys en they- en they both fight ↑eee
		(.......... .....)
	Abe:	Don't Roy he's go'na hurt em
		(...)
	Tad:	Okay:, the zookeeper's go'na get ya
90		(..........)
	Roy:	You wah- you gah be a <u>a</u>nimal you can't get in there
		·hh or you're tra::pped.
		(..)
	Abe:	Uh- uh hu::h, because the zookeeper goes in cages
95		(........)

Tad:	Yeah, duh stop fights, too hhh-
	(...)
Roy:	↑eee
	(.....)
Abe:	I'm one of the zookeeper's helpers
	(..........)
Tad:	I'm a monkey
Tad:	Okay mon-=
Abe:	Gettin in a fight with a monkey is tough when you're a
	zookeeeeper's helper
Roy:	eu, euu.
	(......)
Tad:	Be a good- monkey okay?
	(.......... ....)
Abe:	I take care a m<u>o</u>st of the things and I stay in the cages
	and stuff like that.
	(........)
Roy:	↑eu eu oo
Abe:	I gotta read my checklist
	(.......)
Roy:	hm hm (.) hm (......) hm::.
	((SMACK))
Abe:	Quit i:t (..) Quit it
	((SMACK)) ~
Abe:	Hey, that one's mine, that one's mine,
	(..........)
Roy:	↑eeyuh, eeyuh
	(....)
Tad:	At kids- at monkey↓s fetchin it
Roy:	eeh uh=
Tad:	=Or- or he's a three way d<u>o</u>g.

The line numbers in the left margin are: 100 (Abe), 105 (zookeeeeper's helper), 110 (Abe), 115 (Roy), 120 (Abe), 125 (Roy).

Abe: Yeah, you can say that ⌈again

Tad: ⌊Go get- go get it monkey

Roy: ↑eeh, eeh eeh eeh

130 Abe: He's a one way dog

                    (.......)

Abe: I didn't say he's a three way dog

         I said he's a <u>one</u> way dog.

STUNNING

Alice: D'I show you my new toy, d'I show you my new toy?

                    (....)...

Marie: No you didn't show us your new toy you didn't show us

         your new to:y,

5   Rikki: huh huh ↑hih

                    (..........)

Alice: Cause I'm living alo:ne, (..) I wanted to

         ⌈get myself

Marie: ⌊Uh- please don't play with ⌈that ↑Alice do::n't.=

10   ⌊((ZAP ZAP ZAP ZAP ZAP))

Rikki: =What is that.

Alice: It's c(h)alled a stungun?=

Rikki: =Are those're the stunguns?=

Alice: =And if I touch ⌈someone

15   Marie: ⌊↑Do::n't.

Alice: I'm not gonna do it but if I touch someone, (..) with this,

         (..) and I push this button, (.) it will-

         ⌈shock the living: <u>day</u>lights out of em=

Marie: ⌊It immobilizes em

20   Alice: =and make 'em have ⌈ like a epilep-

Rikki: ⌊That's what we're getting for

New York

Marie: Right.

Alice: ((ZAP ZAP ZAP ⌈ZAP))

25 Marie: ⌊Alice please just don't play with tha:t,=

Alice: =I've taken it out right in the mi(h)ddle a the club like ·hhh

I was dancin the club and I was ⌈goin ((ZAP ZAP ZAP))

Rikki: ⌊Where'd you get it=

Alice: =heh ⌈huh huh

30 Marie: ⌊You're not funny::.

Alice: I thought it was like ·hh a strobe light.

(...)

Rikki: Wher'd you get it.

Alice: My sister gave it to me she didn't wanna have it

35 Marie: Where'd she get it I want one. ⌈for New York.

Alice: ⌊I don't know,

Marie: We, need one

Rikki: We're getting one for New York, for sure,

Alice: I ⌈don't-

40 Marie: ⌊I thought that thing about chick (.) stun that guy where

she's gnn-, went n got arrested.

Rikki: I know, she's getting ⌈charges pressed

Marie: ⌊D'I tell you guys?

(..)

45 This- girl we met at um (......) where were we Toulouse?

(...)

She's from New York she's iss black girl, and she's from

New York and um she's just here for like a couple of

months and she just grew up in New York loves it,

50 everything ·hhh a:nd so sh'e used to New York, in New York

if someone's following you, (....) you get very scared, in

Austin if someone's following you they're probly goin their

		car. (....) So she said she's walkin down Sixth Street by
		herself and this guy's behind her ⌈going some-
55	Rikki:	⌊No cause she was at a
		club and he asked her to dance he said I wan dance with
		you, ·hhh and he followed her out and pulled her arm and
		said, come ↑dance with me.
	Marie:	So she- takes the stungun- (...)
60	Rikki:	st⌈uns him huh huh
	Marie:	⌊stuns him, and she got arre(hh)sted:.
	Rikki:	He pressed charges
		(.......)
	Alice:	Did he go into an eplieptic seizure?
65		~
	Marie:	Did I tell you why I was so attracted to Dan?
	Alice:	Um mm.
	Marie:	I'm sitting at the club, and Dan and Robby and all them
		were sitting around the bar:? (..) and u:m (.) and I was just
70		standing next to Dan they're all talking and Robby- was
		talking about some girl and he goes ·hhhhhh ma:n she was
		as soft as mah hushpuppies and as warm as a
		buttermilk biscuit I go oh my God that's from House Party
		Dan says you- have watched House Party? (..) I go I have
75		watched ⌈House Party hee hee
	Rikki:	⌊uhuh huh huh huh huh ~
	Rikki:	We did it for um- (....) ⌈Shannon Konsky
	Marie:	⌊Shannon Konsky
	Marie:	She was dying
80		Shannon Konsky looks g:orgeous have you seen her
	Alice:	Tell me.
	Marie:	She looks beautiful
		(....)

		Beautiful like ·hhhh Shannon's always been pretty like
85		her face then she lost all of her weight so she was skinny
		andshe still had a pretty face and she was pretty
		·hhhhh she's like st<u>u</u>nning now ⌈I think
	Alice:	⌊Tell me why.

(....)

90	Marie:	Her hair's like <u>r</u>ed (.) but with a lo:t of blonde in it?
	Rikki:	And it's ⌈just so
	Marie:	⌊it's like down to her:e.=
	Rikki:	=And it's curly.=
	Marie:	=<u>A</u>ll curly, one length, (.) she's thin?
95	Alice:	↑Thin.

(....)

	Marie:	She's not ski<u>nn</u>y.
	Rikki:	Right. She's thin ⌈she's this thick
	Marie:	⌊She's like the ↑ta:ll.
100	Marie:	She's real tall looking (..) and she's like you look at her.
		She's the type of girl that would walk down the street and
		you'd look like three times.

(..)

	Marie:	Cause she's very attractive.
105		(......)
	Marie:	Like stunning ⌈I was in shock
	Rikki:	⌊s'lookin s<u>o</u> good.
	Alice:	There's really nothing stunning about me and I've been
		tryin to figure something stunning
110		·hhhh like I know that I'm okay, (..) and everything but I'm
		saying ·hhhh like there's certain people that you look a:t
		(..) and there's something that s- <u>s</u>tands out with them?
		I don't think there's anything wrong with me but I don't
		think I have one thing that stands out, ·hhhh because the

115		only that could is maybe my cheekbones?
		(..........)
		but who notices cheekbones.
		(..........)
	Alice:	You know?=
120	Marie:	I do.
	Alice:	And so my sister told me:, ·hhh that I should stop wearing
		al- all my makeup and like do everything really lightly, and
		then wear bright lipstick.
		(..........)
125		That's what I been trying to do but still doesn't make me
		stunning
	Marie:	Well some people aren't stunning some people your- are
		pretty.
	Alice:	I'm just not st(h)unning. ~
130		(.......... ...)
	Alice:	I don't have an outstanding feature to be seen.
		But I don't mind I mean,
		(..........)
	Rikki:	I think you don't try to figure out what it is
135	Marie:	=Eh heh huh heh=
	Alice:	=I don't have one- I don't have like
		⌈bl:ack black hair
	Marie:	⌊I don't have an outstanding feature.=
	Alice:	=I don't have anything outstanding
140	Marie:	Neither do I:.=
	Alice:	=And not one thing.
		I- I don't like a l:ong legs, that's for sure
	Marie:	Uh heh huh huh ·hh
	Alice:	I look like a football player but other than tha:t,
145	Marie:	I don have anthing outstanding

		(...)
	Alice:	Pretty e:yes.

	Alice:	Pretty e:yes.

Alice: Pretty e:yes.

            (..........)

Alice: Humongous boobs. huh heh ⌈huh heh=

150   Marie: ⌊huh huh but you got your h:air

         huh heh ~

Alice: Can you imagine how much hair I have?

             (..........)

Rikki: I don't really have to ima(hh)gine uh- huh

155   ⌈uh huh huh huh huh huh

Alice: ⌊You can see it with your own <u>ey</u>es.=

Marie: = One time when Alice and I were earlier talking about

         what was the prettyiest and ugliest about us ·hhhh and

         when-

160   I was like telling her (......) the- the best feature you

         have's like your cheekbones and all this stuff and I go

         what about me she goes ·hhhh your best features are your

         eyebrows.

Alice: That is not ⌈what I said

165   Marie: ⌊it is↑too:?

Alice: I never even noticed your eyebrows

Hi Hello Mija

M: Hello

H: Hi mo:m,

M: Hi hello mija

5   H: How're you doing

M: Muy bien (.) está viendo el boxeo

M: ⌈hah hah

H: ⌊Ah:::↑:: Como está de frío alla

	M:	No:↑: está: lloviendo
10	H:	Pero no está haciendo frío
	M:	No: no es- no que yo poquito pero no it's not cold very very no
	H:	⌈Eh yeah
	M:	⌊No-
	M:	Y alla cómo están ustedes
15	H:	Sí:: it's getting co:ld,

(..)

	M:	S- h<u>ow</u> a ver que tal
	H:	Pues- uh right now it's dr<u>i</u>zzling verdad ~
	M:	We made empañadas today?
20	D:	↑My:::::.
	M:	Oye- ·hhh How did you like my (...) c- uh corn bread
	H:	Estaba bien grasoso mother
	M:	Jo si esto mucho mantequilla
	H:	Le puso mucha mantequilla?
25	M:	Sí, yo creo que sí después es ⌈que-
	H:	⌊A:h es like manteca mom it's- it's

ba:d don't- I mean d- that's- that's too thick, I think too

	M:	S<u>í</u> porque le puso ⌈four eggs
	H:	⌊Too greasy mom (.) too greasy
30	H:	·hhh It was- it was okay in the beginning pero no I hadn't throw

it away because I- I really didn't like it after that

(.....)

	M:	No: pues si mucho manteca
	H:	Um huh
35	M:	Y asi no- no I didn't know- I didn't just- taste bad pero es que (.)

quite as strong ~

	H:	A::y c<u>ó</u>mo est<u>á</u> t<u>í</u>a
	M:	Tiene <u>é</u>l tambi<u>é</u>n está mala de la gripa

	H:	Ay pobr⌈eci-
40	M:	⌊De la gripa y Margarita está mal de la gripa y el catarro
		y no fino se le desconoce la vo:z
	H:	Ay⌈: :
	M:	⌊Pero eso es tiempo lo- le- ti⌈El tiempo es-
	H:	⌊Sí, I know
45	M:	Take care of yourself mija
	H:	I know- oye mother what was I going to tell you um=
	M:	=When are you coming
	H:	·hhhh A:::m Wednesday
		(.....)
50	M:	Wednesday or are you gonna- come Thursday morning
	H:	No Wednesday because I have Wednesday off
		(..)
	M:	Sí: ~
	H:	So we're planning to go like sometime in the morning ~
55	M:	·hhh Oye has oído tú esto ·hh e- cuál es tú birthday el del o- el
		del jueves o del sab- el domingo=
	H:	Mo:ther::
	M:	Pues es que me- bueno porque=
	H:	=The twenty third that's that's Laura's: birthday it's
60		Thanksgiving (..) Day =
	M:	O bueno tú qué quieres mija
	H:	⌈M m m m m m m m m m m m m m m m m m m m m m m
	M:	⌊What do you wanted- what would you like to have Or you
		A ver que digas I:- give me this o: you know
65	H:	Mno:: (..) I- I really don't- uh- nothing
		(..........)
	H:	But ye- could- if i- mean if you want to give me a gift don't I
		prefer money

	M:	Ah que bueno (.) very good I read- que bueno que me dijistes
70		mija it's good ⌈it fits
	H:	⌊Uh huh
	H:	=Uh huh=
	M:	=Yeah it's better por que asi (.) you get whatever you have,
	M:	Okay?
75	H:	Yeh-
	M:	Esta bueno
	H:	Bueno Mom ⌈entonces este=
	M:	⌊Okey
	M:	=⌈Say hello to Doug okay
80	H:	=⌊We'll talk to you later eh?
	M:	Sí, andale
	H:	Ue-
	M:	⌈Goodbye ⌉
	H:	⌊Love you ⌋ bub bye:.
	M:	Bye bye ((Kissing sounds)) p

Index

movement
  awkwardness in, 45
  performing sense through, 115–116
multiple effects, 94
"My Last Duchess" (Browning), 144

narrative strategies
  direct discourse as, 181–182
  indirect discourse as, 182
  listening to, 179–180
  pace as, 182–183
  performing, 180–183
  quotation as, 181
  selection as, 181
  sequence as, 181
narratives, 164
  description of world in, 212
  as genre, 166
  as performance, 166–167
  personal, 217–236
narrator
  intentions of, vs. author, 93
  need for, 167
  point of view, 185
  and story, 172–179
  world of, 171
Nash, Ogden, "Parsley for Vice-President!,"
    151–152
Natural Drills in Expression (Phillips), 202
'Night Mother (Norman), 21, 22–23, 29
  narrator's world in, 171
nonverbal communication, 12
Norman, Marsha
  'Night Mother, 21, 22–23, 29
  narrator's world in, 171
"Nostalgia" (Collins), 112–113

observer, narrator as, 173
obtrusive narrator, 185
O'Connor, Flannery, "A Good Man Is Hard
    to Find," 204–205, 206
"An Old Story" (Kelman), 167–169,
    203–204
  intertextual script with, 213–214
Olds, Sharon, "The Elder Sister," 156
"On Smoking" [script], 256–259
"One Home" (Stafford), 61
onomatopoeia, 127

pace, as narrative strategy, 182
paradoxes, 9
paraphrase, 182
parody, 201
Parrish, Wayland Maxfield, 26, 201–202
"Parsley for Vice-President!" (Nash),
    151–152
participant, narrator as, 173
passion, in speaker's characterization, 75
past-tense experiences, performance and,
    52
patterned speech, 139–140
  in conversation, 142
patterns in poetic speech, 141–157
  involving ear, 147–153
  involving eye, 143–147
  involving mind, 153–154
  involving the whole, 154–157
pauses, 25, 240–241
  in conversational transcripts, 4, 5
  in scripts, 238
performance, 2–3, 198
  actions in, 29–30
  as assent, 198–200
  awkwardness in movement, 45
  building on effect, 83
  conversational, 3–5
  good reading for, 28
  language in, 215–216
  live, 10–13
  as method of study, 12
  as method to realize language, 23
  moving from analysis to, 71–73
  multiple levels for, 103
  narrative as, 166–167
  and past-tense experiences, 52
  as resistance, 200–202, 215
  scripts of everyday conversation for,
    237–308
  sense from vocal, 104–109
  solo, 203, 206
performance knowledge, 198–216
performer
  creativity as, 39
  intentions of, 93
  learning from performance, 198
  resistance by, 201
  world in storytelling, 172